EVERYTHING
YOU NEED TO KNOW ABOUT...
Training Your Puppy

Dear Reader,

Is it your first time living with a puppy or have you done this before? Either way, your new puppy is 100 percent unique, and will soon share in special lasting moments in your life that are unlike any others. No matter the number of puppies you have, be it one or more, they become part of the fabric of your family and your life. The goal of this book is to maximize your relationship with your puppy, and all aspects of his or her care are covered. In this, **EVERYTHING** *New Puppy Book*, you'll find answers to some of the most confounding issues you'll face—training challenges, nutrition, basic health care, even behavior problems—all explained in ways to put you and your puppy companion at ease and on track to enjoy many satisfying years together.

We get excited just thinking about puppies—they are the cute, cuddly, happy, joyful, playful, better sides of ourselves. They are, in and of themselves, a gift. They bring love and softness with them, trust and lots of puppy licks. They delight in the simplest of things—and fill our days with many special moments. We hope this book helps you find the same joys in your life with your puppy (-ies), and that your coming years together are the best ever.

Time for a treat!

Carlo De Vito and Amy Ammen

Welcome to the EVERYTHING YOU NEED TO KNOW ABOUT... series!

These handy, accessible books give you all you need to tackle a difficult project, gain a new hobby, comprehend a fascinating topic, prepare for an exam, or even brush up on something you learned back in school but have since forgotten.

You can choose to read an **EVERYTHING** book from cover to cover or just pick out the information you want from our four useful boxes: e-questions, e-facts, e-alerts, and e-ssentials. We give you everything you need to know on the subject, but throw in a lot of fun stuff along the way, too.

We now have more than 400 **EVERYTHING** books in print, spanning such wide-ranging categories as weddings, pregnancy, cooking, music instruction, foreign language, crafts, pets, New Age, and so much more. When you're done reading them all, you can finally say you know **EVERYTHING**!

QUESTION?
Answers to
common questions

FACTS
Important snippets
of information

ALERTS!
Urgent
warnings

ESSENTIALS
Quick
handy tips

PUBLISHER Karen Cooper

DIRECTOR OF ACQUISITIONS AND INNOVATION Paula Munier

MANAGING EDITOR, EVERYTHING SERIES Lisa Laing

COPY CHIEF Casey Ebert

ACQUISITIONS EDITOR Katie McDonough

DEVELOPMENT EDITOR Brett Palana-Shanahan

EDITORIAL ASSISTANT Hillary Thompson

Visit the entire **EVERYTHING YOU NEED TO KNOW ABOUT...** series at *www.davidandcharles.co.uk*

EVERYTHING
YOU NEED TO KNOW ABOUT...

Training
Your Puppy

Choosing, raising, and training your new best friend

Carlo De Vito with Amy Ammen

D&C
David and Charles

Dedication
To my wife, Dominique De Vito, and my sons, Dylan and Dawson.
And to Chief, Cinderella, Sadie, Lulu, Exley, Chelsea, Bentley, Storm, Cheri,
Pepi, Red, Benji, Max, Burton, Timothy, and Jo. They have all taught me a great deal
about puppyhood and dogs, and even more about being a better human being.

A DAVID & CHARLES BOOK
Copyright © 2009 by F+W Media, Inc.

David & Charles is an F+W Media Inc. company
4700 East Galbraith Road
Cincinnati, OH 45236

First published in the UK in 2009
First published in the USA in 2009 as *The Everything® Puppy Book* by
Adams Media, an F+W Media Company
57 Littlefield Street, Avon, MA 02322 U.S.A.
www.adamsmedia.com

Photographs copyright © Mary Bloom

A catalogue record for this book is available from the British Library.

ISBN-13: 978-0-7153-3296-2 paperback
ISBN-10: 0-7153-3296-1 paperback

Printed and bound in Great Britain by CPI Antony Rowe Ltd, Chippenham for David & Charles
Brunel House   Newton Abbot   Devon

Visit our website at www.davidandcharles.co.uk

David & Charles books are available from all good bookshops; alternatively you
can contact our Orderline on 0870 9908222 or write to us at FREEPOST EX2 110
, D&C Direct, Newton Abbot, TQ12 4ZZ (no stamp required UK only);
US customers call 800-289-0963 and Canadian customers call 800-840-5220.

This publication is designed to provide accurate and authoritative information with regard
to the subject matter covered. It is sold with the understanding that the publisher is not engaged
in rendering legal, accounting, or other professional advice. If legal advice or other expert assistance
is required, the services of a competent professional person should be sought.

Contents

Acknowledgments

I want to thank Amy Ammen for writing the training sections of this book in its first and second editions. Amy is one of the most accomplished dog trainers I have ever met, and I admire her commitment to helping puppies and dogs and their owners learn to live together with respect, manners, and joy. Learn more about her at *www.dogclass.com.*

And I would like to thank my wife, Dominique De Vito, who helped me immensely. She is an accomplished and successful pet writer/editor. Her fingerprints are all over it, and the readers and I are luckier for it.

Carlo De Vito

Top Ten Puppy-Raising Pointers

1. Patience
2. A schedule for daily activities
3. The best diet possible
4. Plenty of exercise
5. Plenty of sleep
6. Manners training
7. Plenty of attention
8. A trusted veterinarian
9. Appropriate chew toys
10. A safe and secure home

Introduction

▶ THERE IS NO more exciting or important time in your dog's life than the puppy years. They're filled with a playful wonder and awe-inspiring cuteness, and as you and your new friend enter into a lifetime of companionship and friendship, you will be building great memories. Get your camera ready!

The journey of bringing a puppy into your life begins with a choice of what type of breed or mixture you will choose (or the one that will choose you). And then there are a thousand decisions after that, many of which will set the stage for you and your puppy's life together for years to come. That first decision is a big one. Are you someone who leads a sedentary life? Are you someone who's more active? Are you a type-A personality? Do you have kids? A full-time job? Do you live in an apartment or a single-family home? Do you have a backyard? These are factors you need to take into account when choosing the puppy that's right for you.

From puppy-proofing your home to obedience training, from eating habits to socialization, the puppy years will include certain perils and learning curves as well as lots of puppy kisses. Crating issues and potty training are front and center in the puppy years. Creating a reliable and workable schedule for you and your dog is another thing you'll need to tackle right away. This will set you up to be consistent about taking the pup for walks and bathroom breaks, feeding dinner and treats, and establishing a bedtime. When expectations are set and patterns are developed, the consistency of your schedule is the simplest way to communicate with your pup.

Although dogs come in a variety of physical packages, they are all big where it counts—personality. In the character department, they are all colossal. People who are lucky enough to open up their lives and let in a friend as true and loving as a dog find a bond that transcends the verbal. It does not have the exchange of experience that is characteristic of a human relationship, but it is as open and honest a relationship as exists in the world. There is something in the magically expressive eyes of a dog that is difficult to explain to someone who does not understand. So open, so honest, so loving. If you have a dog, you already understand. If you're thinking of getting one, you're in for the experience of a lifetime.

It would be nice if puppies didn't require instruction booklets, but they do. There are lots of things you need to know, not only for your puppy's sake, but to strengthen the bond between you. Training is key, and that's why Amy Ammen wrote the training chapters. She's an amazing trainer who has trained countless pets privately and in groups. She has trained dogs in each of the AKC Groups to high-level obedience trial titles.

Puppy owners need to know about their breeds' histories and traits, grooming requirements, nutritional needs, basic health care, how to prepare their home and family for a dog, and much more. I am lucky to have met many dog professionals in my life. Thanks to them I understand that the puppy years are more than just feeding an animal and taking him or her to the vet. It's more than just enjoying the unconditional love puppies give. It's about being partners as well as friends.

May your life with your puppy give you the kind of joy and memories that you will treasure for a lifetime, and may this book help you give your puppy everything he or she needs as well.

CHAPTER 1

Dogs and Where They Came From

If you haven't already decided what kind of puppy you want—and hopefully you haven't because there's so much to learn in the first few chapters of this book—you'll soon discover that there are hundreds of breeds to choose from. It's amazing to think that a tiny Chihuahua shares the same genetic makeup as a gigantic Irish Wolfhound, but it's true! And that's why this chapter is in this book. Knowing a bit about how dogs evolved will give you that much more understanding of their nature.

The Beginning of the Human/Canine Bond

The history of dogs is so closely woven in with the history of people that historians and archaeologists cannot agree on when or how dogs were introduced. Prehistoric people may have found many good uses for dogs. Once domesticated, dogs were used as early warning detection devices against human or animal intruders. They would defend people's caves and camps as their own, and so they must have been excellent protection as well as an alarm system.

FACT

Numerous cave paintings depict dogs hunting alongside humans in 4000–5000 B.C., though there are even earlier examples of this partnership. By that time, five primary types of dogs appear in the paintings: greyhounds, pointing dogs, mastiffs, wolf-type dogs, and sheepherding dogs.

Obviously, the greatest use early people had for their canine companions was hunting. Once the dog was part of the human family, and once humans were part of the pack, hunting together became a valuable common interest. There is also conjecture concerning man's early use of dogs to guard livestock. Of course, as a dog fancier, one must wonder in the end, what attracted dogs to people? According to dog experts there were mainly three things—food, fire (for heat in winter), and community.

Lloyd M. Wendt, a noted historian of the human/dog connection who wrote the very detailed book *Dogs*, believes that the relationship between early humans and domesticated dogs can first be traced back 100,000 years to northern Africa and the Middle East. Remains found suggest a communal burial or death, rather than a violent end. Carbon dating has put the most recent findings at 92,000 years ago. He also noted that as little as 10,000 years ago, Algerians were drawing hunting scenes on cave walls, depicting the hunt, with dogs on leashes.

Historians place the working aspect of the human/dog relationship at approximately 80,000 years ago, with the advent of the spear. Spears gave humans a weapon to fend off aggressive animals, as well as something to kill them with. It was probably about this time that humans and dogs began hunting together in earnest.

As humans became more adept at navigation on the sea, they also began to seek dogs that were optimal for specific tasks. Great wolf-like animals were bred for hunting wolves, bears, and lions in Abyssinia and Persia. The largest and best of the herding dogs came from Tibet. And the fastest hunting greyhounds came from Egypt.

The Egyptians

Of course, the dog achieved its first great fame among modern people in Egypt. Dogs played an important part in everyday life—so much so that they were incorporated into the religion. The god Anubis was portrayed as a dog or as a strange mixture of a human's body with a dog's head. It was not uncommon to have the form of a dog sculpted to rest on the sarcophagus of a deceased king to deter grave robbers, and as a symbol of a guide who would lead the entombed through the afterlife. The Egyptians so loved their dogs that theirs was the first civilization with a law to punish humans who were cruel to dogs.

A richly decorated wooden casket dating to 1300 B.C. shows Tutankhamen in his chariot pursuing Nubian soldiers who are being harassed by his Assyrian dogs.

The Greeks and Romans

Alexander the Great and, later, the Roman emperors were also fond of dogs. Because the Greeks and Romans traded with the Egyptians, dogs became popular with Hellenic aristocracy for a variety of purposes. Unlike the Egyptians, who prospered in semi-isolation, the Greeks and the Romans were products of the very heavily populated and mercantile-minded

Mediterranean and Middle Eastern cultures. Life was competitive and land came at great cost.

Learning from the Persians and their other warlike neighbors, the Greeks began to use two types of dogs. One was large and massive in build, with a large, broad face, and was known as the Molossian. The other, known as the Laconian Hound, was also large, but had a rather pointed snout, and was faster and sleeker. Aristotle was a fan of both dogs, saying that the Laconian female was gentler and smarter, but by no means fit for war, and that the Molossian was the dog of choice.

The Molossian was named for the northern Greek tribe that had made it well-known. The Molossian of Alexander the Great's time is the ancestor of today's Mastiff, which for centuries was the ultimate dog of war—large, strong, fearless, and smart. The Greeks and then the Romans used these beasts in war for something like a cavalry charge. The Laconian Hound was developed, it is believed, in Sparta. It was fast and brutal, but of a sleeker build than the traditional Mastiff.

The first literary classic pairing of a man and his dog comes from the Greeks. Dating back to one of the first classic pieces of literature known and studied for centuries, *The Odyssey* features the story of Odysseus, warrior of the Trojan War, attempting the long, treacherous, and adventurous journey home. After many years away from his farm and kingdom, the hero of the story is not recognized by those people who knew him long ago. Despite his claims, he is only believed when his faithful hound—by then old and impaired—crawls to his master, for whom he has been faithfully waiting. Upon greeting him, Odysseus's dog dies, wagging his tail, happy at his master's feet.

FACT

In a dispute among rulers in Norway, when King Eysteinn conquered a particular territory, he put his son in charge. The people killed him, and the King asked them then to chose to be ruled by a slave or a dog. They chose the dog, thinking it would soon die. Instead, it lived an extremely opulent life for three years until descended upon by wolves.

If dog was man's best friend in Greece, another dog was the mother of Rome. According to myth, two men fought over the founding of Rome: Romulus and Remus, who had been raised by a wolf, suckling on her milk. It was the Romans who first outfitted their war dogs with thick leather collars, studded with sharp metal blades to deter other attacking dogs. Dogs were instrumental in Rome's rise. As its famous roads were built and expanded, guard posts along the way were manned by small militia and hosts of guard dogs. The Romans also used their large dogs as beasts of burden. It was not unusual to see dogs, along with cattle, oxen, horses and ponies, pulling carts of all sizes from all different parts of the empire.

The Middle Ages and Renaissance

In the period after the fall of the Roman Empire, the bubonic plague, or Black Death, was one of the galvanizing events. It was during this time that the dog acquired its more negative lore. During the plague, in which fleas transported the deadly disease, historian Mary Elizabeth Thurston points out in her book, *The Lost History of the Canine Race*, that the dog, "with its inborn resistance to the plague bacillus," was now on its own. Most livestock was killed by the disease—cattle, sheep, chickens and others. People were killing each other over food. Few people during this period kept pets. Ownerless, dogs ran wild, usually in packs, eating corpses and killing in groups.

During feudal times, the aristocracy assumed ownership of many fertile lands, especially the great forests in which animals and other natural resources were still abundant. During this time, the hunt became ritualized, and dogs were used to pursue various kinds of game. Lords and barons had different dogs to take down deer, bears, bulls, wolves, large fowl, and foxes, and preferred other dogs for small game, mostly vermin. Others were bred for specific duties, such as tracking, coursing, and retrieving on land and in water.

Thurston points out that Henry I of England had a kennel of 200 dogs for huntsmen to train, care for, and deploy. As the aristocracy grew, so did their land claims. And unless you were someone of rank, you could not take game from a claimed preserve.

It was not until after the fall of the French king in the late 1700s, during the French Revolution, that ordinary people were allowed to hunt in the largest and most heavily stocked game forests. In the early 1800s, many lands across Europe were opened up in an attempt to dissuade the masses from overthrowing various monarchies. These policies were part of larger political agendas, which all worked to varying degrees. However, one thing was an absolute success—hunting became popular to the extreme.

The Victorian Era

Queen Victoria was a devoted dog fancier, and when her husband, Prince Albert, suddenly sickened and died in 1861 at the age of forty-two, the saddened Queen grew even fonder of her gentle pets. In her lifetime she raised more than fifteen different breeds of dogs. According to noted historian Paul Johnson, "She formed passionate attachments to animals when a child, and the vehemence with which she fought for their rights persisted to the end. At her various jubilees, prisoners were released all over the Empire provided that she personally signed their remission. There was only one category she refused: those convicted of cruelty to animals, which she called 'one of the worst traits in human nature.'" The Queen was especially fond of a favorite spitz, who was actually allowed to jump on the Queen's breakfast table.

Due to Victoria's love of canines, the dog reached an all-time high status. Your choice of dog conveyed whether you were a sportsman or a true lady. Dogs helped people fulfill their aspirations toward a higher station in life. Indeed, it was in this period that many dog classifications began. It was also a time in which many new dog breeds were bred by varying groups, especially hunters.

In the 1700s and 1800s, many of the sporting breeds, such as the German Shorthaired Pointer, Weimaraner, Vizsla and other hunting dogs, were bred because middle-class Europeans had more time for hunting as recreation, and they wanted one dog to perform a series of functions for which the European aristocracy could previously afford to keep several breeds. Likewise, smaller, toy breeds also became more popular, and many breeds which were hitherto unknown came to the fore.

The different species we are so familiar with today are the result of the continuing quest during this time to find the perfect dog. In many cases throughout history, people have bred dogs for different characteristics such as size, speed, hunting abilities, and others, to produce dogs for a variety of uses. This period became the golden age of the dog.

FACT

The United States may not be known as the country where dogs are especially cherished—for example, In France almost all dogs are welcome in restaurants, whereas in the U.S. only registered service and therapy dogs are—but that doesn't mean it doesn't have its share of people who adore their canine companions. In fact, dogs have been alongside the settlers of the United States since the country's infancy.

Today's World of Dogs

In today's world, there is a different kind of dog for every lifestyle. There are tiny dogs and giant dogs, hairless and shaggy, pedigreed and mixed breed. Dogs who sniff out narcotics or explosives, dogs who search for missing people, dogs who excel at certain sports, dogs who hunt, dogs who are assistants for those with handicaps, and dogs who are simply dogs.

The popularity of dogs is booming all over the world. The clubs and organizations dedicated to certain breeds are helping newcomers to these breeds not only learn more but do more with their dogs. Small dogs, easier to transport and care for, are becoming increasingly prevalent in urban areas. Dog owners have more options than ever to select not only their breed of dog, but everything their dog(s) need, from food to accessories to health care. For many beloved canines, it is a great time to be a dog.

FACT

Upon her death in 2007, the late hotelier Leona Helmsley left $12 million to her Maltese, Trouble, and also requested that the dog be interred with her in her mausoleum upon its death.

On the other hand, it's a fact that caring for a dog is not for everyone. In the end, a dog is still a dog—a living being whose genetic makeup dictates that it behave in certain ways that are not always compatible with ours. In countries where divorce rates are near 50 percent, is it any surprise that family dogs are often turned over to shelters for reasons as absurd as a new dwelling not allowing dogs or a persistent housetraining problem? As spoiled as many dogs are today, there are also many who are languishing (or dying) in shelters.

It is our responsibility to be conscientious and compassionate caregivers to the animals we bring into our lives. *The Everything® New Puppy Book* can be your resource to making the right choices that benefit you and your puppy. Perhaps you, too, will contribute to the wealth of art and literature that helps constitute our relationship with dogs.

CHAPTER 2

Before Getting a Puppy

You've decided that you want a puppy. That's a fine decision, but just remember that what you're really bringing home is a dog. Puppies are very cute and cuddly and small, but they can grow up to be large adult dogs. Bringing home that little bundle of energy and fur is a long-time commitment to another being. You are saying that you want the responsibility of caring for and loving and training an animal: grooming, walking, feeding, taking him to the veterinarian, and paying the bills. This chapter is a reminder of all that goes into sharing your life with a puppy.

Are You Ready for a Puppy?

Of course, you can't wait for that cute little devil to turn your best pair of shoes into the most expensive doggy toy ever created. You can't wait for an accident that permanently scars your off-white rug in the living room. And you can't wait to go home at night instead of hanging out a little later at your favorite nightclub or restaurant with your friends. And of course, most of all, you can't wait for fuzzy-wuzzy to someday slip his leash and make a mad dash across the road, in heavy traffic, so he can finally catch that tasty, tantalizing squirrel. Okay. Okay. You're still reading, you must really want a dog.

Let's be honest, there is nothing better than coming home from a hard day's work and finding that tail-wagging, sloppy-tongued mop of a dog who can't wait to greet you when you arrive home. Dogs are so bouncy and loving and wonderful; there's no getting around it, dogs are wonderful companions. They are fun, friendly, love attention, and most of all, love you—no matter what. They love to play, go for long walks, and be mischievous.

In fact, because of their potentially naughty sides, there are thousands of dogs that are left homeless each year and are sheltered in dog pounds and rescue homes all across the country. Often this is no fault of the dog; instead, it's usually because the cute puppy turned eight months old and started showing an ornery streak, and that was the last straw. When an over-obliging owner suddenly finds himself with a dog who growls when he's told to get off the bed, well, the dog may become a casualty.

People give up their dogs because they didn't fully understand doggy behavior, and all the things that need to be done to keep a dog healthy and well-behaved. They find out that Dalmatians require too much exercise; they didn't know St. Bernards grew *that* big; those tiny Maltese are mischievous balls of fire. Suddenly old Rover finds himself at the shelter with a haunted look on his face, cowering at the back of his pen, as countless strangers pass by and he remains alone. Unfortunately, dogs pay for being disposable with their lives. In fact, every year, thousands of dogs are put down because of neglect or homelessness.

This speaks volumes about how many people don't think through the addition of a dog in their lives. Don't let this happen to you! Ask yourself some important questions before you go running out to get the dog your kids are screaming for or that you think will fill the gap in your life:

- What kind of life do you lead?
- How much room do you have, and what kind of house do you live in?
- What kind of attention do you think you can offer the animal?
- Will someone be home to housetrain and socialize a puppy?
- Do you have a fenced yard?
- How old are your children?
- Does everyone in the family want a dog, or are you caving in to a demanding child?
- Do you want an active dog, a laid-back dog, a big dog, a small dog, a hairy dog, a hairless dog, a slobbery dog, a neat dog?

These are just some of the questions that need your attention before you bring home a puppy. Take this time to think about what you and your family want. Be responsible, and enjoy the comfort, love, and happiness that owning a dog can bring for a long time to come.

A puppy is so adorable that adding one to the family can seem like an easy thing to do. This Cardigan Welsh Corgi is irresistible. But caring for your pup demands time and commitment —are you ready?

Puppies are little bundles of joy. But just remember, junior will grow up. A ten-week old puppy will probably weigh less than 5 to 10 percent of its final body weight. For example, a Labrador Retriever puppy will weigh approximately 5 to 10 pounds. A full-grown Lab might weigh anywhere from 65 to 100 pounds.

Which Puppy Is Best for You?

This is a question most people don't stop to think about, but should. Most of the time when people think of getting a dog, they think about getting a puppy. They think of the cute ball of fluff running around the house making the family laugh. They want to nurture and raise the dog from a pup.

There is nothing that inspires adoration like a young puppy. No matter the breed or mix of breeds, there's something about a puppy that's a few months old that is just, well, precious. With their big, innocent eyes and puppy fur, their spastic movements, and the way they will fall soundly asleep at one moment then bounce to life the next, they are endlessly entertaining and adorable. It can be pure pleasure to nurture and raise a little ball of fluff into a confident and trusted companion.

But think about it: Do you really want a puppy? Is a puppy the best fit with your family's lifestyle? Having a puppy is like having a two-year-old in the house. Puppies want to get into everything, and they use their mouths to explore. They need to chew, and if you don't supply a variety of toys, they'll chew what's available. Puppies need to be kept on very strict schedules in order to be housetrained. That means taking the puppy out first thing in the morning, several times during the day, and last thing at night. It means monitoring the puppy during the day to try to prevent accidents from happening. It means making a real commitment to training and socializing, because when your puppy gets big and he doesn't know what's expected of him, he'll make the rules.

It may be cute to have your puppy curl up on the couch with you or sleep in your bed or jump up on you to greet you, but then don't be surprised if you meet with resistance when your pup's grown up and you don't want him doing those things anymore.

What Older Dogs Have to Offer

When you get a six-month-old youngster you obviously miss the utterly adorable stage of twelve to twenty-four weeks. But let's be honest, a six- to twelve-month-old puppy is still pretty darn cool—and cute. These slightly older puppies are generally a bit calmer, they're usually house-trained, sometimes they've been taught other aspects of basic obedience, and they have a sense of what to expect from people. While the circumstances of their needing a new home may have left them feeling anxious and insecure, in the right home with the right kind of attention and rules, they will soon relax and settle in.

There's also the feel-good part of getting a slightly older puppy, because whether you adopt one from a shelter or a purebred rescue group or just take one in from a neighbor, you are essentially saving that dog's life. Yes, you are inheriting behaviors that the dog has learned from its previous owners or circumstances, but contrary to the old saying, you can teach an old puppy new tricks.

YOUNG PUPPIES VERSUS OLDER PUPPIES: PROS AND CONS

	YOUNG PUPPIES	OLDER PUPPIES
PRO	Cute	Easily (if not already) housetrained
	Playful	Doesn't usually require lots of training
	Cuddly	Playful
	Bonding between you and your dog establishes pack position early	Active Still cute
CON	Needs to be housetrained, socialized, and obedience trained	Miss the early puppy stage
		May inherit someone else's problems

You should always remember that you really don't want a puppy before it is eight to ten weeks old. Puppies younger than eight weeks risk missing a critical development period that takes place in a litter with the mother. The lessons they learn from their littermates and mother at this tender stage help set their temperaments later in life.

Bringing Home More than One

In the search for your new canine family member, you may meet a litter in which more than one of the puppies is available. You may also work through a rescue group that has a pair available that in their opinion shouldn't be separated because they are so close. In either of these scenarios, you are faced with the tough question of whether you should take on the care of not just one, but *two* puppies (or older pups or dogs).

The prospect can be daunting: Double the supplies, double the training, double the food, and double the vet bills. Then again, the prospect can be encouraging: The dogs will always have each other for company; if there are several children in your home, having more than one dog can reduce possessive feelings; you become an instant extended family.

John Whalen lives with his wife and three sons in Maine. When it came time to finding a dog for their family, they all wanted to start with a puppy. They decided on the kind of breed that would be best for their lifestyle (an English Labrador Retriever), and they found a breeder with a litter to choose from. When they got to the breeder's, there were just two puppies left. One appeared to be shy, and the other was obviously very attached to it and somewhat protective. "We had to take both," John said, "It just didn't seem right to separate them."

The Whalens' Labs—Maggie and Gracie—are now nearly five years old. How has it worked out? John describes their companionship as "remarkable"—they are still practically inseparable. The family is not sorry that their girls came together; in fact, they describe puppyhood with two as "double the fun." They say the pluses of having two dogs includes that they always have each other, which makes it easier when they need to leave them with a pet sitter for a few days, and that they entertain each other, which takes some of the pressure off of the family to provide it all themselves. There is less possessiveness among the boys, too. The biggest challenge, according to John, is the training, because they want to be together. For the Whalens, life wouldn't be the same without their sister dogs.

Looking and Learning

The only way to get a realistic grasp of what a specific dog is like is to actually see the dog in action. From veterinarians to breeders to trainers, there are numerous professionals who are usually more than willing to share their wisdom. Asking knowledgeable people will lead you to information you may not have considered, which could help you avoid getting into a bad situation.

QUESTION?

Are all breeders the same?
In general, most breeders are reputable and helpful. However, there are some in the business only for the money. You should try to check as many references as you can about the breeder. Ask for several references, and see what types of responses you get.

The best way to find out about the idiosyncrasies of various breeds, and to really get a good look at them, is to go to dog shows. You'll find representatives of just about all the AKC breeds at a dog show and, best of all, you'll find their breeders—the people who understand them best. Not only that, because you'll get to look around and talk to so many people, you may leave with a completely different idea about what kind of dog you want than you had before you went to the show.

For example, you may think a Beagle will suit everyone in your family. He'll be small enough for the kids, solid enough to be played with, active enough to go on family outings, and not so big you feel he'll take over your small house. When you go to the dog show intent on meeting some local breeders and finding out if they have puppies available, you may see the Beagles in the ring and decide that something about them doesn't appeal to you at all. They always have their noses to the ground; they bark at other dogs too often; they seem aloof. And just as you feel your heart sink, your son tugs your sleeve and says, "Look, what's that?" and you fall in love with a West Highland White Terrier.

Seeing is believing, and being able to talk to breeders is invaluable. Breeders are used to dealing with people in the same situation as you. Also, they want to find the right homes for the dogs they breed. A Husky breeder would not recommend that one of her pups go to a home in which the primary caretaker was wheelchair-bound. That wouldn't be fair to the person, and it wouldn't be fair to the dog.

How do you find dog shows to attend? It's easier than ever with the Internet. Just go to *www.akc.org*, click on Events, and search for Conformation Events in your state. Or you could call the American Kennel Club and ask for show information. The AKC's customer service number is (919) 233-9767.

Many dog shows will feature puppy sweepstakes. No, you won't win a puppy. These are competitions for breeders to show some of their younger dogs. The puppies will be six to eighteen months old. This is an excellent opportunity for prospective dog buyers to see their breed of choice up close. It's also an excellent way to see what these dogs are like as puppies.

Your Lifestyle and Schedule

Puppies can be one of the most difficult things you can add to your life. While they are absolutely adorable, they can also be fur-covered wrecking balls. Plants, throw pillows, carpets, oriental rugs, furniture—absolutely anything is open season. So, whatever dog you choose, you should make sure it fits into your version of what life is like.

When you consider your lifestyle, think about what you do every day. For example:

- What is your idea of fun? Is it rollerblading? Riding your bike? Watching a movie or sports on television? Hiking? Going on day trips in the car? Visiting the park or beach and lying out in the sun?
- Do you work? Part-time? Full-time? Do you put in seventy hours a week? Do you like to come home, shower, and go back out to dinner and the movies or to your favorite bar?
- What about how you keep your home: Are you obsessively neat? Are you allergic to pets? Do you have small children whose toys are all over the house? Do you like to entertain a lot?

You have to ask yourself these kinds of questions when you are choosing the best dog for you. It's important to think about your life before you buy your dog, so that six months later poor Fido isn't back out on the street looking for a new home. Many times people who don't think about what kind of dog they really want are at cross purposes with their dog. You don't want a pet that's going to cramp your style. And of course, you don't want to pick a dog whose life you're going to make miserable.

If you're a rollerblader, you want to know that when you come home, you can suit up, put a leash on Rover, and bring him along. Obviously, you can't do this with a puppy. To find a dog that will want to share in that fun, you need an athletic dog with the stamina and explosive energy to keep up with you. You don't want some sedentary hound who's panting after the first half-mile. Likewise, if you like going for an evening stroll, you don't want some drooling half-lunatic pulling you around the block like a crazed demon. You want a good dog who shares your pace and enjoyment of the evening air.

Maybe you need a dog who can keep up with your children and one you can trust to watch over them. You need your dog not to be a substitute parent or some kind of living, unbreakable toy, but a companion and playmate for your kids to share in their well-behaved fun.

Evaluate Your Lifestyle

If you are a career person, working tons of hours per week, you should probably put your dog-owning desires on hold until your life settles down. If you have roommates or family living with you who are willing to give your dog the attention it needs, then you probably could get a dog. However, a dog will perceive those who show it the most attention as its closest "pack members." Would you really like to own a dog that perceives you as a semi-stranger?

A young married couple who both work and have no children should determine how much time at least one person can be home. A dog cannot be left alone for long periods of time, especially as a way of life. Children can often be an asset in caring for a dog. However, if the child is not old enough to help with caring for the dog, a young couple might find themselves raising two babies!

The main thing to consider is how often your home is empty. If you can afford a dog walker who can take out your dog in the middle of its "home alone" period, that can be a help. Remember, your home is not empty only when you are at work. How often do you like to go out at night? How many weekends do you spend out of town? Does your job send you on a lot of business trips? The less time you can spend at home, the less likely you are ready for a dog.

Your Activity Level

There is a dog for every activity level. But it is extremely important that you match your activity level with the dog you choose. It is all well and good to think: "I should get a dog that will force me to walk more often to get more exercise." In practice, however, most people will revert to their old habits and create an unfair environment for a dog that has been bred for a specific energy level that you knew about well in advance.

On the flip side, if you are a very active person who enjoys outdoor activities, you should get a dog that can keep up with you. A breeder is usually a good person to ask if his or her specific breed of dog is a good match for you. Following is a simple chart that should give you a basic idea of what breed might suit you best.

IF THIS DESCRIBES YOU . . .	THINK ABOUT THESE BREEDS:
I am very active. I like rollerblading, biking, hiking, and swimming.	Dalmatian, German Shorthaired Pointer, English Springer Spaniel, Jack Russell Terrier, Weimeraner, Vizsla, Irish Setter, Doberman Pinscher, Brittany, Alaskan Malamute, Airedale Terrier
I am somewhat active. I jog short distances, I often go on long walks, I like light exercise.	Golden Retriever, Labrador Retriever, German Shepherd Dog, Beagle, Rottweiler, Standard Poodle, Boxer, Siberian Husky, Cocker Spaniel, Shetland Sheep Dog, Australian Sheepdog, Great Dane, Collie, Chinese Shar-Pei, Chow-Chow, Saint Bernard, Mastiff, Chesapeake Bay Retriever, Newfoundland, Bloodhound
I am less active. I like to watch movies, go for a nice stroll, garden in the backyard.	Poodle (Toy or Miniature), Dachshund, Pug, Boston Terrier, Miniature Pinscher, Scottish Terrier, West Highland White Terrier, Cairn Terrier, Bassett Hound, Maltese, Bulldog, Pekinese, Bichon Frise, Lhaso Apso, Corgi (Pembroke and Cardigan)

Consult with a breeder who can help you with specific nuances, such as which dogs will do better with certain types of exercise. You can also look at the same chart in reverse to learn which dogs are a poor match for specific activity levels.

Your Environment

Just as there is a dog for every activity level, there are several dogs that can fare well in all sorts of home environments. Truth be known, pretty much any dog can do well where there's some room to run—whether it be the most active Border Collie, or the tiniest Chihuahua—but certain dogs just fit in certain places better. Following is a chart to help you choose a dog that will fit with your living environment.

IF THIS DESCRIBES YOU . . .   THINK ABOUT THESE BREEDS:

IF THIS DESCRIBES YOU . . .	THINK ABOUT THESE BREEDS:
I live in an apartment in the city.	Poodle (Toy or Miniature), Dachshund, Pug, Boston Terrier, Miniature Pinscher, Scottish Terrier, West Highland White Terrier, Cairn Terrier, Maltese, Bulldog, Pekinese, Bichon Frise, Lhaso Apso, Corgi (Pembroke and Cardigan)
I live in a townhouse in a city.	Any of the above, as well as Basset Hound, Rottweiler, Standard Poodle, Boxer, Cocker Spaniel, Australian Sheepdog, Chinese Shar-Pei, Chow-Chow, Chesapeake Bay Retriever
I have a suburban home.	Golden Retriever, Labrador Retriever, German Shepherd Dog, Beagle, Rottweiler, Standard Poodle, Boxer, Siberian Husky, Cocker Spaniel, Shetland Sheepdog, Australian Sheepdog, Great Dane, Collie, Chinese Shar-Pei, Chow-Chow, St. Bernard, Mastiff, Chesapeake Bay Retriever, Newfoundland, Bloodhound
I live in a rural area.	Dalmatian, German Shorthaired Pointer, English Springer Spaniel, Jack Russell Terrier, Weimaraner, Vizsla, Irish Setter, Doberman Pinscher, Brittany, Akita, Alaskan Malamute, Airedale Terrier, any of the Herding or Working breeds.

The Cost of Acquiring and Keeping a Dog

While it's true that when you want something badly enough you will do whatever is necessary to take care of it, that emotion can often blind you to the very real financial commitment involved. Another truth is that each dog is an individual, and as such it is difficult to generalize about the variable expenses relative to its care. For example, if you get a Poodle, you won't have to factor in the cost of an especially strong vacuum to cope with shed fur, but you will have to factor in regular trips to the groomer's to keep him or her from looking scruffy. The same is true for most terriers.

Another example is health care. You could have a pure-bred dog whose only visits to the veterinarian are for routine checkups or a mixed breed with a persistent problem—or vice versa. The kind of food you choose to feed will vary tremendously in cost, and the kinds and quantity of "stuff" you get for your dog will vary, as well.

This begs the question: Is it possible to determine the cost of dog ownership? Fortunately, there is an organization that helps with just that. It's the American Pet Products Manufacturing Association (APPMA), and it regularly calculates and approximates the costs. According to the APPMA, Americans spend over $40 billion a year on their pets, with food and veterinary care consistently topping the charts. You can learn more about pet spending at *www.appma.org* and searching for Industry Trends.

CHAPTER 3

Exploring Different Breeds of Dogs

Even if your puppy is a mixed breed, you can learn a lot about his behavior by reading this chapter. The way your puppy acts has a lot to do with how he looks. That is, if he looks like a hound (and he's either a purebred hound of some type or he has some hound blood in him), he's going to act like a hound. By learning how hounds act, you're going to understand his behavior that much more. This section is intended to help you better understand your dog, or to help you shop for the kind of dog you think would best suit your lifestyle. But remember, every dog is an individual. That's why it's important to talk to other owners of the kind of dog you have or are interested in.

Where to Begin

There are several hundred breeds of dogs from around the world—and many encyclopedias that show pictures of them. This book will base its discussions on the classification system established by the American Kennel Club (AKC). Kennel clubs around the world use similar systems of breed classifications; in fact, the American Kennel Club's is based on one developed by The Kennel Club in the United Kingdom.

FACT

The largest registering organizations for purebred dogs around the world include the American Kennel Club (AKC); Canadian Kennel Club (CKC); The Kennel Club (KC) in the United Kingdom; Federation Cynologique International (FCI), based in Belgium and also known as the World Canine Organisation; and the United Kennel Club (UKC) in the U.S.

The AKC categorizes the different breeds by groups to make understanding the big picture a little easier. Each breed group has distinguishing characteristics that are shared by all the breeds in it. Currently, there are seven breed groups recognized by the American Kennel Club. They are as follows:

- Herding
- Hound
- Non-Sporting
- Sporting
- Terrier
- Toy
- Working

The American Kennel Club also has a Miscellaneous Class, a sort of "holding" group for breeds that have not met all the criteria for full registration (of which there are many), and recently the AKC instituted a Foundation Stock Service (FSS) category to assist rare breeds in gaining recognition. More on the breeds in these groups at the end of the chapter. For now, here's a profile of the seven AKC breed groups and some of the most popular breeds in them.

The Herding Group

The herding group is a relatively new group, having been established in 1983. Herding breeds were originally part of the working group, but when it became large and unmanageable, breeds were subtracted from it and the herding group was established. Some of the oldest dogs known are in this group; their early jobs were guarding and managing the livestock of our nomadic ancestors.

These are some of the smartest, most trainable, and energetic dogs. It is important to remember that they have been bred to herd, and it is in their genes to perform that job. While you are walking down the street they will want to circle you—especially if you are with a friend, loved one, or family. The bigger the crowd, the more they want to shape you into a nice group.

The herding group tends to have dogs who bark a lot. These are dogs with natural instincts to communicate—with one another and with people. Having been used through the centuries to generally guard sheep and cattle, it is not above them to nip and snarl to get their charges to move where they want them to.

This Australian Shepherd puppy is a member of the herding group, known for intelligence, protective instincts, and devout loyalty.

These breeds are generally happiest in homes with large yards, and should be given plenty to do. In general, they are very active, so you need to be able to keep them busy. These dogs really, really want to work; they have the bodies and minds to do jobs and do them well. That's why you find so many herding breeds in obedience, agility, herding, and flyball competitions.

They usually make excellent guard dogs. Herding dogs were meant to guard the sheep and cattle as well as herd them. They were an especially important part of keeping away other predators. Many of them are aggressive, ferocious fighters, who are strong and willful. Herding breeds have long been employed as police dogs, as well. Some have even been trained as guide dogs for the blind. Not all of these dogs are for the novice owner. Indeed, many of these dogs were developed to think on their own, or do the bidding of their human counterpart. When you are unsure, you will either fill them with confusion or they will fill the breach, and make decisions for themselves. You need to be the lead dog—and they will follow. Many dogs in this group respond quickly and easily to obedience; in fact, they excel at it.

The AKC herding breeds are:

- Australian Cattle Dog
- Australian Shepherd
- Bearded Collie
- Beauceron
- Belgian Malinois
- Belgian Sheepdog
- Belgian Tervuren
- Border Collie
- Bouvier des Flandres
- Briard
- Canaan Dog
- Cardigan Welsh Corgi
- Collie
- German Shepherd Dog
- Old English Sheepdog
- Pembroke Welsh Corgi
- Polish Lowland
- Puli

- Shetland Sheepdog
- Swedish Vallhund

Many are surprised to learn that there are two distinct Welsh Corgis—the Cardigan and the Pembroke. Renowned as the beloved dogs of Queen Elizabeth II of England, Pembrokes are more familiar. It is actually the Cardigan who is the more ancient breed. He is typically dark-colored and he has a tail (whereas the Pembroke does not). It is believed the Cardigan migrated to Wales with the Celts around 1200 B.C.

The Hound Group

The hound group has in it some dogs whose ancestors were man's earliest companions and assistants. Alexander the Great hunted with hounds. This category also offers the widest range in size of any group. The smallest hound is the Dachshund, which is the only dog in this group that is neither a sight- nor a scenthound, but rather a dog that was bred to hunt smaller game "to ground," going gamely into burrows and dens for small mammals like a terrier. The largest dog in the group is the Irish Wolfhound, a giant bred to fearlessly pursue and bring down wolves.

Hounds generally are grouped together because they will actually hunt down prey and either corner it or kill it. They will not wait for the hunter but will let the hunter know where they are by various types of barking ("giving voice"). Hound people make a distinction between a hound barking (meaning just your average dog bark) and when a hound is "baying" or "tonguing." These terms refer to the different types of barking that a hound makes when on the trail, hot behind some fast-moving game.

Hounds are generally categorized into two distinct groups. The first are the scenthounds. These are the trackers who hunt with their noses. The best known of these are Beagles, Bassets, Bloodhounds, and Foxhounds. The other group is sighthounds. These are the hounds bred to pursue swift game by keeping their eyes on it. Popular breeds of sighthounds include the Greyhound, Afghan Hound, and Basenji.

This short-haired Dachshund puppy is a member of the hound group, known for its breeds' exceptional abilities to track and pursue quarry.

All hounds were bred for very specific purposes, and many date back either to the feudal hunts or back to ancient Egypt. The Irish Wolfhound hunted wolves; the Beagle and the Petit Basset Griffon Vendeen hunted rabbit; the Otterhound hunted otter; the Scottish Deerhound hunted deer; and the Rhodesian Ridgeback hunted lions.

The most popular hounds (by AKC registrations) are the Beagle, Dachshund, Basset Hound, Bloodhound, and Rhodesian Ridgeback. Most scenthounds have loud voices—and they like to use them! The sighthounds are more cat-like and aloof. All hounds share the characteristic of being independent thinkers, even though many hunt in packs. In a pack, each hound's duty is to nose up the game and keep on the trail, or, as a sighthound, to outsmart the prey by matching it swift turn by swift turn, simultaneously closing in for the kill.

Scenthounds tend to be social and easygoing, though their noses so dominate their lives that it can be hard for them to pay attention to anything but what's around to be sniffed. And since a dog's sense of smell is infinitely better than ours, your scenthound may become distracted by something you didn't know was there. He will seem to spend his every waking moment engaged in sniffing the floor, sidewalk, yard, kitchen—his whole environment. When you feel like your scenthound puppy is being inordinately stubborn, remember that he's from the same family as the Bloodhound, a dog whose whole reason for being is to find a trace of scent that could be months old and find its source. You've got to have one amazing nose to do that!

The more the merrier! Two popular hounds, Beagles and Dachshunds, come in multiple sizes. Beagles can be under 13 inches in height, or 13–15 inches in height; Dachshunds can be Standard (16–32 pounds), and Miniature (11 pounds and under). Dachshunds also have three coat types: smooth, longhaired, and wirehaired.

Sighthounds seem particularly aloof to strangers, but those who live with them know that like all hounds, they are motivated by good food and soft beds. For breeds that can achieve some of the fastest speeds of all land animals, sighthounds can be the biggest slugs around. The fact is, their top speeds and intense pursuits only come in bursts. The rest of the time they're happy to sit in your lap—even the mighty Irish Wolfhound! Hounds may not demand the most from you in terms of exercise requirements, but their independent natures can occasionally try your patience.

These are the members of the AKC hound group:

- Afghan Hound
- American Foxhound
- Basenji
- Basset Hound
- Beagle
- Black and Tan Coonhound
- Bloodhound
- Borzoi
- Dachshund

- English Foxhound
- Greyhound
- Harrier
- Ibizan Hound
- Irish Wolfhound
- Norwegian Elkhound
- Otterhound
- Petit Basset Griffon Vendéen
- Pharaoh Hound
- Plott
- Rhodesian Ridgeback
- Saluki
- Scottish Deerhound
- Whippet

ALERT!

Not all hounds bark, they bay. Baying is like a loud, prolonged bark combined with a howl. This trait proves very useful to hunters who need to follow their dogs while they're on a scent, but might not be very pleasant to you or your neighbors. It's important to teach hounds that their voices aren't appreciated by all from an early age.

The Non-Sporting Group

These dogs have one thing in common—none of them fits neatly into any of the breed groups. While some of them were working or sporting dogs in previous lives, their jobs have been so long outmoded that they have primarily been companion dogs for almost a century, in some cases longer.

Other than that, let's be honest, this is a miscellaneous crowd as far as the AKC and other breeders are concerned. But in here you have some very popular, if disparate, dogs. You have the Poodle (originally one of Europe's finest hunting dogs); the Dalmatian (the ubiquitous coach dog); the Bulldog (used to bait bulls centuries ago); the Bichon Frise (a companion dog too big for the Toy Group); and many, many others.

The Bulldog is one of the most distinct members of the non-sporting group, which is an eclectic mix of breeds. Representing courage and tenacity, he is a popular mascot for sports teams.

All of the dogs in this group are very much worth looking at—especially so, because the dog world lumped them together for no better reason that they couldn't pigeonhole these iconoclasts! Deciding on a breed from this group is even tougher than the others because you won't have those common traits you can refer back to when you're trying to explain your breed's behavior. Discovering the pros and cons of these dogs is even more fun! The histories on these breeds are usually fairly extensive, so you can be assured you're getting a dog with characteristics that have been mulled over for a long, long time.

The members of the non-sporting group are:

- American Eskimo Dog
- Bichon Frise
- Boston Terrier
- Bulldog
- Chinese Shar-Pei
- Chow Chow
- Dalmatian

- Finnish Spitz
- French Bulldog
- Keeshound
- Lhasa Apso
- Löwchen
- Poodle (Standard and Miniature)
- Schipperke
- Shiba Inu
- Tibetan Spaniel
- Tibetan Terrier

FACT

So thoroughly associated with courage, strength, and resolution is the Bulldog, that he is the mascot of numerous sports teams and—of highest distinction—the United States Marines.

The Sporting Group

The AKC sporting group is made up of some of the oldest and most popular breeds registered by the AKC. Many of the dogs in this category were bred for hunting. Specifically, they were bred for either one or two of the following purposes: to point, retrieve, or flush game birds. That is why the sporting group is composed of pointers, retrievers, and setters—specific examples are the German Shorthaired Pointer, the Labrador Retriever, and the Cocker Spaniel.

While many people who own sporting breeds will never need them to do anything but be the family pet, they will get to see their dogs using their hunting instincts around the house. These traits can be some of the most enjoyable aspects of owning a sporting dog. For example, it's wonderful to see your Weimaraner go on point while running along a hedgerow; it's fun to have your Lab or Golden tirelessly retrieve a tennis ball from a lake or the ocean; it's reassuring to have your English Springer Spaniel go back and forth in front of you on a walk (this is called quartering in the hunt field). But be forewarned: your dog is a dog, and one day he may come back with not just a ball or toy, but with the real thing:

a dead animal. Generations of breeders instilled the pointing, retrieving, and quartering instincts in the sporting breeds so that their dogs could do their part to bring food to the table. Your purebred sporting dog has that in his blood—and he's proud of it!

Another characteristic of the sporting breeds is an outgoing personality. As dogs who worked singly or in pairs with their masters, the sporting dogs needed to be enthusiastic, responsive partners. For example, if a spaniel or pointer flushed a bird and then took off after it, the hunter would not be able to take a shot at the bird. Therefore, the sporting breeds were trained to find the game, then hold their ground while the hunter took his shot, then go gangbusters to find and bring back the game with as little damage as possible. Sporting dogs had to be able to do this all day, if necessary; strength and stamina were highly desired. The better and longer the dog worked, the more prized it was.

With this in mind, what can you expect from your sporting breed? A never-say-die attitude (whether you're ready to quit or not); a passion for the pursuit of game, whether it's to retrieve or dash through fields and woods; an in-your-face enthusiasm for everything you do; an athlete who thrives on sharing the great outdoors with you.

This Labrador Retriever pup is a classic example of a sporting breed, a group known for its enthusiasm, responsiveness, and athleticism.

In the United States, the American Cocker is simply called the Cocker Spaniel; in England, the English refer to what we call the English Cocker Spaniel as the Cocker Spaniel.

Here are the breeds in the sporting group:

- American Water Spaniel
- Brittany
- Chesapeake Bay Retriever
- Clumber Spaniel
- Cocker Spaniel
- Curly-Coated Retriever
- English Cocker Spaniel
- English Setter
- English Springer Spaniel
- Field Spaniel
- Flat-Coated Retriever
- German Shorthaired Pointer
- German Wirehaired Pointer
- Golden Retriever
- Gordon Setter
- Irish Setter
- Irish Water Spaniel
- Labrador Retriever
- Nova Scotia Duck Tolling Retriever
- Pointer
- Spinone Italiano
- Sussex Spaniel
- Vizsla
- Weimaraner
- Welsh Springer Spaniel
- Wirehaired Pointing Griffon

The Terrier Group

The dogs in this group are by turns tenacious, lovable, energetic, and downright funny. Terriers are basically a group that is mostly made up of a number of wire-haired, smaller dogs that were originally bred to help landowners and gamekeepers keep undesirables off their properties—namely raccoons, foxes, rats, weasels, and badgers.

The word terrier finds its root in the Latin word *terra*, which means earth. And that's what many of these dogs were and still are used for. They were bred from way back to start digging to either kill or chase out animals that went to ground for cover or safety. They would bark and dig simultaneously, driving away vermin, or fighting their adversaries right there in the den's entrance. Indeed, many dogs in the terrier group have short, strong tails that many a gamekeeper or huntsman used to pull the little fighter out when it seemed he might be getting the worse of the scrap, or when the accompanying man thought that the contest had already been decided.

For the most part, terriers are well suited to urban, suburban, or rural life. However, they are determined little dogs, and require kind and consistent training to keep them on the straight and narrow. Like some of their larger brethren, these dogs need obedience and love; they need a real leader to keep them from ruining the house or backyard.

There is another thing that must be stated here: Don't be fooled by the package. Just because some of the terriers are small doesn't mean they are suitable apartment dogs. Terriers are opinionated, scrappy, feisty, fun-loving, high-energy animals that require extensive exercise, attention, and time. Their wiry coats also need special grooming. Many of them don't shed, and left to grow, your should-be-sleek terrier could look like a poor bedraggled orphan of a dog.

Terriers have been the steadfast companions of sportsmen and women for centuries. They thrive on being part of the action, and were common escorts in country carriages or urban avenues. In *The Wizard of Oz*, Toto is a Cairn Terrier who never leaves Dorothy's side, come tornado, wicked witch, or scary lion. Many of the terriers originated in the British Isles and are said to share the characteristics of their peoples: the stubborn but lovable Scots, the impish and wise Irish, and the adventurous, self-confident English. Study the history of these islands and you'll learn a lot about your terrier.

Terriers are steadfast and passionate companions who have a never-say-never attitude. This Norwich Terrier puppy has the sparkle in its eyes typical of terriers.

The AKC-recognized terriers are:

- Airedale Terrier
- American Staffordshire Terrier
- Australian Terrier
- Bedlington Terrier
- Border Terrier
- Bull Terrier
- Cairn Terrier
- Dandie Dinmont Terrier
- Glen of Imal Terrier
- Irish Terrier
- Kerry Blue Terrier
- Lakeland Terrier
- Manchester Terrier
- Miniature Bull Terrier
- Miniature Schnauzer
- Norfolk Terrier
- Norwich Terrier

- Parson Russell Terrier
- Scottish Terrier
- Sealyham Terrier
- Skye Terrier
- Smooth Fox Terrier
- Soft Coated Wheaten Terrier
- Staffordshire Bull Terrier
- Welsh Terrier
- West Highland White Terrier
- Wire Fox Terrier

The Toy Group

The AKC toy group is comprised exclusively of some of the smallest dogs in the canine world—and also some of the cutest! Many of these cuddly little rascals have been bred purely for companionship, and were never intended for anything other than being a pet. Some of them come from very obscure backgrounds, but make no mistake—these are dogs.

The most amazing thing about little dogs is that they think just like big dogs. They mark territory; they are loving; they are protective; they are great watchdogs; and they will bite, too, if they feel threatened. The best thing about them is they get away with a lot more because of their size and cuteness, and guard their privileges jealously: they are usually welcome on the couch to sleep in your lap; they're usually allowed in public places and on transportation, where their larger cousins are absolutely forbidden; hotels even sometimes turn a blind eye to them. At the very least, they're so small, they're easier to hide!

Some of these dogs are so small, that many centuries ago in Europe they were called sleeve dogs, because ladies of means hid the dogs in their sleeves! Many of these breeds have stories about them regarding royalty. Many is the breed whose vigilant watch over his master included warnings in the middle of the night of shrill barking, announcing approaching assassins.

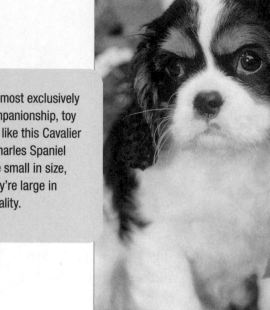

Bred almost exclusively for companionship, toy breeds like this Cavalier King Charles Spaniel may be small in size, but they're large in personality.

Toy dogs tend to be smart and feisty. They can be trained easily for the most part and many do not require too much exercise. These are all good house and apartment dogs. They love attention and they expect to get it. They also require grooming, and they love that, too.

If toy dogs are small, imagine how small toy puppies are! This is why many breeders discourage households with small children from getting a toy breed puppy. Even well-meaning and well-behaved children can cause serious damage to a tiny toy breed puppy. But because toy breeds don't necessarily think of themselves as "toys," many of them can handle the youngest members of a family just fine. If a toy breed is for you and you have very young children in the house, talk to other owners and breeders before bringing a puppy home. This is a good time to remember that there are often older dogs that need homes; perhaps a rescue toy is best for your family!

The dogs in the toy group in the American Kennel Club are:

- Affenpinscher
- Brussels Griffon
- Cavalier King Charles Spaniel
- Chihuahua
- Chinese Crested
- English Toy Spaniel
- Havanese
- Italian Greyhound
- Japanese Chin
- Maltese
- Manchester Terrier (Toy)
- Miniature Pinscher
- Papillon
- Pekingese
- Pomeranian
- Poodle (Toy)
- Pug
- Shih Tzu
- Silky Terrier
- Toy Fox Terrier
- Yorkshire Terrier

ALERT!

If you are a parent, it is important that you consider the following before you undertake buying a toy breed. They are delicate little animals that will be easily injured if handled roughly, and may also bite if cornered or mistreated. If you're not sure how your children would handle a toy breed, you should consider something a little bigger that can take the tussle and playfulness of small children with confidence.

The Working Group

Most of the dogs in the working group were bred for specific jobs other than hunting. Many of the breeds date back to Roman times, where guarding valuables, like property and family, was often a daily necessity. However, there were other jobs to be done. The Greater Swiss Mountain Dog was used to drive cattle and was the most popular dog in the Alps until about fifty years ago. The Portuguese Water Dog was the fisherman's dog, used to retrieve items, or people, that had fallen overboard or to carry messages from one boat to another. The Newfoundland was bred for hauling in huge fishing nets laden with fresh fish. Saint Bernards were rescue dogs, saving lives throughout the Alps. And of course, the Alaskan Malamute and the Siberian Husky were sled dogs, pulling men and their families back and forth across frozen tundra.

There are many popular dogs in this group, most notably the Rottweiler, Doberman Pinscher, Akita, and Mastiff, which were bred primarily as guard dogs. They are powerful dogs, and when properly trained and socialized, make invaluable friends. These dogs will risk life and limb to protect their families, and are a great source of pride and love. However, there are many people who have given these dogs a bad name. Because they are powerful, large dogs, if they are not trained and socialized with other dogs properly, they can become a menace. It is not in their nature to be—it is in the nature of people who buy these dogs and then encourage them to be that way.

These oh-so-cute Samoyed pups, who now resemble stuffed toys, will grow to be large, strong, and hard-working dogs who demonstrate unwavering companionship all day every day.

Things can and should be much different for your puppy, whose family is part of the honorable working group. Owners of breeds like Bernese Mountain Dogs and Siberian Huskies now delight in training their dogs to pull sleds or wagons laden with people and things. Samoyeds make great hiking companions, able to nimbly carry packs with supplies along steep mountain trails. The athletic and noble Boxer excels in almost all canine performance events. Your working group pup will soon grow into his feet, and he'll be happiest if he can put them to use assisting in the daily enjoyment of his family unit.

The breeds in the AKC working group are:

- Akita
- Alaskan Malamute
- Anatolian Shepherd Dog
- Bernese Mountain Dog
- Black Russian Terrier
- Boxer
- Bullmastiff
- Doberman Pinscher
- Dogue de Bordeaux
- German Pinscher
- Giant Schnauzer
- Great Dane
- Great Pyrenees
- Greater Swiss Mountain Dog
- Komondor
- Kuvaz
- Mastiff
- Neaoplitan Mastiff
- Newfoundland
- Portuguese Water Dog
- Rottweiler
- Saint Bernard
- Samoyed
- Siberian Husky
- Standard Schnauzer
- Tibetan Mastiff

Rare Breeds, Designer Dogs, and Mixed Breeds

Most certainly there are other breeds. This chapter has only skimmed the surface of the most popular breeds in the seven AKC-recognized groups. There are many dogs in the world that are not recognized by the AKC—including the now-trendy "designer dogs," and mixed breeds, the perennial favorite of many.

Rare Breeds

Why are there so many purebred dogs that are not registered with the American Kennel Club? It's not because they're unworthy; it's simply because they don't have a large enough representation in the United States, or a well-organized breed club, or a proven breeding record.

Until they are recognized (at which time individual dogs and litters may be registered with the AKC and the breed may compete in all AKC-sanctioned events) the breeds are accepted for recording in the FSS, and if they reach a particular benchmark, are considered part of the miscellaneous class (MC). MC breeds may compete in select AKC events until they achieve full recognition. Visit *www.akc.org* to learn the status of a breed you might be interested in, as it can happen slowly or quickly. The FSS breeds (which include some MC breeds) are:

- American English Coonhound
- Appenzeller Sennenhunde
- Argentine Dogo
- Azawakh
- Barbet
- Belgian Laekenois
- Bergamasco
- Berger Picard
- Bluetick Coonhound
- Boerboel
- Bolognese
- Boykin Spaniel
- Bracco Italiano
- Cane Corso

- Catahoula Leopard Dog
- Caucasian Mountain Dog
- Central Asian Shepherd Dog
- Cesky Terrier
- Chinook
- Cirneco dell'Etna
- Coton de Tulear
- Czechoslovakian Wolfdog
- Entlebucher Mountain Dog
- Estrela Mountain Dog
- Eurasier
- Finnish Lapphund
- German Spitz
- Grand Basset Griffon Vendéen
- Icelandic Sheepdog
- Irish Red and White Setter
- Jindo
- Kai Ken
- Karelian Bear Dog
- Kishu Ken
- Kooikerhondje
- Lagotto Romagnolo
- Lancashire Heeler
- Leonberger
- Mudi
- Norrbottenspets
- Norwegian Buhund
- Norwegian Lundehund
- Perro de Presa Canario
- Peruvian Inca Orchid
- Portuguese Podengo
- Portuguese Pointer
- Pumi
- Pyrenean Shepherd
- Rafeiro do Alentejo
- Rat Terrier

- Redbone Coonhound
- Russell Terrier
- Russian Toy
- Schapendoes
- Sloughi
- Small Munsterlander Pointer
- Spanish Mastiff
- Spanish Water Dog
- Stabyhoun
- Swedish Lapphund
- Thai Ridgeback
- Tosa
- Treeing Tennessee Brindle
- Treeing Walker Coonhound
- Wirehaired Vizsla
- Xoloitzcuintli

QUESTION?

What about the American Pit Bull Terrier?
The popular American Pit Bull Terrier is registered by the United Kennel Club and is a very close relation of the AKC-recognized American Staffordshire Terrier. Unfortunately, like the Rottweiler or the Doberman in the past, the Pit Bull has gotten a bad rep as a vicious breed by people who use him as a guard dog.

Designer Dogs

This is a relatively new designation of purebred dog crosses that have caught the public's attention. They've been named after the breeds that produced them and put into the category of "designer dogs." Here you'll find popular Poodle crosses—the Labradoodle, Goldendoodle, and Schnoodles (to name a few)—as well as Puggles (Pug/Beagle), Morkies (Maltese/Yorkshire Terrier), and Imo-Inu (American Eskimo/Shiba Inu). In fact, the American Canine Hybrid Club, based in Harvey, Arkansas, registered over 400 breed crosses at the time of this book's writing. (Go to *www.achclub.com* to see the full listing.)

This curious puppy is a Schnoodle—a cross between a Miniature Schnauzer and a Poodle —one of many "designer dog" breeds that have become increasingly popular.

Mixed Breeds

There is a lot of information written about purebreds because they've been selectively bred to look and act in particular ways. This should simplify choosing your family dog. But it can also make it seem quite complicated! There are so many choices, so many things to think about. After investigating all the breeds, you may find that none especially fits you.

If you're worn out on the purebred route, or it simply doesn't matter that much to you how much you know about your dog's genetic makeup, you may want to adopt a mixed breed dog. (These dogs used to be called "mutts" but it is agreed that they deserve a title that's less pejorative.) While these dogs are sometimes not the most beautiful dogs you have ever seen, and you may never be sure whether their instincts are coming from retriever blood or terrier blood or perhaps a bit of everything, mixed breeds can make superlative pets.

Mixed breed puppies come in all shapes, sizes, colors, coat types, and personalities. Sometimes you'll know their parentage, sometimes you won't. This can be a risk, but for those who take them in, it is usually well worth it.

Mixed breed dogs often marry the best traits of the dogs they're descended from. It is fun to try to guess what breeds went into making your dog. In some cases you'll know, like if your Lab bred the Australian Cattle Dog next door by mistake, but in many cases you won't know at all. The British magazine *Dogs Today* runs a monthly contest for its readership to try to guess the parentage of a mixed breed dog. It's fun!

In the end, neither a purebred nor a mixed breed is going to be a better dog than the other. Both are dogs. The important considerations are, again, how well your lifestyle accommodates your dog's basic needs. If he's a big, hairy purebred or a big, hairy mix and you're a neat freak who lives in a fifth-floor walkup, things might not work out.

Whether you choose purebred or mixed, you have to realistically assess the amount of time and energy you have to take care of your dog the way he deserves (and needs) to be taken care of. Remember, while quality breeding is important to keep the various breeds alive, dogs, unlike humans, don't differentiate between breed and non-breed. Dogs only care that you are their primary caregiver and leader. What kind of dog will you choose?

CHAPTER 4

Where to Get a Puppy

Buying a dog isn't like buying a new shirt. Even if you are dead-set on getting a specific breed of dog, you should not rush into this kind of purchase. Although careful breeding makes each individual in a breed share a set of common traits, there are still subtle and not-so-subtle differences between individual dogs. In addition, some less scrupulous breeders have over-bred and inbred many purebred dogs, creating low-quality specimens. You may think it's simply too time-consuming to work with a breeder—your kids want a puppy now!—but the research you do and time you spend to find the right puppy can spare you the heartbreak of bringing home the wrong one.

Breeders

Be forewarned: Not all breeders are nice. Remember, though, that where puppies are concerned, this is a good thing. Would you expect a mother putting her child up for adoption to want her baby to go to just anyone? If she did, how would you feel about her? Now transfer that to a responsible, reputable dog breeder. This is someone who cares about her dogs and the puppies they produce for their lifetimes. This is someone who knows that if a puppy goes home with a family whose kids are involved in all kinds of after-school activities, where the parents work full-time, they enjoy extended holidays, and they just moved into a big house that doesn't have a fenced yard, the puppy is going to be at risk for neglect. Long hours alone, an unsafe place to play, and regular visits to a boarding kennel are in this pup's future. It may be a financially secure and harmonious family, but it's not a home for a puppy.

It is a breeder's job to secure the safest and most compatible homes possible for their puppies. You must understand and respect this going into the deal. For your efforts—and those of the breeder—if you are the right person for one of her pups, you can practically guarantee that raising your puppy will be much easier than you thought. The breeder is your go-to person for any and all questions you may have at any time.

ALERT!

While there are many excellent and qualified breeders around, there are always a few who are not as reputable. Be suspicious of any breeder who doesn't want to show you health records of the parents, who won't introduce you to the parents, or who wants you to take a puppy before it is eight to ten weeks of age.

Here are some questions you should ask a breeder:

1. How long have you been breeding these dogs?
2. Did you breed any dogs other than these? If so, for how long?
3. When is the last time you showed one of your dogs?

4. Are either the sire or the dam finished champions? May I see their pedigrees?

5. Do either of them have working titles earned in obedience or other performance events?

6. Have the dogs been tested for hip dysplasia, eye problems, heart problems, or whatever genetic conditions relate to the breed? (Breeders should be only too happy to show you pedigrees and health certificates. If they're reluctant or say they'll show you when you come to pick up the puppy, don't trust them. These documents should be readily available.)

7. Are either of the parents on the premises, and if so, may I see them? (Ask about other siblings, too.)

8. Have the puppies had their shots? What shots and when?

9. Is the litter registered? Will I go home with my puppy's registration? (If not, again, suspect trouble.)

10. May I have the names of references to call?

When considering your selection of a puppy —and a breeder—ask lots of questions, visit the pups, and be mindful of all aspects of the breeder's care of the pups and the pups' parents.

Your Purebred Dog's Papers

Besides being ambassadors and safe-keepers for their breeds, reputable breeders are also businesspeople. When you purchase a puppy from a breeder, you should be supplied with the following:

- The puppy's pedigree
- A registration form
- The puppy's health records from birth
- A recommended feeding plan and diet
- A list of recommended supplies
- Anything else the breeder deems relevant to the puppy's care

The pedigree and registration papers can seem confusing, and the breeder should explain what to do with them. Basically, the pedigree tells you the dog's family (genetic) background, and usually goes back five generations. In short, it's a family tree that shows you who's who in your dog's life. Many times the dog has champions in his bloodline. Of course, the nearer the champion to your dog, the better your dog is supposed to be as a representative of the breed. The pedigree is optional, but most breeders include it.

The registration form must be turned over to you the very day you purchase or acquire your puppy. This form allows you to officially register your dog with the American Kennel Club (or another registry if the breed isn't AKC recognized). The breeder should have registered the entire litter that included your puppy when it was born, at which time he or she received individual registration forms for each of the puppies in the litter. Breeders are responsible for keeping all their paperwork up to date, and have to record the sale of each puppy. It is then up to you to fill out your pup's registration form and send it in with the required fee to the registering body.

Remember, just because your dog is a registered purebred does not mean his health or worth are guaranteed in any way. You will know the value of your dog by discussing his pedigree with your breeder. If there are no champions or dogs who've earned working titles in his line, then you shouldn't consider breeding him. In fact, your breeder will probably insist you sign a spay/neuter contract. If you want to show your dog, you need to find as much out about showing as possible before you try it, otherwise you may come away frustrated and broke. Find a breeder who can be your mentor should you choose to compete in this exciting sport.

FACT

Responsible breeders understand the dynamics of early puppyhood and use the information they gain from watching the puppies to help pair them with future owners. The breeder may decide that a family with active, assertive children may intimidate a lesser-ranked pup and want to pair that family with a more confident puppy who can take care of himself. Similarly, a more gregarious pup in a reserved, quiet family may grow to dominate them.

Purebred Rescue

A rescue dog is a purebred who has been "rescued" from a former home or from a pound or shelter and is currently homeless. Most AKC breed clubs sponsor purebred rescue groups. When a dog is dropped off at the shelter or taken into the dog pound, if that dog is believed to be purebred, that local shelter calls the contact person for the local rescue group. If the rescue coordinator believes the dog is a purebred of the breed in which he or she is involved, that dog is taken from the pound and housed in a foster home until the rescue organization can find the dog a home.

Many of the dogs in rescue groups tend to be mature, older dogs, but you may be surprised to learn many dogs are actually under eighteen months of age! Rescue is run generally by breeders who are very concerned about dogs in general. They make no money from this, and usually work on a volunteer basis. Much of the cost of fostering is picked up by the family who is sheltering the dog in their house. Each breed has a specific network of these people who have extremely big hearts, and only want to see the dogs find a good home.

Do these dogs have something wrong with them? Generally speaking, no. Sometimes they end up in rescue because their owners have not been able to adjust to having a puppy in their lives. Or, they have been housed by people who no longer were able to properly care for their animals, because of difficult circumstances or a death in the family. Rescue coordinators bail out abandoned or unwanted dogs and evaluate them before seeking new homes for them. Many rescue dogs need some stability to help regain their self-confidence, and foster owners spend a lot of time working with such animals to ensure that they'll adjust to a new home.

They then list the dog with a national or regional network, where the dog will eventually be placed. All kinds of dogs pass through this scenario. Generally speaking, they tend to be a little older than puppies, usually from eighteen months to ten years old. They come in all shapes, sizes, and temperaments. The only thing they have in common is that they are all purebreds.

Because they are rescue dogs, they also tend to be less expensive up front—though cost is no guarantee of the quality of a pup or dog. The rescue associations usually ask you to make some kind of donation to defray the costs of operating the rescue group and caring for the individual dog. These groups are run by loving individuals who are looking earnestly for the right home for the right dog. You should seriously consider this venue as a means to getting a dog.

Humane Societies and Animal Shelters

One place you can always find either new puppies or slightly older puppies is your local animal shelter. These are in operation all over the United States. Some dogs are brought there by their current owners, or by the families of those persons. Sometimes the dogs are found on the side of the road by a concerned citizen who can't shelter the animal, or they are brought in by the local animal control department.

They may be perfectly fine animals who just need a home. In many cases, the animals take a little time to adjust when you first bring them home. Dogs want to be part of a pack. Being moved from pack to pack undermines a dog's self-assurance. A pack position is very important to a dog, being separated and then situated into a new pack definitely plays games with poor Rover's head. The longer period of time a dog spends with you, the more secure it will become in its surroundings and the more comfortable it will feel with you.

The puppy that's right for your family is one whose background has been thoroughly researched so that its innate instincts as well as its individual characteristics are suitable for its new home (your home!). Chances are much higher that such a pup will fit in with and be loved by everyone, which is what a puppy most needs.

Sometimes the shelters have lots of information on a particular dog, and sometimes they have none. But many of the people who work in shelters are there because they love animals and spend great amounts of time with them. They are often the best judges of what these dogs like and don't like. In short, if you don't care about purebred versus mixed breed, there are plenty of puppies that need a good home. They will need a little extra loving and some space before they can become more confident, but will make it up to you with love and admiration. Later chapters will talk about the special needs of rescue and shelter dogs when you first bring them home.

Questions to Ask at the Shelter

Make sure you learn as much as you can regarding the puppy you want to adopt from the shelter. Questions to ask include the following:

1. Why is the puppy up for adoption?
2. Who were the previous owners?
3. Was the animal abused?
4. Are its littermates present? If so, may you see them together?
5. Is the mother here? If so, may you see her as well?
6. May you spend more than a few minutes with the puppy in order to decide?
7. Has the puppy been checked by a veterinarian for potentially serious illnesses?
8. Has the puppy been vaccinated?
9. Has the animal shown any signs of antisocial or aggressive behavior?

Pet Shops

Are the dogs you can buy in a pet shop any different than the ones you can buy from a breeder? More times than not, absolutely. A breeder takes care that they have bred two dogs who complement each other in order to breed the best possible dog that would be most emblematic of the breed standard or ideal. Responsible breeders ask you a lot of questions before they agree to sell you a puppy, and they try to match yours and their puppies' personalities.

Many pet shops get their dogs from puppy mills. These breeders produce dogs with little or no concern about breed standards, temperament, or health problems. As a result, unsuspecting buyers don't know what they're getting. These dogs are as purebred as the dogs you get from a breeder, because purebred only means that the mother and father are registered purebreds. These puppies are also as cute as the ones you'll see at a responsible breeder's, though they may lack the energy or robust appearance of the responsible breeder's pups.

Pet shops know that puppies are most appealing when they're six to eight weeks old. That means that to get them to the store by that age they are usually separated from their mother and littermates at four to six weeks of age—far too early. These pups miss the nutritional and behavioral benefits of staying in their first family for as long as they should, and their new families pay the price in health and behavior problems later in life.

Does this mean good dogs don't come from pet shops? No. And with the media attention on the plight of puppy mill pups, more of them are either not selling puppies or host adoption days where local shelters come in so people can get their dogs from the shelter. This is valuable PR for the pet shop and good business for the shelter. It also makes people feel better about the dog they're acquiring.

While some pet shops are negatively labeled, because they use breeding farms called puppy mills to supply them, many pet shops do in fact use better suppliers. Regardless of whether you buy directly from a breeder or from a pet shop, ask for as much information as possible. Also, make sure there is a return or money back policy. Many breeders will take back their dogs if you find they have any health defects in any way. Good pet shops do the same.

If you do buy a puppy from a pet store, ask the staff a lot of questions about its background and whether the store provides any guarantees on the puppy's health. Take the puppy to a veterinarian right away for a first physical, and if the vet suspects any problems, speak with the store staff immediately.

Friends and Neighbors

This is probably one of the most unlikely places you will or should go to get a dog. Think about it: How much does your friend know about breeding dogs? Maybe he has great fashion sense, hangs out with cool people, has a great job and family, but what does he really know about dogs?

You also have to ask yourself, "Is my friend really good to his dog? Did he read up on what to do with a pregnant dog? Did they go to their veterinarian and get his or her advice? Do I like my friend's dog? Have I spent enough time with that dog to know whether or not I like it?"

Perhaps your friend found a stray and is trying to find it a pleasant home. This is more common than you think. If this is the case, make sure to ask as many questions as you can. Try not to be moved by the sad story. You need to find yourself a dog that you can live with for a long time. In short, real friends won't try to sell you a dog you don't need. Think about the person who's trying to give you the dog as well as about the dog itself.

Picking the Best Puppy for You

Obviously, this is the moment of truth. What kind of animal will you choose? There are several important things to remember when picking a new puppy, especially if the puppy is part of a large litter.

First, break down the decision process into two stages. The first stage is observing the puppy with the rest of the littermates. This can tell you a lot about the puppy's personality. The second part of the process involves you and the puppy alone together. This is also very revealing if you know what you're looking for.

FACT

There are three things to remember when evaluating puppies before choosing: position in the pack, sociability with humans, and intelligence. These three things are key in helping to establish the dog you should choose.

Watching how a puppy interacts with other dogs, especially its littermates, can tell you a lot. Judging a puppy's position in the pack is extremely important. Is it the dominant puppy? Is it the weakling? These personality extremes are best for novice dog owners to avoid. Why? As appealing as their rambunctiousness may seem, dominant puppies usually turn out to be dominant dogs that can be difficult to control and train. They may bully their new "littermates," who will be your kids and your kids' friends.

Many people are moved by watching the litter's weakling puppy. They want to rescue it from the rest of the pack and nurse it because they feel sorry for it. These dogs present their own problems. They usually lack confidence, both in the canine and the human world. This can lead to trainability problems and problems with human interaction later on.

Are either of these two dogs ever going to find a home? Yes. A more experienced person can better understand these puppies' needs. For newcomers to dog ownership, a more stable-tempered, middle-of-the-road pup is best. Such a pup is neither pushed around too easily nor overly dominant with its littermates or mother.

The next thing to judge is how the puppy responds to your presence. You probably shouldn't go for the first one who comes rushing at you. Neither do you want the one who won't come at all. You want one of middling temperament. A follower? That's a good dog. You certainly don't want your dog to be a leader. That's your position.

A little pup too busy to come over to you or too afraid to come over to you probably isn't a suitable pet. While socialization with dogs is important, socialization with people is also key, since your puppy is going to be living night and day with you and your family, and not his.

The pup's relative intelligence is probably the most difficult trait to figure out. You want a pup who will make the effort to understand you. Calling the puppies in a friendly voice is the best way to get their attention. Do not command them, as you will probably frighten them. Using a friendly tone to entice them, which puppies turn their attention to you and return your interest? The ones who don't understand your entreaty are probably not for you. Again, do your best to judge not the boldest, but the smartest.

Remember that even if you weigh less than 100 pounds, you are a giant to a young puppy. Just the sheer size of you can be scary to them. The best way to entreat a little puppy to approach you is to bend on one knee and place your hand lower than its head. The idea is to offer something that is not so intimidating. You're trying to get a real read of the dog's personality. You are not trying to scare the heck out of it.

What you're really trying to judge here is how well these puppies will take to obedience training. You want a puppy that is interested in human interaction—not just playing, but understanding.

Just You and the Puppy Alone for a Minute

This is the second part of the choosing process. What is it about? The idea is to see if the puppy responds to you alone, when it is not being distracted by its littermates. What would be best is if you can either go out in the yard or at least in a separate room for a moment, so that you spend some quiet time alone. Some breeders will want to be with you and the pup, and that's fine. When you're alone and quiet with the pup, here are some questions to consider:

- Is the puppy responding to you?
- Is the puppy too distracted by other things to interact with you?
- Is the puppy responding to your entreaties?
- Is the puppy willing to play with you?
- Is the puppy too shy to respond to you?

The conclusions you draw based upon the answers you get will help you to be better prepared to make a final decision.

Final Comments on Choosing a Puppy

What you must do is think about what you need instead of what you like or find cute. While you may be attracted by personality to the dominant dog, or the submissive one, or the litter clown, you should be choosing none of these. Are these bad dogs? No, but you may not be the best person equipped to deal with the personality traits being exhibited by those dogs.

Certainly one of the things most important is the energy level. Again, you should not look for the least or most active dog. Consider the puppies of moderate tendencies.

With the help of a trusted breeder or experienced rescue person—or even store owner or friend—you can take the time to find the pup that will best fit into your life and the life of your family for many years to come.

CHAPTER 5

Preparing for Your Puppy

You've actually picked a dog and the arrival date is near. Now comes one of the most important parts: preparing for your newest little bundle of joy. This is a tougher job than you'd imagine. But it's also fun. The excitement of bringing home your new puppy is thrilling. Whether you've done this before or not, it's important to review the materials you'll need to own a dog. The basic things are obvious—leash, collar, ID tag, crate, food, and bowls for water and food. And don't forget toys! However, you need to know about each of these before you go out and buy something and then find out it doesn't work for you.

Naming Your Puppy

Choosing your puppy's name is fun. Your pup's name will help define who he or she is—and how you and the rest of the world relate to the puppy. A serious name like Beazely or Mrs. Melinda will evoke a very different response than a more casual name like Fred or Muffin. If the puppy is for one particular member of the family, it is most appropriate for that person to name him or her. That doesn't mean that the pup should get saddled with a name no one else likes; it's better to go back to the drawing board with name choices than to settle for something that makes any one in the family cringe any time they say it.

While odd or complicated names are certainly, well, different, they are not the most practical for the canine species. Why? Because dogs, more than most animals, require interaction. So before you name your dog Phidippides (the guy who ran the first marathon), or Bacchus (the God of wine) remember that your dog needs a name that will be simple to respond to, that has a sharp, clear sound, and that you will be comfortable saying over and over again. Something short—no more than three syllables—is generally a good idea.

FACT

A dog will actually be able to recognize a two-syllable name better than a single syllable. One of the reasons is that single-syllable names often sounds like other common words or requests from you that your dog will hear. So if you want to name your dog Sam, for example, consider calling him Sammie as a general rule.

Changing the Name of an Adopted Puppy

Puppies and dogs from other families or situations already have a name. It may be a name you really dislike. If you know you won't be able to live with the name, you will need to retrain the pup to his or her new name as soon as you bring the dog home with you. Remember, too, that dogs are not actors or rock stars. You cannot constantly change your dog's name. Changing it once in a lifetime is probably enough. Constant name changes will lead to confusion and difficulties where training and obedience are concerned, as well as a host of other problems. This doesn't mean you can't refer to your dog as Smoochie or Bun or Little One or Smarty Pants as time goes on and these terms of endearment present themselves to you. But just as you would address a child or spouse as Honey but also use their name, the same is true of your pup.

If you get your pup from a breeder, she may have a kennel name that she wants you to use as part of your dog's formal name. The Beagle that won the 2008 Westminster Kennel Club dog show is officially named Champion K-Run's Park Me In First, but to everyone he's known simply as Uno. K-Run is the breeder's kennel name, and Park Me In First was added for him specifically. But Uno was selected as his "call name"—the one people use on a daily basis. If your purebred pup has a long name, worry not. Simply keep it on his or her registration certificate and call your pup something more practical.

Essential Supplies

The number and variety of supplies for dogs and puppies can be somewhat overwhelming. Don't sweat about it too much. You will also find that different dogs will need different things. Consult with your breeder for any special items your puppy may need. To get you started, though, you should have supplies on hand before your puppy comes to your home. Remember, you want to make the transition to your home as easy as possible for your pup, and that means the fewer distractions, the better. With the following supplies on hand and assigned their places, you'll be prepared:

- Appropriate food
- Bowls for food and water
- Collar and leash
- Bed
- Crate or carrier
- ID tag
- Toys
- Grooming supplies (brush, nail clipper, toothbrush and paste, shampoo)

Your puppy must have at least one dog bed that is hers alone. You may find it's helpful to have one in each room where you spend a lot of time so there is always an appropriate place for your pup—like this Shetland Sheepdog—to snuggle up beside you.

As far as food goes, if you really want to understand what's best to put in your puppy's bowl, read Chapter 8. In it you'll learn how to understand the multimillion dollar business of dog food and how to navigate the choices to provide what's healthiest for your puppy.

In the meantime, if you're getting your puppy from a breeder, that person will most likely insist that you continue feeding the food your pup has been eating all along. This will make life easier for you and for your pup, as you won't have to worry about upsetting his tummy (and the consequences of that). Study your options before switching.

Of course, your pup will need a bowl out of which to eat—and choosing one can feel as overwhelming as finding the right food! There are so many types and styles. You bought this book to find out what's best, so here's the deal: buy stainless steel or crockery. Stainless steel is lightweight, durable, and very easy to clean. For messy, inquisitive puppies, stainless steel bowls are often the only ones with a wide, slip-proof base and a rim that's not too high—the last thing you want is a bowl that the pup can push all over, that tips easily, or—worst of all—can be chewed. A crockery (pottery) bowl is usually heavy enough that it can't be pushed around, and it's certainly easy to clean. These can be quite attractive, too.

Their only drawback is that they can have high rims and food can sometimes get stuck along the inside edges.

Avoid plastic dog bowls. They are often the least expensive and may appear to be perfectly suitable for your needs. You'll regret your decision, though, should your puppy develop a habit of chewing on the bowl, or when he steps on it the wrong way and it goes flying because it doesn't weigh much. Worst of all, there are now warnings about the phthalates in plastics that can be potentially hazardous to one's health—but especially that of puppies (and children).

A Collar, a Leash, and a Tag

There are many types of collars. The three most popular are the traditional buckle collar; the choke chain or slip collar; and the pronged training collar. For your pup's first collar, you should choose a sturdy buckle collar. You can find them made out of everything from the finest leather to patterned or plain nylon and, for the eco-conscious, organic cotton or hemp or even recycled rubber.

Your pup's first collar can be thinner, too, as you won't want something too heavy around his delicate (and growing) neck. Collars are measured in inches, and to buy the size that's best, be sure to measure your pup's neck. Buy a collar that's slightly larger than that so you can adjust the size if necessary.

How tight should the pup's collar be?
To fit properly, your pup's collar should be neither too snug nor too loose. The generally accepted rule is that it should fit well, leaving enough room for two to three of your fingers to easily slip between the collar and the puppy's neck.

If your puppy has a tendency to back out of his collar, you may choose to use a slip collar or choke chain as it tightens and loosens with the pressure of your leash, sending clear signals to your pup. This collar is a slip-knotted, smooth metal chain that comes in various sizes. The idea is that as the dog pulls harder and moves away from you (his trainer), the collar tightens and inhibits his breathing. When he stops and the collar loosens, he can breathe normally. Because of its potential to choke a dog, it should only be used as instructed and only when training. If left on as a permanent collar, should it become stuck on something and your pup panics to get away, he can accidentally choke himself.

A pronged collar operates like a choke chain in that it tightens around the dog's neck as he pulls harder. But the pronged collar has dulled metal prongs that poke him in the neck the harder he pulls. Many people use this when walking powerful dogs they can no longer control with a simple buckle collar. While the pronged collar can be a helpful training tool, if you feel you need one to just walk your dog around the block, it's time to see a trainer before the problem gets even worse.

The simple metal identification tag you can make yourself at a machine in a pet store can literally save your pup's life. Get one right away and keep it on your pup's first collar, then transfer it to his next collar. It should include your name, your home phone number, and your cell phone number. Proper identification is extremely important.

Leashes or leads, like the collars they often pair with, come in a variety of colors, textures, and styles. It's fun to outfit your pup in a color that reflects his or her gender, like bright blue or pink, or personality, like flowery or plaid. Just as the advice about choosing a collar emphasized a practical decision for a growing puppy, the same has to be said for a leash. Puppies love to chew on leashes—something they should and need to outgrow. Until yours does, go practical. Your leash should be about six feet in length, and one that's made from sturdy cotton weave is truly best. Nylon can be slippery, leather is almost irresistible for a teething pup, and metal is out of the question.

For Slumber and Security

Every pup and dog needs a bed of his or her very own. This can be as simple as a collection of old towels shredded into an old cotton laundry bag (for the truly eco-conscious), or as deluxe as a miniature sofa just for your pup! Beyond the choice of what kind of bed to get, it's critical to know where you will want your puppy to sleep in your home. If you're bringing home a young pup, his accessibility to the house should be limited until he's housetrained, in which case having a bed (or crate) in the kitchen or family room is the best choice. Puppies are very social, and will not want to be left alone at night. Provide a comfy bed or crate in a bedroom with a family member for night time. The person with whom he sleeps for the first month or so must be willing to take him out late for his last walk, and get up early to take him out in the morning. Otherwise, accidents *will* happen! (But more about housetraining in Chapter 10.)

Though your pup may float in it at first, get a bed that will accommodate him as he grows. Be sure it has a washable liner! You may want to remove the stuff and line it in plastic and then put the cover back over it for the first few weeks so accidents don't penetrate the bed's filling. Supplement with an old towel or blanket laid on top of the bed—anything that's easy to wash. Pups and dogs are suckers for comfy spots, and if the beds you provide fit the bill, they'll take to them with no problem and sleep comfortably.

QUESTION?

Do you need a crate?
While some people call crates "cages"—with their association of entrapment—for den animals like dogs a properly used crate provides a reassuring, safe enclosure. Crate training is explained in detail in Chapter 10, and it's a subject you'll definitely want to read more about.

You're getting to the bottom of the list of absolute essentials for your pup, and though these are near last, they are certainly not least. What are they? Toys and grooming supplies. Your pup needs both.

Now that you have a pup or puppies, you will also need a selection of toys, as dogs need these for entertainment and exercise. These Ibizan Hound pups are enjoying playing with a chew toy made from a sock.

Puppies need toys they can sink their razor-sharp puppy teeth into. Rubber or plastic toys designed for chewers come in all shapes and sizes, and are specially made to safely satisfy a variety of sizes and ages of pups (and dogs). Buy wisely, and be sure the material won't rip or puncture, exposing your pup to dangerous substances such as squeakies or toxic stuffing. Your pup's breeder, trainer, or veterinarian can recommend the proper toys for your particular pup.

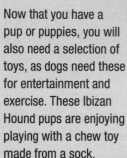

ALERT!

Toys you don't want to buy include those meant for children, action figures, plush, any plastic object with a liquid center, footballs, basketballs, soccer balls, kickballs (they will puncture and destroy these), baseballs (they'll rip the hide cover off and then who knows what'll happen to all the insides), anything made of glass, and balls of twine.

Some grooming supplies are essential. These include a brush that's appropriate for your dog's fur type (short, long, double-coated, curly, etc.); nail trimmers (get your pup accustomed to these as soon as possible so nail-clipping isn't a dreaded event); a gentle dog-specific shampoo; and a doggy toothbrush and toothpaste made for dogs. Chapter 9 covers all aspects of grooming your puppy, and you'll want to set up a routine for doing it so your pup enjoys and looks forward to its benefits throughout his or her life.

Interesting Extras

Now that dogs are considered members of the family, all sorts of products are being manufactured to make their lives with us (and vice versa) more comfortable, appealing, decorative, and special. There isn't room in this book to catalog all those products, but it's worth mentioning some of them. While these items might not be used on a daily basis, they can become equally "essential" in their own way.

- **Housetraining aids**—baby gates for limiting access to the rest of the house; enzymatic cleaner for dealing with accidents; special training pads; a pooper scooper and/or baggies for picking up after your pup (preferably biodegradable).
- **Training aids**—healthy treats for rewarding good behavior; whatever equipment your trainer suggests for humanely working with your pup; appropriate chew toys; anti-chew sprays (Bitter Apple, for example) to discourage chewing inappropriate items.
- **Accessories**—everything from sweaters to booties to hats to special-occasion collars and leashes, etc.
- **Travel items**—specially outfitted car seat or harness; portable bowls for food and water; a first-aid kit for your vehicle; etc.
- **Home supplies**—a lint/pet hair remover; a decorative and washable throw for a favorite sofa or chair that your dog likes; a mat to go under your pup's bowls; etc.
- **Medical supplies**—a first aid kit; veterinary approved supplements; etc.

All of these are items you will accumulate over time. They are also discussed in greater detail in the relevant chapters on grooming, health, feeding, and so on.

Bringing Your Puppy Home

Don't be in too much of a rush to pick up your puppy. Arrive prepared and everything will go better for everyone. Have a supply of old towels in the car, as well as paper towels and a trash bag. Take along the new collar and leash you've selected for the pup. If the trip will be a long one, you may need a crate or some way to keep the pup safe and secure over a long distance.

The first thing you and your puppy will do together is drive from the breeder, foster home, or shelter to your home. Remember, this will not only be a strange new environment to the puppy, but will also be the first lengthy period of time away from everything he or she has ever known. You and your family are sure to be very excited about this event; for your puppy's sake, you want to manage it as calmly as possible.

When you arrive for your puppy, plan to spend some time just hanging out so the pup gets somewhat used to your attention and the smells of you and your family. Let your children interact with him (under appropriate supervision) while you take care of the final details. Go over any questions or concerns you have. Put the new collar you bought on the pup, and let him sniff the new leash.

The day you bring your puppy home from the breeder's is one of the happiest and most exciting—so long as you are prepared for his homecoming.

If he's old enough, take him for a short walk. It would be best if he eliminates just before getting in your car. Although dogs rarely suffer from what we call motion sickness, the noise, vibrations, and sudden movements can cause lots of anxiety. Some dogs will develop lifelong anxiety associations with driving and will vomit or urinate in a car even before the engine starts.

Travel with someone else who can drive so that you can tend to the puppy during the trip. Don't trust this to your kids, who will be too excited and may drop or otherwise mishandle the puppy—and purely by accident, which is something they shouldn't experience.

ALERT!

There is nothing cuter than children and puppies. But children, especially young children, are not experienced in handling such small animals. They don't know their own strength and how delicate puppies are. Puppies are not stuffed animals. You really need to tell your children not to squeeze too hard and hurt the newest member of your family.

Stop at convenient rest stops or about every half-hour to an hour to allow your pup to relieve himself if he needs to. Don't linger on these visits; they're for doing his business only! If he doesn't have to go, be on your way. If he does, tell him what a good puppy he is before scooping him gently back into the car. Don't do anything to compromise the safety of your puppy. Stay away from other dogs, don't let your kids run around with the pup, and don't feed him junk food even if you're having some. Keep him on a secure leash and close to you so he is not exposed to anything that could harm or upset him.

When you get home, allow your pup to explore the outside of your home. Be absolutely sure that any other dogs or pets you have are securely confined to another room before bringing him inside. The last thing you want or need is for your other beloved dog(s) to suddenly attack your pup. If you think it couldn't happen, think again. Let your new pup explore on his own before introducing any other pets. (Chapter 7 explains introducing new pets to each other.)

The All-Important Puppy Schedule

It is so, so important to get your puppy on a schedule! Of course the schedule needs to work for you and fit in with how you spend your day, but it also needs to accommodate the physical and social needs of your puppy. As a baby, she needs to eat regularly, go out regularly, play, spend time with you, and sleep. Each of these is very important and can't be neglected. Here is a sample schedule to help you plan yours:

Daily Schedule

6:00 A.M.—take puppy out

6:10 A.M.—feed first meal

6:30 A.M.—take puppy back out (if she does her business, allow her to spend more time outside; if she doesn't do it right away, bring her back in and take her out every five minutes until she does—only then go for any kind of extended walk/outside time)

7:00–8:00 A.M.—confine puppy to kitchen while household gets up and ready and out the door

8:00 A.M.—take puppy outside

8:15 A.M.—confine puppy to her room or put her in her crate

8:15–11:30 A.M.—do something that doesn't involve the puppy

11:30 A.M.—take puppy outside

11:35 A.M.—feed another small meal

11:45 A.M.—take puppy back outside, as per 6:30 A.M.

12:00 P.M. and through the afternoon—spend time playing or interacting with the puppy

3:00 P.M.—take puppy outside

3:10 P.M.—feed another small meal

3:30 P.M.—take puppy back outside

4:00 P.M.—confine puppy for an hour or so

6:00 P.M.—take puppy outside

6:15 P.M.—feed last meal of the day

6:30 P.M.—take puppy back outside

6:45 P.M.—play and interact with puppy in other parts of the house with supervision to prevent accidents

9:45 P.M.—take puppy outside before bed

10:00 P.M.—bed time

This can seem daunting, especially if you don't have anyone to help, but if you stick to it, it will work. If you have other family members who are responsible enough to participate, assign them portions of the schedule. For example, if you have a child in high school who gets home around 3:00 P.M., she can take over the afternoon portion of the schedule.

Who to Call for Help

Just as you will want to post your puppy's schedule on your refrigerator so that it is prominently displayed and easier to follow, do the same with the phone numbers of people you can call if you have any concerns about your puppy. Put these numbers on your cell phone, too, so you can reach them at any time. This list can include:

- Your puppy's breeder or, if your pup is a rescue or adopted, the former caretaker
- Your veterinarian
- A neighbor or friend who can pinch-hit for you should you get stuck in traffic and be late to let your pup out
- A poison hotline should you suspect your pup has eaten something dangerous (888-426-4435)

CHAPTER 6

Puppy-Proofing Your Home

When you are firmly set on getting a puppy, you must take special care to make sure your living area is safe for your new arrival. You may decide to restrict your puppy to a few choice areas at first, which is highly recommended. However, dogs are master escape artists, so even if the new fella is restricted to just a couple of rooms at first, you should take the time to make sure the entire house or apartment is safe.

The Puppy's Own Space

Remember that part of a successful and reassuring transition for your puppy is the need to feel secure. When your pup comes into your home, nothing is familiar to him. You can show him around your house and yard so that he is exposed to it all, but once he's had the tour, the best thing to do is confine him to one room that is as safe and secure for him as possible. The room he will come to know very well and feel truly comfortable in.

You will notice by living with your pup that dogs are den animals. They like to find cozy corners into which to snuggle. They like to be close to others who are in the same room with them. Pups are more secure in a smaller space rather than a larger space (so long as it isn't *too* small, of course!).

Another reason you want to confine your pup is for your own benefit: The fewer rooms he has access to, the less trouble he can get into. This chapter will explore various areas in your home and yard and tell you how to make them safe for your puppy, so that you won't feel your pup has taken over your home. There are puppy proofing considerations for all areas. If you decide you want your pup to be able to wander the house at will, follow the simple suggestions here and at least you will know he'll be safe.

Kitchen and Bathroom

If you're crate training (and you should), the kitchen is a great room in which to situate the crate. If you're not crate training, then the kitchen is the best choice for keeping your puppy safely confined. Why the kitchen? For several reasons: it has a floor surface that's easily washed and usually pretty durable; it is a room where other members of the family congregate, so your pup won't feel he's being isolated (which is a very horrible thing for a puppy or any animal); there is a sink for easy access to running water; cleaning supplies are typically close at hand. All of these make taking care of and cleaning up after your puppy much easier.

Like the kitchen, a bathroom has access to cleaning items and running water and has a floor that's easy to clean. If your bathroom isn't centrally located, though, your pup will feel isolated in it. If it's just off the kitchen so that the pup can feel part of the household's activities, then it can be an option.

ALERT!

There are many jokes about dogs drinking out of the toilet bowl, but in fact this is a potentially deadly habit and should be strongly discouraged. While toilets are flushed and fresh water fills them, there is still a chance that bacteria or other harmful items can be present in the water. Also, the cleansers used for toilet bowls are toxic!

You'll need a baby gate to block off any room. The best kinds are the wooden ones that stay closed through pressure on both sides of the wall. When positioned properly, they are quite difficult to knock down and your pup can see through them. It will be much more comforting for him to be able to look and smell through the gate instead of feeling completely trapped behind a solid door or partial wall.

For the safety of your pup and the protection of your home, there will be times when you will need to confine your puppy to a particular room. You can do this by putting him in a crate, or by putting up a baby gate.

Once you've put up the baby gate (or gates), you need to look around and ask yourself the following question: If you were a dog, what would you chew on? Don't hesitate to answer in this way: Everything. And that's the problem. If there are exposed wires, cover them up or otherwise secure them, or they will be readily chewed, causing damage to not only your electronics, but possibly your puppy! Do you have antique chairs around the kitchen table? Don't trust them with your puppy; put them in the attic for now. Be sure that any cleansers and other potentially toxic substances are locked away.

To decrease damage to cabinets, chair legs, or other things that may seem like ideal chewing objects for your pup, spray them with a substance called Bitter Apple. If your pup gets it in his mouth, the taste is extremely bitter—an immediate deterrent that usually keeps the pup away.

Be absolutely sure you keep the garbage out of your pup's reach—put it away under the sink, in the pantry, or in the basement. Don't leave anything out. No large, tall container. No covered can. Your puppy will find it. Put the garbage somewhere that your pup absolutely can't access it, or come home every day and wonder what condition your house and your dog are going to be in, because if he can get into it, he will.

While deciding which things may be hazardous to your pup, consider towels, rags, and other cloth items. You may notice you have a lot of these kinds of things in the kitchen—dish towels, paper towels, tissue boxes, aprons, oven mitts, etc. To a puppy, all are great chew items. If you don't want them destroyed (and your pup harmed by ingesting them), put them securely out of reach.

As for the bathroom, anything that smells nice—soaps, perfumes, shampoos, shaving cream—must be kept out of reach. Remember that even though you may try to keep the bathroom door closed and the puppy out, you will most likely forget once in a while, so it is better to be safe than sorry. You need to be extra careful with sponges and body scrubs because their chewy texture make them very fun for puppies of all ages and they can harbor residual chemicals and bacteria. The toilet seat should be kept down—a small puppy might be able to crawl in and be unable to get out. Rubber duckies and other bath toys may look like doggy toys, but they won't withstand a puppy's chewing and can pose a choking hazard.

Toys, Glorious Toys

When you leave your pup alone while you go out, provide things that are appropriate for him to chew on. Teething puppies don't chew to be spiteful or purposely damage your possessions; they chew because they need to. Like teething babies, their chops ache while their teeth and jaws are growing. And being creatures who explore with their mouths, they can't help but get their teeth involved.

Examples of appropriate chew toys are durable rubber chews (often with cavities into which you can put cookies or peanut butter to make them extra yummy), a chew hoof, a sterilized bone, etc. Make sure there a few of these things to distract your puppy from the things you don't want him chewing on. Rotate the toys, too, because your pup can become bored with the same toy day in and day out.

FACT

There is nothing more exciting or interesting to a young puppy than a houseplant. It's natural. It's leafy. There's dirt! If you have any houseplants on the floor, get rid of them now! They are an accident waiting to happen. Some houseplants are also toxic for dogs. For a list of potentially poisonous items you should keep out of reach of your dog, see Chapter 18.

Living Room and Family Room

Whatever you call it, the place where you and your family spend the most time will be where your dog wants to be. The family living room is a place where all kinds of potentially dangerous items can find their way into your pup's mouth (and stomach). Knitting materials, game pieces, other kids' toys, remote controls, magazines, ashtrays, pens and pencils, electronics paraphernalia, and any other small items should be put where your pup cannot reach them. You may need to redecorate for a while, finding secure containers for these items while your pup grows. Remove dangerous items before your pup enters the room, and train all family members to think about putting their things out of your pup's reach if they don't want them chewed or destroyed.

Things like potted plants and delicate end tables will get knocked over. It might be a good idea to store them away for the first few months until your puppy can learn to behave properly. Electrical cords need to be coiled and sprayed with Bitter Apple to prevent chewing. Anything wooden or seemingly chewable should also be protected from chewing.

Even with these precautions, it is recommended that you only let your puppy into your living and family rooms with supervision. Keep him on a short leash so his movements are restricted, and keep him close to you. This way, you can properly teach him how to behave so someday you can move some of your finer and more delicate furniture back where you want it and not have to worry about leaving the remote on the coffee table—or finding another set of iPod headphones mangled.

Bedrooms

As tempted as you might be to let the new puppy hang out in the kids' rooms, you must take extra care. A child's room is usually the most cluttered, especially with little things that may have been handled by fingers sticky with ice cream and other treats (this makes the most basic little doodad seem like a tasty treat to a mouthy puppy).

This can work to your advantage. Most children will do just about anything to be able to have the dog in their room. Let them know it will be okay so long as the entire room is puppy safe. Be sure to stress that it is for the puppy's health, otherwise your child might not think it such an important task, and will simply stuff things under the bed where just about any puppy will be able to get them.

Posters should be tacked up high. A low-hanging poster can be pulled down, possibly letting loose a tack which could be harmful if stepped on or swallowed. Deflated balloons and other small, soft items have a texture that will make you puppy think they are edible and could cause serious problems.

As for the adult bedrooms, loose change, pantyhose, makeup, and medications can all pose serious risks to a dog's health and should be kept safely out of reach. Night tables, especially ones with lamps, should be made as sturdy as possible.

If you are going to allow the puppy to sleep in someone's bedroom (which is a great idea), find a spot that will be just for the puppy's bed or crate. For the first month or so this might be right next to your bed so that you can reassure the pup when he wakes up at night—or get him outside quickly should he need to do his business! When he's a bit older and knows the routine, you can move the bed to a far corner of the room. This way he's with you but not right beside you, so that if you need to go to the bathroom in the middle of the night yourself, you won't be the one waking him up.

ALERT!

Under no circumstances should a puppy be allowed on the top of a bunk bed! A puppy's curious nature and inexperience in terms of coordination will almost guarantee a fall.

Basement and Attic

Many of today's homes have finished basements, making them the new family rooms or kids' playrooms. As discussed already, these rooms tend to be filled with the stuff of everyday life—and your pup will want to get his teeth into it! Follow the advice given in the section on living and family rooms if you have this kind of basement.

The basements in some houses may be strictly utilitarian—dark places used for work benches, storage, laundry rooms, etc. You'll want to keep your puppy out of these kinds of basements. They're probably not places you want to spend much time in, and there's no reason your puppy should, either.

Don't bring your pup up to the attic with you, even if he cries at the bottom of the stairs because he wants to be with you. Give him a favorite chew toy if you think he'll be upset by your disappearance.

However, in the event he might sneak by you and get into the attic, you should consider puppy-proofing this space. If you have an attic with a large amount of stored items—holiday decorations, old baby items, and lots of junk you just haven't been able to let go of yet—they should be stored in secure containers and placed out of your puppy's reach. Small spaces between boxes or boxes and walls should be avoided, your puppy will try to squeeze into small spaces and might not be able to squirm out.

Garage

This is another area that should be kept relatively off limits to the four-legged members of your family. Dogs love both the smell and taste of antifreeze, which is deadly in even small amounts. Also, many rat poisons and other pest control products are designed to kill without tasting bad.

Nails, screws, paint, petroleum products, fertilizer, sharp objects, tools, electrical outlets, and things that could be knocked over—like bicycles, motorcycles, ladders, and furniture—are all serious hazards that need to be secured before your puppy can be allowed to roam this area.

The Yard

The backyard is a place you'll want to spend a lot of time with your puppy, yet it, too, can be one of the most dangerous places for a dog. Common yard plants like rhododendrons, azaleas, laurel, crocuses, daffodils, lilies of the valley, irises, amaryllis, and delphiniums are all poisonous to your dog.

This doesn't mean you need to rip out any plants, but keep a careful eye on what your pup takes interest in while in your yard (and on walks). Dogs are survivors, and most won't be interested in these plants in the first place. But for bored or stressed pups, especially, discrimination is not a faculty of theirs, and danger can ensue.

In our quest to have perfect lawns, Americans resort to the use of plenty of dangerous chemicals to promote growth, kill bugs, and rid a lawn of weeds. Have you ever noticed the flags that lawn companies put around after they've treated a lawn? They usually show a dog in a circle with a bar through it, indicating that pets should not be allowed on the grass for a certain amount of time.

Before you let your pup (or pups) outside in your yard off-leash, be sure you have examined it for any places where they might escape or get into something harmful or dangerous. Even then, you'll want to keep a close eye on your pups —like these young Airedales—while they're exploring the great outdoors.

Because dogs are basically bare-footed all the time, and they clean themselves by licking (often their paws and also sensitive areas like their genitals or anus), it is easy for them to ingest and expose sensitive tissue to dangerous substances. If you want your pup to grow old with you, reconsider how important a picture-perfect yard is to you and your family.

The All-Important Fence

While it isn't absolutely essential that your yard is fenced in, it is safer for your dog and a whole lot more practical. The idea of the fence is to keep your pooch safely enclosed. For this to work, the fence must be high enough and either extend into the ground or at least reach the ground and be difficult to push through.

Just as it is cruel and potentially harmful to imprison your dog in a room by himself for long periods of time, it is equally cruel and harmful to leave your dog outside by himself for any length of time. Without proper supervision, your pup is free to explore and get into any number of things. He may also take to running the fence out of boredom, chasing down or barking at others passing in the street. He may dig or claw his way out of the yard, risking becoming lost or being hit by a vehicle. Children and neighbors who should know better may intentionally or unknowingly taunt your dog. And there is nothing sadder than the sight of a dog tied to a rope that only extends a certain distance from a dog house.

As horrifying as the thought may be, many dogs are abducted out of fenced yards. The fate of these poor creatures is grim, including being sent to a puppy mill or even sold to an animal research lab. If you live in an area where you think dog theft is a possibility, never leave your pet outside unsupervised, especially at night. These areas include any heavily populated areas, or any area with a history of pet theft.

On the other hand, a safe yard is a truly wonderful place for your dog. He can sniff and explore off-leash for short periods of time, play with your children, and you can let him out at night while he does his business (without having to put him on a leash and walk him). It is the place where naps in the sun and family picnics will be enjoyed and special memories will be made. Now that's the life!

CHAPTER 7

Your Puppy's First Month

The most important thing to remember during your first month with a new puppy is to establish a routine immediately. Everything from where your dog will sleep, to when she is first fed, to what behaviors are acceptable should be set in stone from day one. You must also set it in your puppy's mind that you are the leader of the household. This doesn't mean you're a hard-hearted drill sergeant; instead, it means you demonstrate the responsibility of a true parent by setting fair limits, acting responsibly, and being firm in the face of trouble. Spoiling your puppy can give her a sense of superiority that can cause problems later on, including aggressiveness.

The First Day Home

The first time you bring your puppy home it's the equivalent of the Oscars for the puppy. The excitement is palpable. The oohs and aaaahs begin. There's lots of laughter and cooing. Everyone wants to handle the new arrival. Plus there are the sights, sounds, and smells of the new house. All of this can be a little overwhelming for a very young animal recently removed from her mom, siblings, and any caretakers she's ever known.

One of the first things you want to watch out for is not to overstimulate the puppy. While everyone will want to hold the little one, one of the best things you can do is to minimize this tendency and let your puppy initiate the greetings. Letting the puppy explore and understand her surroundings is the best way to establish a relationship with the little pup. It will also help to solidify his confidence in himself and his surroundings.

Establish Routine Immediately

Remember the discussion about a schedule in Chapter 5? Refamiliarize yourself with it, because it's critical. You will be tempted every which way to stray from your routine—by visiting family members, by staying up too late, by feeding treats that may cause digestive upset, etc.

Remind yourself and all your family and friends that there will be plenty of time in the puppy's life for these indulgences. For the health of your puppy (and your own sanity), make the first day one of paying particular attention to the schedule and practices you've decided will be best for your puppy.

Here's a sample first day:

- Late morning: Arrive at your home with the puppy.
- With the puppy on a secure leash, let her explore your yard and home, encouraging her to eliminate outside, and keeping a close eye on her so she doesn't grab and swallow anything harmful or eliminate in the house.
- After going through the house with your pup on her leash, bring her outside again to see if she needs to eliminate. Then, bring her to the room where you will confine her, put the baby gate up, and let her off the lead.

- Have a bowl of fresh, cool water waiting for her.
- Prepare a small meal for her. She may be too excited to eat, but she may very well need to eat. Follow her lead.
- After she eats, take her back outside.
- Bring her back to her room, and sit quietly with her. If your family wants to be in the room with you, ask them to be quiet. Your puppy will probably need to nap.

While she's sleeping, you can do some household chores quietly.

- When she's up, take her out first thing. Depending on the time of day and weather, consider playing gently with her outside if possible. Have family members sit in a circle and call her to them one by one. Entice her with a special toy.
- Follow a pattern of going out, feeding, playing, and napping until it's time for bed.
- Take her out one last time, and then bring her upstairs with you, settling her into her new bed/area. You may need to sit with her in the new place until she falls asleep.

As exciting as it is to have a puppy in the house, remember that all of you need to establish your routine together as soon as possible. This must include times for exercise, feeding, playing, and of course, sleeping. This tiny Chihuahua is ready for a nap.

That First Night

You will be oh, so tempted to bring your puppy to bed with you. The adorable, vulnerable little ball of fluff is the perfect snuggler, and you want to reassure her and help her feel loved. It's a very strong temptation, and you may in fact spend many nights of your lives together sleeping side-by-side. But for the first night (and for at least a month), avoid this temptation. Your pup needs to know right from the start that your sleeping area and hers are separate.

QUESTION?

Why can't my puppy sleep on my bed?
When a dog sleeps on your bed, right beside you, they consider you a peer, not truly a leader. They think you must be the same as them. A young puppy, especially, needs to know you are her leader, not her littermate. You can be close by her, but you are not to share the same bed.

This is where crate training comes in handy again. A crate (complete with super-comfy padding for a bed) makes a great cozy sleeping spot where distractions are minimized. Many crate-trained dogs sleep in their crates with the door open at night—like a bed with curtains around it; sounds nice, doesn't it?

If you don't have a crate for the bedroom, do have a dog bed positioned where you want it. The best place for the first few nights, at least, is just beside your bed. Your pup will crave another warm body beside her if she's been sleeping with littermates until now. Consider filling an old tube sock with with rice and warming it in the microwave for about a minute. Wrap this warmed tube in a towel and secure it so it won't fall out—you don't want the pup to chew on the sock and cause the rice to spill, nor do you want the warm sock to burn her—and then put it beside your pup on the bed. Sit with your pup while she settles in and gets to sleep.

The Big Cry

Now, regardless of how wonderful you are, and how wonderful your family and home are, your puppy is going to be miserable on the first night. It will dawn on your little puppy at the end of the day that his brothers and sisters and mother and former owner are not with him. She is alone with strange people in strange surroundings. At some point during the night, she will most likely awaken and begin to cry.

How you handle the crying will make a difference for the pup in the days, weeks, and months to come, and will establish a pattern of what she can expect from you when she is upset. This is a difficult situation to deal with, because you have other family members whose sleep may be disturbed if you can't quiet the pup. You don't want her to cry inconsolably, yet if you pamper her too much she'll come to expect that any time she whimpers she will get your attention.

The other consideration is that your puppy needs to go to the bathroom. If that's the case, you certainly want to get her outside. Very matter-of-factly, take her out on a leash so you can monitor her, give her a minute to get to it, and then bring her back inside. Reheat and rewrap the rice warmer if you think that will help, then bring her back to her bed and get her settled in. What you want to do is take care of her physical needs without indulging her social needs. She has to learn that sleeping through the night is what you expect of her.

Some experts suggest a different cure for crying: For the first week or two, let your puppy stay downstairs until she's worked out this whole crying thing. She'll eventually settle down and go to sleep. When she's learned that the morning comes and brings you with it, she'll feel secure in sleeping through the night. Then you can bring her upstairs.

The First Week Home

Three words are the key to making it through the first week with your pup—and the rest of your dog's life: Schedule, schedule, schedule. Just as you did the first day, you need to stay focused and keep your pup on the schedule you established to the very best of your ability. Will there be distractions and will you stray? Of course. Recognize these digressions as errors and get back on track as soon as you can.

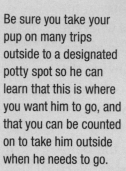

Be sure you take your pup on many trips outside to a designated potty spot so he can learn that this is where you want him to go, and that you can be counted on to take him outside when he needs to go.

Because you want your puppy to settle into a routine in your household, this should involve her being able to cope with you or your family's absence. This doesn't mean you can all leave for school and the office and keep your puppy confined alone to a crate or the kitchen for eight hours or more. Would you do this with a human baby? Certainly not. So why would you consider doing it to your puppy?

Fortunately for you, a puppy is not a baby, and you have a lot more leeway. You could consider doing half days at work the first week. Leaving your pup alone for about four hours at a stretch is reasonable. Not longer than that, and only once you have made sure that her environment is safe and that she has an appropriate chew toy with which to occupy herself.

If all you have to give to your new pup is a weekend before you have to get back to work, then you must get help. You need to hire someone trustworthy and reliable to come in and check on your puppy several times a day for the first few weeks and then, as she gets older, at least once a day.

Your veterinarian or breeder can probably recommend a dog-walking service. You can also research local services yourself, though it's always better to have a recommendation. Meet in advance with the person you select to care for your pup so you're comfortable with each other. Exchange all the necessary emergency contact information, including your veterinarian's phone number. Ask the person to visit when you bring home the puppy so they can meet and you can review the schedule together. You want to limit surprises all around.

FACT

Don't allow bedtime to be pushed later and later for your pup. Don't get off the feeding regimen. Make sure to get your puppy out often and reinforce proper housetraining (see Chapter 10). And be sure your pup gets enough sleep during the day.

If you're the one staying home, begin preparing your pup for what lies ahead when you do return to your normal schedule. Use this week to find a dog walker, since you will definitely need one if your pup is to spend any long hours at home. Start expanding the range of your walks. Take your pup for the first veterinary visit. Do some very basic training of Sit. Consider getting a crate and training your girl to use and enjoy it. And most important—stick to your schedule!

Handling Your Puppy Properly

The easiest way to pick up your puppy without risking injury is to reach under her chest (brisket) between her front legs with one hand and place the fingers of your other hand between her two rear legs, keeping your thumb under her tail. As you straighten your knees to stand, smoothly bring her into your chest so she is leaning into you. Puppies can get wiggly when you least expect it, so make certain her weight is fully supported by your hands, fingers, and forearms. Young children and awkward people shouldn't pick up the puppy and, instead, should either get down to her level or let her sit on their lap if she is small and calm enough. Many puppies do not like to be carried, but all should learn to tolerate being picked up and held.

As for general handling by you and others, gentleness is key. Rough handling, even under the guise of play, can hurt even the sturdiest-looking puppy, and can create bad habits in the future. Another aspect of handling that is important for your puppy to get used to is being touched all over her body. It's hard to find a dog that doesn't enjoy being petted on the head and back, but it can be hard to find a dog that *does* enjoy having her feet touched, her legs picked up, her head repositioned, her teeth checked, and so on. Being touched in these ways feels unnatural to your puppy or dog, but she must learn that she must allow you to do so—and that it is not painful.

What you don't want to do—and be sure the other members of your family know this, too, especially children—is grab or twist any part of your pup's body. Never force a situation. Rather than think, "Okay, now I'm going to accustom my puppy to having her feet touched," and make it a job you need to do, approach the touching as a very slow but steady learning curve for you and your pup.

With some tiny treats in your pocket, sit down next to your puppy and just interact normally with her. As you're doing this, reach for and gently hold a paw for just a second. Produce a treat and give it to her if she doesn't struggle. If she tries to pull her paw away instantly, let her, but don't give her a treat. As you're petting and interacting with her, try touching the sensitive areas—paws, ears, lips, under the tail—for very short times (just a second or two), and reward any positive response.

Handling Nipping

Remember that puppies explore with their mouths. Her natural way of interacting with you will be to want to mouth you, and she has sharp teeth! Don't hit her for accidentally nipping you, as she will be confused and scared by this. Instead, go into defense mode: Lower your eyes, put your hands into a fist so it is harder for her to get a grip on any part of them, and whimper loudly like a hurt puppy. This should startle your puppy and evoke a natural response to stop and observe you. If she backs off, reach out gently for her, and if she doesn't respond with her teeth, resume petting and gently playing. If she tries to go for you again, whimper again and get up and walk away from her. She needs to understand that using her teeth on you is unacceptable.

Keeping Your Cool

Puppies (and dogs) are experts at reading body language. They are all too aware of when you are upset. There will be times when your dog will do things that greatly upset you. If you fly off the handle at every incident, she will come to think of you as unpredictable, which is not reassuring for a dog. The stress you put on her will come out as excess chewing, nipping, excitement, and possibly even aggressive behavior. Read the behavior and training chapters for more information, but try to remember that she is a pup (or a dog), and accidents happen. Get help. Give yourself a time out to cool off. Understand and appreciate that you, your pup, and your family are going through a major transition. Anyone who said this would be fun and easy is wrong—it is hard, it is tiring, and it will be full of ups and downs. Enjoy the ups, and do your best to cope with the downs.

Time goes by so quickly, and soon the puppy months will be behind you—and when they're gone you'll probably wish they were back. If you're really at your wit's end, bring in a qualified trainer as soon as possible. You owe it to your puppy. The Association of Pet Dog Trainers is one place to start. Go to their website to find a trainer near you (*www.apdt.com*) or call them at 1-800-PET-DOGS. Another is the International Association of Canine Professionals. The IACP's list of recommended trainers can be found at *www.dogpro.org*. Or, better still, ask your veterinarian for referrals to the best trainers in town.

CHAPTER 8

Feeding Your Puppy

Welcome to one of the most contentious aspects of dog care—what to put in your pup's bowl. There are many products on the market, all packaged to appeal to you. There are also those who feel a raw diet is best for dogs, and still others who claim that cooking for your pup is the safest and healthiest route. So what are you, the new puppy owner, to do? First, continue to feed your pup whatever he was being fed by his previous caretaker. Keep him on it for at least a few weeks while he adjusts to his new home and family. A change in diet along with all the other changes will only upset his tummy.

A normal puppy has a healthy appetite and will look forward to mealtimes. It is your responsibility to provide the healthiest diet possible. This Welsh Springer Spaniel pup is enjoying his breakfast.

Understanding Dog Food

The commercial dog food industry was born in the late 1800s when an American man named James Spratt developed the first "biscuit" for dogs by mixing ground vegetables and flour and cooking it to form hardened bits. In the early 1900s, F.M. Bennett developed his formula, which went on to become Bennett's Milk-Bone Dog and Puppy Food. These pioneers of the industry wanted to create a product that provided a high-quality food for dogs that was also convenient and easy to feed. Dogs, of course, literally ate it up, and thus was born the commercialization of dog food.

FACT

For years, Kal Kan was one of the best-selling dog food brands in America. As the industry became more competitive, higher-quality foods hit the shelves and Kal Kan lost market share. The company refocused its efforts and reformulated their product, finally recasting the food as an upscale brand—and thus Pedigree was born. Today, Pedigree is one of the best-selling dog foods in America.

With market demand comes variation, and as you'll learn as you continue with this chapter, dog foods have developed over the years to include wet, dry, and semi-moist formulations and much more.

Necessary Nutrients

Now that you've been introduced to the business of commercial dog food, the next step is to learn to understand what your pup (or dog) needs from food to remain healthy for many years. You're looking for some nutritional essentials here: proteins, carbohydrates, vitamins, minerals, and fats. They are all contained conveniently in commercially prepared foods.

The ingredients are listed in descending order by weight—that is, how much of the ingredient is actually in the product. Therefore, if a pure meat source like chicken, beef, or lamb is right up there at the top, you can be sure you're buying a protein-rich food.

Proteins are present in all kinds of meat and meat by-products, such as chicken, lamb, beef, or chicken meal. These are the best sources of protein for your dog. Many foods use vegetable proteins such as soy. These are harder for your dog to digest, so although you will invariably find them in his food, make sure they aren't major ingredients. A dog's need for protein varies—most notably for age, size, and activity level. Puppy foods have high levels of protein, whereas senior foods contain lower levels.

Carbohydrates, which are necessary for energy, also make up some of the primary ingredients in dog food. Their sources are typically rice, corn, or some other grain, though more and more frequently vegetables such as sweet potatoes are being used as well. Wheat and soy can sometimes trigger an allergic reaction in dogs, which is why more and more formulas use rice as their starch. Some dogs aren't affected at all, however, so it's always wise to monitor your dog's overall health.

Dogs need vitamins and minerals to keep their bodies functioning. A lack of iron means not enough hemoglobin to pick up red blood cells in the lungs, which means a less energetic dog. A lack of vitamin E can result in brittle skin. Vitamin C has been called a wonder vitamin for its curative powers. Several commercially available foods on the market add special vitamins and minerals to the food to compensate for certain conditions. One of the most popular is the addition of glucosamine and chondroitin in foods for senior dogs to promote joint health. If you note a substantial amount of an unfamiliar ingredient in your dog's food, do some research and, most important, observe your dog for the potential side effects (hopefully good ones).

Fat is a necessary part of any dog's diet. Fat is what keeps the skin supple and the coat shiny. Too little fat, and your dog will end up with a dry, brittle coat and dry skin; too much fat, and you'll end up with an obese, "well-greased" dog. Fat is extremely palatable to dogs, as well, so manufacturers use it for nutritive and taste values. This can lead to problems with storage, as fats tend to oxidize and go rancid when exposed to air or heat. They must be properly preserved in order to hold.

QUESTION?

What about preservatives?
Manufacturers use preservatives to maintain freshness, taste, and texture. In the 1980s, dog breeders raised concerns about the adverse effects of a common chemical preservative, ethoxyquin. It and the chemicals BHA and BHT were thought to contribute to numerous health problems. Now these are rarely used, though it's important to check for them. Instead, most manufacturers use natural preservatives—tocopherol, a form of vitamin E, and ascorbic acid (vitamin C).

Canine nutrition is a hot topic, and this chapter only skims the surface. The bottom line is: How does your dog do with the food you feed him? If you select a premium brand and feed according to the guidelines in this chapter, your dog should show all the signs of being healthy: clear, shiny eyes; soft, supple coat; pink gums; normal stool and urine; and appropriate energy level. If he doesn't seem healthy to you, speak with your veterinarian and research a dietary change.

All-Important Water

No discussion of what to feed a dog is complete without mentioning water. This is a nutrient as important to dogs as it is to other living things.

Dogs can go longer without food than they can without water. To stay hydrated, and to cool off, dogs need a constant supply of fresh, clean, cool water.

It's absolutely necessary to leave out a clean bowl of water at all times for your puppy or adult dog. Never regulate the water supply. Dogs can't tell you when they're thirsty, so it's vital that you leave water for them at all times. When they're thirsty, they'll drink. Change the water in your dog's bowl a few times a day, and clean the bowl thoroughly once a day. Attention to the water bowl may also alert you to any changes in how much—or little—your dog is drinking, which can be an indication of a serious medical condition.

Don't let your dog drink out of the toilet. This is not a substitute for a water bowl, and in fact could be contaminated with bacteria and residue from the toxic cleaning products that could seriously harm your dog.

Feeding a Commercial Diet

Commercially prepared pet foods come in three standard forms: kibble (dry food), canned (wet food), and semi-moist (burger-type foods). If each claims to be nutritionally complete, do you feed one instead of another or combine them?

Again, think about and look at what's in the foods. Kibble is the most economic food choice, but it is also the least palatable (by comparison). Canned food, on the other hand, is quite palatable, but it can't provide the hard crunchiness that benefits a dog's teeth and gums. Semi-moist, burger-type foods are the most comparable to human junk food. They're loaded with extra sugars and preservatives. Sure your dog will eat them, but at what cost to his health?

Kibble-Canned Combos

If you're confused about whether to feed kibble or canned, ask your pup's breeder what he feeds. After all, he will have spent years developing a feeding plan that works for that particular breed—what a great resource! But it doesn't mean you have to stick with his recommendation. Many owners feed their dogs a mix of kibble and wet food that's approximately three-quarters dry and one-quarter wet. Both these foods are formulated to provide your dog with the same types and mixtures of proteins, fats, carbohydrates, vitamins, and minerals. While dry food contains the same thing canned food does, it's different because all the water (and often blood) has been taken out of it.

Many breeders and dog experts feed their dogs commercial, name-brand dry dog foods and supplement those foods occasionally with canned food and fresh foods. There's no denying that canned food adds great flavor to a meal, and a little added meat, which dogs love. The dry food is beneficial not only for its nutritive value, but because it's hard and crunchy. This causes your dog to chew more, and eating the kibble helps clean his teeth by scraping off bits of accumulated plaque or tartar. Wet food, like human soft foods, can accumulate along the gum line and between teeth, contributing to poor oral health.

It's important to store kibble in as airtight a container as possible to help ensure freshness. You will find a variety of containers at your local pet supply store. When you bring a new bag home, open and pour it into the airtight container as soon as possible. Also, buy the appropriate-sized bag for your dog or dogs. Don't think you'll be saving a lot of money if you buy the giant bag when you're only feeding your Chihuahua a cup a day. Freshness is more important.

Feeding an Alternate Diet

With the growing awareness of what some commercially prepared foods lack, a lot of research began into a more natural diet for dogs. The research concluded, in a nutshell, that the dog's ancestor, the wolf, and today's feral dogs occasionally bring down their own food (another animal) and other times scavenge for food (pick off the remains of someone else's kill). Their food sources, then, are fresh meat (including organ meat), and the digested food of the other animal. Today's raw diets are based on this premise and are centered around feeding fresh (uncooked) meat and partially digested (steamed) vegetables and grains.

Proponents of raw diets say their dogs exude good health—no allergies, no chronic conditions, few parasites, fresh breath, healthy joints, and so on. There are many books and magazine articles on how to formulate and feed a raw diet, and they're fascinating.

For others who don't want to risk the potential ill effects of a commercial diet, there is the option to feed a homemade diet. Again, there are many books detailing what to include in the meals, as dogs do have nutritional needs that are different from humans, and simply giving leftovers from the family's table will not provide for all of them. A successful homemade diet needs to contain the necessary proteins, carbs, vitamins, minerals, and fat that a dog needs. The nice thing is that these proportions are under your control when you make your dog's food.

Typically, owners who feed homemade diets prepare large batches and freeze portions, often adding fresh ingredients as the individual meals are prepared.

Supplementing Your Dog's Diet

For years, books recommended against supplementing your dog's commercial food in any way, claiming that the supplements could harm in ways as seemingly inconsequential as giving your dog diarrhea, to potentially deadly—such as causing debilitating growth spurts or disrupting the overall balance of a food.

While these fears can be valid, canine nutritionists, veterinarians, breeders, and pet owners have come to find that not only does smart supplementing do more good than harm, it can actually significantly improve your dog's health. Note the word "smart" before supplementing. That's the key. Your dog's bowl shouldn't be a garbage can for every leftover you have in your refrigerator. At the same time, there are lots of things you and your family eat that are really good for your dog. Some of these are fresh vegetables; fresh fruits; organic meats; fresh fish; omega-3 oils; and other fresh and natural foods.

It's critical to understand what you're supplementing your dog's food with and why. For example, if your dog is taking an antibiotic, you should add some plain, organic lowfat yogurt to his meals. Antibiotics can destroy the beneficial bacteria in the intestine, and the live, active cultures in yogurt can help reestablish a healthy balance. If your dog has itchy or dry skin, add an omega-3 oil such as fish or flax oil. Adding steamed fresh vegetables to your dog's food provides the same benefits from an excellent source of carbohydrates and fiber as it does to your diet.

Besides the health benefits of certain supplements, your dog will appreciate the variety that supplements can provide. I suspect that everyone is guilty of feeding part of their Thanksgiving dinner to their dogs; after all, shouldn't they enjoy the bounty, too? The key to feeding human goodies to your dog is moderation and consideration. Excessively fatty, over-processed foods aren't good for people or for dogs. But small pieces of pizza crust, the last slice of lunch meat, the occasional potato chip— these will not hurt your dog *in moderation* and using common sense.

ALERT!

If your dog stops eating his dog food because he's waiting for you to give him something tastier, it's time to take a step back. Unless you want to research how to feed a nutritionally sound homemade diet, your dog needs the nutrients that are in commercially available foods. His kibble should make up 95 to 98 percent of his meal. Cut out the supplements until he is eating his dog food again, and then proceed with caution.

When and How Much to Feed

Puppies need to eat more because their bodies are growing at an astounding rate. This doesn't just translate into quantity of food, however. Their active systems require more frequent meals, not just larger meals. As outlined in earlier chapters of this book, a young puppy's schedule includes about four feedings—one in the early morning, one around midday, one in the late afternoon, and one in the evening.

The quantity of food your pup should receive will vary depending on several factors. One is, obviously, the size of your puppy. In general, the larger the dog, the more food it will need. Adding to the complexity is individual need: Two puppies from the same litter may eat completely different amounts. One may seem to gobble up food while another barely touches it. Just like people, dogs are unique creatures.

Your pup's breeder should have given you a guideline for getting started relative to how much to feed your pup. For the first few days, his excitement and nerves may cause him to lose his appetite. Start off feeding about half of what your breeder recommended so that you aren't wasting food. If your pup eats it all, give a little more.

Here is the recommended timeline for cutting back on the number of meals you feed your puppy during the day:

- Age one to six months, four times a day
- Age six to eleven months, three times a day
- Eleven months and older, two times a day

QUESTION?

What if my pup doesn't finish his food?
If this happens within the first few days of coming to your home, and everything else appears normal, then you might attribute a lack of appetite to nerves. If your pup is eating all of his food and then stops for some reason, suspect a medical condition. If he's cleared by the veterinarian and still doesn't finish, he may be trying to tell you he doesn't like the food.

One of the reasons you should feed a certain amount at certain times of the day is so you can monitor your pup's health. For most dogs, food is a primary motivator, and they are enthusiastic about meal times. Wanting the food and finishing the food in a certain period (ten to fifteen minutes), indicates that the pup's appetite and energy level are normal. If a pup is typically enthusiastic about food and suddenly declines a meal, you can be sure something is bothering him. Take the food away and keep a close eye on him, ready to call the vet if his condition doesn't change or you notice anything else unusual.

This French Bulldog puppy has a healthy appetite and is eager to eat his food. Discourage fussy eating, and if your pup refuses food, suspect that there is a health issue.

Feeding for Different Life Stages

It might not seem possible now, but your pup will soon be an adolescent, then an adult, and before you know it, a senior. As he grows up, his nutritional needs change, and there are foods that are targeted to meet the requirements of those different life stages. This is an overview of those foods.

Puppy Food

You may think so, but in fact not all dog foods are the same. Puppy foods are specially formulated to help develop strong bones and good muscle mass. If you read the ingredients, you'll see that puppy foods tend to offer more protein and vitamins than maintenance-formula dog foods, and are formulated for excellent health at this very important developmental stage.

Maintenance Diet

When your puppy reaches about eighteen months of age, you'll want to switch him over to an adult (or maintenance) diet. At this stage his body needs less protein, and certainly less fat. In this category, though, there are a multitude of choices from high-protein formulas for working dogs; natural formulas; formulas based on certain protein and carb sources, like lamb and rice or sweet potato and rice; and more. Talk to your veterinarian if you have concerns about switching your puppy to one of these foods. Staying with a brand you have come to trust makes the most sense, but if you've become a student of the ingredient list, you may find a food that seems even better for your growing pup. Give it a try!

Lite Diet Formula

If you and your veterinarian agree that your pup could stand to lose a few pounds, invest in a lite-formula diet. You can keep his helping size relatively the same, but instead of calorie-laden proteins and fats, these foods contain more fiber and less fatty carbs. These can fill your dog's tummy while keeping off the extra pounds.

ALERT!

Please note that a lite-formula diet is not a substitute for the exercise your dog needs to stay in shape. Part of his diet should include longer walks, more play time, and a reduction in the number of treats you feed, as well.

Senior Formulas

When does your dog become a senior? That question is sometimes difficult to answer. It ranges from breed to breed and from dog to dog, though there is a general understanding that dogs aged seven or older are considered seniors. Some breeds, however, don't even reach that age, and are considered senior before then. Your dog's breeder, your veterinarian, and other owners of your breed can help you determine when switching to a senior food would be right for your dog.

Aging means the loss of vigor and ability to perform feats once thought normal during the adult years. Seniors can't run or walk as fast. They sleep more. Their systems begin to deteriorate just as humans systems do. Senior dogs need a food that gives them as much energy as possible without making them heavier and slower. Many senior formulas contain the extra nutrition older dogs need, like glucosamine and chondroitin or extra vitamin C.

Hypoallergenic or Therapeutic Diets

Hypoallergenic foods fill a need for owners of dogs with allergies. Your veterinarian can determine if your dog might be allergic to any ingredients in his maintenance diet. A switch to a fish-based food, for example, or supplementing with flax oil, may do wonders for your itchy dog. A particular, recurring health concern may lead your veterinarian to prescribe a therapeutic diet for your dog. Several manufacturers now make these diets, which are prescribed by veterinarians to assist in the treatment of problems associated with particular organs or body systems and conditions, like the kidneys, heart, metabolism, diabetes, obesity, and so on.

Feeding Treats and Bones

From organic cookies cut in fun shapes to beefy chew sticks and beyond, dog treats come in every size, shape, color, and flavor imaginable. There are animal parts (ears, noses, feet, etc.) that dogs love, and the venerable Milk Bone, which dogs have been crunching on for years. Dogs love treats, and we love giving them. However, when it comes to feeding them these goodies, keep moderation in mind.

Many treats are full of artificial ingredients, dyes, extra sugar or salt—many of the things that are in the junk foods people find so tasty. These can affect your dog's overall health, causing everything from gas to itching to weight gain. Reduce the amount of dog food if you feed several treats a day, or consider going healthy with treats.

FACT

Dogs can enjoy healthy treats as much as commercially processed treats. Next time you want to reward him with something special, consider a baby carrot, a small piece of apple, a nibble of lowfat string cheese, some steamed broccoli, or even meat (no sauce). These are treats in more ways than one.

Rawhide chews are a popular treat with dogs, and this Italian Greyhound is certainly interested! Don't overfeed rawhide, and monitor your pup's chewing so that he won't accidentally choke on a large piece.

The quintessential image of a happy dog is one chewing on a large, meaty bone. There's a reason for this: because it's true. Dogs love (and need) to chew, and a bone satisfies this need along with the desire for food. Contrary to what you may have heard or read, giving a dog a bone isn't a huge no-no. In fact, raw diets *include* bones! That said, giving your dog a bone could be disastrous if you don't give him the right kind of bone.

What makes a bone a bad bone is one that can splinter while being chewed or one that is sharp in any way. When swallowed, the sharp edges can perforate your dog's insides. What makes a bone a good bone is one that's either uncooked and fed as part of a raw diet (and you should do your research on this before just going ahead and giving it to your pup), or one that's large enough and strong enough that it won't splinter as it's being gnawed on. A popular choice is a beef marrow bone. These hard bones are filled with fatty marrow. When frozen, they can be given as a chew toy/treat that can keep even an aggressive chewer occupied for a long time. As the frozen bone is worked by the dog, the marrow slowly melts and is eaten for an extra treat.

The first time you give your dog a frozen marrow bone, be sure you can keep an eye on him as he eats it. Make sure it can't be swallowed whole, or that he doesn't gobble it down too fast. Throw it away after it's been worked over and he loses interest.

CHAPTER 9

Grooming Your Puppy

Grooming your puppy is very important. Why? Because the more time you spend taking care of your dog, the happier, healthier, and hopefully longer life he will have. You may look at your puppy and think that you don't have to worry about most of the grooming chores until he's older. Not true, especially if your puppy is a double-coated or long-haired, or a terrier. All of these dogs need lots of attention.

Elemental Grooming

It's a good idea to start grooming your puppy immediately. A puppy is very easy to handle, and since the initial grooming will be very light, you can be extra gentle. This will allow the puppy to become used to the activities, and will provide both of you some bonding. The idea here is that grooming is not only about making a pretty puppy, it's about health maintenance and making the experience enjoyable.

The time you spend going over your puppy with a brush, cleaning his ears, tending to his paws, looking inside his mouth, and even bathing him occasionally will help him feel more comfortable at the veterinarian's office when a stranger may need to take hold of his paw or leg, or look inside his mouth. All those pleasant associations with you will keep the puppy from feeling scared when someone else needs to do it.

The old saying "an ounce of prevention is worth a pound of cure" is what grooming is all about, too. If you didn't regularly groom your puppy, you might not notice new lumps or scratches; you might not realize his toenails are so long that they are affecting the way he walks; you might not smell that cheesy odor in his ears indicating that an infection is brewing. When you do groom your puppy regularly, all these situations would be taken care of, reducing the time and costs of care involved in remedying them.

Your Grooming Kit

To make the job easier on yourself, too (since you already have too much to do), start with a box or container to store the items you'll need to thoroughly groom your puppy or dog. These include:

- A selection of appropriate brushes
- A hound glove or curry comb for short-haired pups
- A flea comb
- A pair of clippers and attachments for long- or curly-haired pups
- A pair of blunt-edged scissors
- Rubber bands or bows if you have a toy breed who needs these to keep the hair back
- Ear cleanser
- Nail clippers (made for dogs)

- Styptic powder
- Toothbrush and toothpaste (made for dogs)
- Cotton balls
- Puppy-friendly shampoo
- Alcohol to clean your tools when you're finished

It won't be part of your kit, but something you should consider using for regular grooming sessions is a grooming table. These are lightweight and portable, and allow you to put your dog on a non-skid surface on a raised platform. It is so much easier to be sure you've gone over your pup or dog thoroughly when you use a grooming table. A second-best option is to place a large rubber mat on your kitchen table and put your dog on it.

Having an established spot where you will do the grooming makes the association easier for your pup, and it also keeps the mess focused for easier cleanup.

Brushing Your Puppy

Why do you suppose that many dogs would stand beside you all day long and let you pet them, yet not let you brush them for even a few minutes? If this is happening with your puppy, consider that you might be using the wrong kind of brush, or one that's poorly made and possibly hurting your pup's sensitive skin.

There are many kinds of brushes available, and the kind you choose should depend on the type and length of fur your pup has. Short-coated dogs need to be gone over with a nubby glove first (commonly called a hound glove or a curry comb) to loosen dead hair and dirt, and then brushed out with a soft-bristled brush. A brush with wire bristles, or one with hard-tipped nylon bristles, may scratch a short-coated pup's skin.

Meanwhile, a long- or double-coated pup is going to need to be brushed with something that can penetrate and separate that fur. For particularly fine-coated dogs, that might be a slicker brush (with small wire bristles set at an angle) or a shedding rake designed to "rake" away dead hair. Having lots of fur doesn't mean these dogs can't have sensitive skin, and no brush should be used to poke a dog, but the right tool is important to do the best job of grooming. If you're not sure which kind to use on your pup, ask the breeder or the folks at your pet store.

A longer-haired pup like this Labradoodle can benefit from more frequent brushing—and learn to enjoy it when it's done gently and carefully.

Brushing is also a way to work with your dog and examine more closely his coat and skin. If there are inconsistencies or infections or rashes, you'll see them a lot more quickly and be able to counteract them much more effectively if you treat your dog to regular brushing. In many cases, brushing is the time when owners find out about things that are seriously wrong with their dogs, like tumors (usually in older dogs) as well as melanomas.

ALERT!

Burrs and matted fur are the two enemies of long-haired dogs. When you spot either of these on your pup, tackle them immediately. Burrs can be loosened and picked at until they come out. Depending on the severity of the matted fur, it's usually easiest to cut the mat away and let the fur grow back.

Puppies don't have a lot of hair, so make sure to use a soft brush. Some experts use very soft human brushes, especially in the beginning. Remember that during these sessions, you want to be making as many happy, cooing noises as possible. Hollering and spitting out commands is a bad way to try to get your pup to work with you on this. And as the puppy grows up, you want him to have a good experience so that the grooming process is not a struggle throughout both of your lives.

FACT

Long-haired dogs are often shaved in the summertime by well-intentioned caretakers who feel that all that hair must make their dogs even hotter. While all dogs feel the effects of summer heat and humidity—and without being able to sweat have a harder time staying cool—the truth is that the thick fur has an insulating property. It is now believed that clipping the fur makes no difference in helping to cool a coated breed in hot weather.

Bathing Your Puppy

Even dogs who love the water rarely enjoy being given a bath. Since this is going to be something your pup will have to live with and undergo fairly regularly, you want to make the experience as pleasant as possible.

The best way to do this is to have everything prepared before you bring your pup to the sink or tub (depending on how big she is). Have extra towels on hand, the shampoo, a conditioner if you're going to use one, a large plastic pitcher for pouring water over the pup, and a slip lead that can help you steady the pup but not interfere with the bath. Run the water until you know it'll be warm when you turn it on. Place a nonskid surface on the bottom of the tub or sink.

With everything prepared, leash your dog, bring her into the bathroom and close the door so she can't beat a hasty retreat. Working calmly and using pleasant and soothing tones, place your dog in the tub and turn on the water so it's running gently. Use the pitcher or a detachable shower attachment to wet the pup all over.

Then start with a big gob of shampoo on your hands and work from the base of the neck along the body toward the tail, rubbing in a circular motion. Don't be too rough. Make sure to work the dog thoroughly under the chest and his hindquarters. Make sure you get the tail. You don't want to use too much shampoo as it will take forever to rinse; use just enough to lather and clean. Be sure to wet his head before applying a small amount of shampoo that you have rubbed between your hands. Do his ears, forehead, and snout gently.

Once you've lathered him all over, begin rinsing. Use your pitcher or the shower attachment, and be sure the water isn't too hot or cold. As you rinse, run your hands over your pup to push off the soapy water. Use as much water as you need to in order to thoroughly rinse the soap out of his fur. Not getting it all out can make your puppy itchy. Don't pour or spray excessive water on her face. You may want to use a washcloth around her eyes, ears, and nose.

When rinsed, you can scoop up your pup in a large, dry towel, and put her on the bath mat to begin toweling her off. Get as much of the water off her fur as possible with towels. Your pup will be excited to be out of the sink or tub, and will want to shake and play. Rub her down with a towel at least once before she shakes or the whole bathroom can get wet. Your pup deserves a good shake or two, though, so let her do it and tell her what a good girl she's been.

Depending on how long your pup's fur is or the time of year, you can complete the drying process naturally or with a hair dryer. If you choose the first route, just be sure your pup won't go roll in the mud while she's still damp. Put her in the kitchen with a baby gate up to confine her until she's dry.

When using a blow dryer on a puppy or dog, be sure to keep it on the lowest setting and don't allow the airstream to blow at her head or ears. Also, hot air can really hurt the skin, and if your pup becomes afraid of the dryer, you're in trouble. So don't hold it too close to the pup.

When your dog is dry, brush and comb him out so he looks extra special. Consider putting a bow in the hair or a bandanna around his neck. Give your pup a special treat and tell him how great he looks.

Ear and Eye Care

These two parts of your dog's body need to be kept clean so your dog can feel good. Dogs with long, floppy ears are prone to ear infections. Since the air can't get inside the ear, bacteria can build up or parasites can find a dark, warm home, and next thing you know, your pup has a full-blown infection. Some of the first signs of ear problems are:

- The dog is shaking his head constantly.
- The dog is scratching his ears often.
- You can smell those ears from across the room

If your pup has any of these signs, get her to a veterinarian to make a proper diagnosis and treat the problem fully. To help prevent the situation, keep your pup's ears clean. Whenever you brush her on the table, take a few minutes to do her ears.

Lift and examine the ear. With a cotton ball soaked in a mild ear cleanser, gently rub the outer ear and as much of the inner ear as you can without poking into it. Do not use cotton swabs as they can push dirt farther into the ear canal.

After the ears have been cleaned, you might want to squirt a little cleaning solution into the ears and rub the ear, then remove the excess with a clean cotton ball. Let your puppy shake out the extra.

It's important to note that dogs who suffer from problem ears tend to be repeat offenders. In other words, if your dog has ear problems once, they are likely to recur. So, keeping your dog's ears clean is very important.

Keeping the area around your pup's eyes clean is simple: With a soft tissue, just work your way around them, clearing off any built-up gunk. If you notice any excessive redness or if anything seems sore, take note, and if it doesn't improve, make an appointment with the veterinarian.

Dogs will wipe their own eyes on carpeting and furniture if the crusty buildup becomes unbearable. This is not only unpleasant for you, but it can cause more problems for the dog. Dirt and scratches may result. Some breeds, such as the Pekingese, can have their own facial hair actually grow to the point where it pokes them in the eye. This is painful for the dog and can result in infection. If you see this happening with your dog, very carefully use a pair of blunt-ended scissors to trim away the hair near the eyes, trimming parallel to its eyes.

Clipping Toenails

Yes, even you can do it! The secret to being able to manage this scariest part of the grooming process is to take baby steps when you start, and always keep it positive for your pup (and you). Don't leave this important part of grooming to the very last. Alternate clipping the nails of a paw with brushing different parts of the body. Keep your pup guessing about what you'll be doing next.

Okay, so if you're going to do it, here's how: Use a high-quality pair of nail trimmers, as the less expensive ones have blades that take longer to cut and often get stuck on a nail, only prolonging the odd feeling for your dog. Many nail clippers have a safety feature that can obstruct your vision and cause you to inadvertently cut into the quick. Avoid relying on it. You only want to take off the very tip.

As you're brushing or petting your pup, get out the nail clippers. Start petting your pup's legs, then feet. Lift a paw gently and as quickly as you can, position the clippers around the tip of a nail and clip. Then stop. Give her a hug and a treat, and move on to grooming another part of her. Keep going back to the nails until they're all done. Even if they still look long after cutting off just the tips, don't worry, ten days later you can have right back at it, that's because as you cut the toenails, the quick will recede within a week's time.

QUESTION?

What is the "quick" of a dog's toenail?
The quick is the soft, fleshy part of a claw. It resides within the nail, near the base. It's a little easier to see on dogs that have white nails (it's the dark shading about half way up the nail). Black nails hide the quick. Light or dark nails, you don't want to hit the quick, so only clip the very tips of the nails.

Should you accidentally cut into the quick on your pup's nail, it will bleed profusely. It will also hurt your poor pup, and you'll have a hurting dog and a bloody paw on your hands. Try to position an old towel or a paper towel on the paw to absorb the blood, and try to keep your puppy still. Apply styptic powder as soon as possible. She'll get over the hurt paw, but she may never forget the association between the clipper and the pain, in which case your job just got a lot harder. You may need to ask a groomer or veterinary assistant to clip the nails if you find yourself struggling over it too much.

Dental Care

Proper dental care can add as much as five years to your dog's life. In addition, the quality of your dog's life will be much higher, especially in her later years. Proper dental care will also do wonders for eliminating doggy breath. Ideally, for the best dental care you should clean your dog's teeth every day and have his teeth professionally cleaned at least once a year.

ALERT!

If you try to examine your older dog's teeth for the first time, use caution. As a general rule, dogs don't like anyone messing around with the inside of their mouth. If there is a problem in there somewhere, and you poke at a tender spot with your fingers in the dog's mouth, the pooch may inadvertently bite down.

It is best to ease your dog into this routine. Even puppies will show their best squirming talents during a tooth brushing. Start by just using your finger tip by itself to gently rub doggy toothpaste onto the surfaces of your dog's teeth. Once your puppy seems okay with this (the toothpaste should taste good to him), start using a damp, soft cloth or a piece of damp gauze to apply the paste. From there you should begin using a regular dog toothbrush.

In addition to regular cleaning, take care to observe the dental health of your puppy. Though most problems won't show up until later in life, it is a good habit to get into from the start. Once a week, you should check to make sure none of your dog's teeth are loose. You should also look for discolorations of the teeth and gums, as well as lumps on its tongue. Any of these problems can be serious. Dental infections can quickly spread to other parts of your dog and can cause death.

When to Use a Professional Groomer

Especially for long-haired breeds, you will want to use the services of a professional groomer at least twice a year. They are experienced and will make sure all the proper things are done to your dog. They are expert at cleaning ears, clipping the coat to achieve the desired look for his breed, trimming his nails, and in general making sure he looks like the dog you want him to be. There is no shame in leaving your dog with a groomer; in fact, when you pick up your coiffed dog and he looks and smells great, you will realize what a pleasure it is. Do it for your puppy and for yourself.

Use caution, however. There are great dog groomers, and there are those who should really be doing something else. Working with a dog while he's stressed (which is common at the groomer's) takes a certain someone. You need to be sure the groomer who handles your dog takes the time to get to know him and handles him properly. Ask for references from any groomer you're considering and call them. Groomers use sharp and hot objects when they work, and the last thing you need is to have your dog mistreated when he is in the groomer's care. A puppy who's been spooked or mistreated will behave differently, often badly, and this can have all kinds of repercussions for you and your family.

On the other hand, a groomer who enjoys working with your dog and really takes the time and effort to make him look good—and who also shares concerns with you about his coat quality, for example, or some other problem she sees—is a gem. Be sure to let her know how much you appreciate her service and attention to your dog by tipping generously when she does a great job. Knowing your dog is being well taken care of by this person is worth every penny.

CHAPTER 10

Housetraining Your Puppy

The first thing every new owner should know before bringing a puppy into the house is how to teach him where to relieve himself. The good news is that all puppies can be housetrained. The bad news is that a puppy rarely becomes housetrained by just letting him out several times a day. This comprehensive housetraining plan requires dedication—but it's simple and foolproof.

The Eight Essentials of Housetraining

This is your to-do list to get started. There are only eight items on it, so it's not too difficult. If you can keep to it, you will be amazed at how well housetraining goes. If you get off track, resolve to get back on as quickly as possible. You can do it!

1. Confine your puppy to his crate when you can't watch him so he won't relieve himself where he's not supposed to or while you're not looking (if you prefer, use a baby gate to confine him to the kitchen or laundry room while you can't watch him—just make sure the room is puppy-proofed).
2. Supervise your puppy when he is out of his crate.
3. Feed him a high-quality diet at scheduled times, and limit treats.
4. Take him to his potty spot as soon as you return home, soon after meals, and when he wakes up from a nap.
5. Teach him to eliminate on command by saying Go potty, Good puppy! in an excited voice while he's doing his business.
6. Clean up his accidents immediately (remove debris or moisture, then treat with neutralizer and cleaner).
7. Never correct him after the fact.
8. Keep a log of his habits (when and where he pooped or peed, and when and how much he ate and drank).

You will need to be diligent about this for several months, so be prepared.

Using a Crate

Until a puppy is perfectly trained, he needs a safe place in which he can do nothing wrong. So when you can't keep your eyes glued to your puppy and monitor his every move, confine him to a place where inappropriate behavior—soiling, stealing, shredding, chewing, or scratching—isn't an option. This book suggests crating because it eliminates the risk of him damaging woodwork, flooring, wall covering, or cabinetry.

Assuming you ultimately want your puppy to enjoy freedom in the house, crating is almost a rearing necessity. Crating is widely accepted by behaviorists, puppy trainers, veterinarians, and knowledgeable puppy owners as a humane means of confinement. Provided your puppy is properly introduced, you should feel as comfortable about crating him in your absence as you would securing a toddler in a highchair at mealtime.

Crates are not cruel. Remember, dogs are naturally den animals. They normally take to crate training very naturally, if you take care to properly set up the crate.

Whether the enclosure is a room, hallway, kennel, or crate, it should be:

- **The right size.** It should be large enough that when your puppy is a full-grown dog he'll be able to stand without his shoulders touching the ceiling of the crate. This sized crate will be far too large for your puppy at first. Use a divider to limit the amount of space your puppy has; for the first month or so, one-third to one-half the crate should be fine.
- **Safe.** Homemade enclosures may save you money, but you would feel awful if he poked himself in the eye, stabbed or hung himself, or swallowed wood splinters or material like wallpaper or blankets because you ignored potential dangers. Make sure there are no protrusions or sharp edges, and no ingestible components.
- **Puppy proof.** If he is prone to chewing, scratching or jumping up, prevent access to any woodwork, linoleum, furniture, counters, garbage, or windows so your home doesn't become a victim of your puppy's destructiveness during his training period.

Though your puppy will come to think of his crate as his sanctuary because it satisfies a puppy's denning instinct, he may not like the idea of going in the crate at first. If you reinforce his objections to the crate by making his early associations with it unpleasant, he may never adjust to it. Go slowly, and praise every positive step along the way.

Make the crate a safe and cozy place for your puppy. Put it somewhere your pup will have some privacy, but not where he'll feel all alone. A corner of the kitchen is usually a good spot. Line the bottom of the crate with newspaper for extra insulation from the cold floor, then put a soft blanket or piece of fleece on top of the newspaper. Hopefully your puppy will never eliminate on his sleeping material in his crate, but don't bet on it, especially not in the first few weeks. The blanket or fleece should be machine washable, and of course, the newspapers can be thrown away.

FACT

One sure way to ruin the crate training method is to use the crate as a means of punishment. If you lock up your puppy as punishment, you will soon lose the advantage of rewarding him with the comforts of his own room in the house.

Get your puppy into a good chew toy habit right away by putting an appropriate chew toy in the crate. Puppies need to chew, so unless you want them to go to work on your shoes, furniture, floor—whatever—turn them on to puppy-appropriate toys early.

When his crate looks like something you might want to curl up and nap in, call him over to it. Let him sniff it. Don't push him toward it or into it. Let him discover it in his own time. Make it interesting for him by putting some small bits of something really tasty like cold cuts or cheese near the entrance. When he shows interest, toss a goody into the crate. If he runs in and gobbles it up, tell him what a good puppy he is. Get excited about it!

Don't shut the door on him the first time he goes in the crate. Let him go in and out a few times, continuing to praise when he shows interest. After all this stimulation, take him to his potty spot. This is his first introduction to the crate.

Later, feed your puppy in the crate. Place him and his food inside and sit with your back blocking the doorway of the crate. Don't close the crate

For your puppy, a crate can be a very special and favorite place to call her own away from the hustle-bustle of the rest of the household. When crate-training is a positive experience, she will love her private place.

door. Sit there and read a book or magazine until he's finished eating, then take him out. For his next meal, prop the crate door and sit at the opening with your puppy. Keeping his food in the bowl, place a few pieces of kibble in the crate, then feed him a few pieces from your hand outside the crate. This way he associates being fed as something that happens in the crate and out. Feeding your puppy from your hands is also an excellent way to teach him that your hands mean good things. Your puppy (and later, your dog) should always associate your hands (and any person's hands) coming toward him as a good thing. There may be times when you have to grab his collar or take his food away or when strangers want to pet him. A puppy who's not afraid of hands will not want to bite when that happens.

Next, teach your puppy to enter and exit the crate on command. Put his paws right in front of the opening. With one hand on his collar and the other pointing into the crate, say Bed. Gently guide him in by the collar as you place your hand under his tail and behind his rear legs to prevent him from backing away. If necessary, gently lift him in. Immediately invite him out by saying Okay and praising him for coming out to you.

Practice several repetitions of this routine three times or more every day so he goes to bed on command—without being enclosed. If you shut him in and leave him every time he is put in the enclosure he may develop a bad association with crating. But when he learns to go in the crate on command as a result of frequent practice, he is more likely to also accept being enclosed.

If you reserve his favorite toy for the times he spends in the crate, he may actually look forward to crating as an opportunity to play with it. Leave food and water out of the crate; puppies don't need it in there and most will dump or scatter it instead of eating or drinking. Create a peaceful environment by covering the crate with a sheet or, if his tendency is to pull it in, surround the crate with a couple of stiff panels for a more enclosed, den-like atmosphere.

FACT

A crate is not a cage unless you make it so. Crate training relies on your making the crate into a den. To crate train successfully, you need to remember to make the crate a comfy room. The crate is not a house of punishment. The more den-like it is, the happier your puppy will be. Make sure it is clean and properly covered. This will make your puppy naturally enjoy its crate.

What to Do if Puppy Barks in the Crate

Sometimes a puppy will bark, yodel, whine, or howl when crated. Unless he is trying to tell you he has to go potty, ignore any noise he might make. Most pups will quiet down if you ignore their pleas. If yours doesn't and you or your family members are losing sleep or sanity, startle him into being quiet, use a word for it (Shush) and praise for the quietness.

To startle your barking or crying puppy, your timing has to be accurate. While he's in full voice, clap your hands sharply twice. You can also create an earthquake by attaching the leash to his crate and giving it a quick jerk as he barks. Do these things where your puppy can't see you. You don't want him to associate you with things that startle or scare him. You may need to do this a number of times before he learns what Shush means. He'll still try to get your attention by barking or crying. Combine ignoring the noise and startling him until he's settled down.

If your puppy sleeps in your bedroom in his crate, you must res his crying in the middle of the night, otherwise you're teaching him the you will respond to that noise and he'll continue to make it. To make the crate more accommodating for him, use the suggestions given in Chapter 7 about handling the first week at home. Covering the crate with a sheet at night can also help. If none of these things work, consider keeping your puppy crated in the kitchen where his cries won't reach you as loudly. Remember, your puppy is not trying to torture you. He wants to be with you. It may take him a few nights, but he'll eventually quiet down.

A crate-trained puppy is not housetrained. Your puppy is likely to do things you're not going to like when loose in the house and, therefore, needs plenty of supervised exploration to learn the house rules. If your puppy is out of his crate, keep your eyes glued on him or, better still, umbilical cord him so when you can't follow him, he'll follow you; this affords you the opportunity to curtail misbehaviors before they become habits.

Here's how umbilical cording works: Tie his leash to your belt on your left side. Give him only enough slack to keep him at your side without your legs becoming entangled. If he attempts to jump up, chew, bark, or relieve himself without your approval, you'll be able to stop him instantly by tugging on the lead to distract him. You'll also be able to tell him what a good puppy he is when he trots after you or sits by your side as you work around the house or sit down to do something. Umbilical cording is a fantastically simple technique and important training tool, which every able-bodied household member should use. You can even umbilical cord two puppies at once. Or when one pet is trained and the other isn't, you can cord the untrained puppy while giving the reliable one his freedom.

Although dogs normally won't mess in their crates, some do. Occasional accidents shouldn't concern you, but if it happens every other day or more, try these suggestions:

- Remove all bedding in hopes he'll be repulsed by having nothing other than his body to absorb the mess.
- Use a smaller crate so he only has enough room to turn in place.
- Teach him to enter and exit his crate on command (Go to your spot).
- Put his food and water in the open crate to encourage a better association about being in there; remove it when he's enclosed.

The Importance of Schedules

Most puppies leave their litter to enter their new home at about two months of age. At this age, the pups eat and drink a lot, and have limited ability to control their elimination, and no comprehension that that might be important. Feeding and potty times should be adjusted to help puppy reach his potential in the housetraining department as quickly as possible. At two to four months of age most pups need to relieve themselves after waking up, eating, playing, sleeping, and drinking—perhaps as often as every thirty to forty-five minutes, depending on the type and amount of activity. At four months, the puppy may be developed like an adult internally, but expect him to behave like a puppy.

To housetrain effectively, you need to establish a schedule that works for your family and will help your puppy learn the rules quickly. You will be amazed at how quickly your puppy learns if you stick to a schedule that has fixed times for eating, sleeping and exercising. Now is a good time to review the sample schedule in Chapter 5 and prepare one that will work for you.

ALERT!

Puppies can dehydrate very easily and very quickly. It is extremely important that you give your puppy ample access to water. Restricting your puppy's water as a means of potty training should only be done as a last resort and only after consulting with your puppy's veterinarian.

Training to Use a Potty Spot

Teach your puppy to eliminate on command. This lesson is handy both when he is too distracted and won't potty or when he's on a surface that he's inclined not to potty on—for example, a kennel run, wet grass, or where other puppies have been. Others will go potty only if they're in a particular area or taken for a walk. By teaching your puppy to eliminate on command, you can get him to go where you want, when you want, and simplify the housetraining process. Here's how to do it.

Sticking to your schedule of getting your puppy out for regular walks will help immensely in your housetraining efforts.

Leash your puppy and take him to the potty spot. When he begins the sniffing and circling ritual that immediately precedes elimination, start chanting a phrase like Potty, hurry up. What you say is unimportant, but it should sound melodic and should always be the same phrase. Use the same words for defecation and urination. When your puppy starts to go, praise him profusely (What a good puppy dog!) and give him a special treat, like a sliver of hot dog or cheese. After a week of chanting while your puppy is relieving himself, begin the chant as soon as you enter the potty area. Always praise when he does what you want and give him an extra-special reward of playtime in the yard or a stroll around the block.

If you take your puppy to his potty spot and he doesn't eliminate right away, take him back inside for a few more minutes until you're certain he needs to. Don't take your puppy outside, ask him to do his business, and take him for a walk whether he does or not. Teach him that going potty right away means getting a walk. If you dash back inside after puppy's gone potty, he'll learn that the only way to get a walk out of you is to hold it—and the only way for you to take him out is to go in the house. Remember, reward him for doing the correct thing: pottying in his spot when you ask him. Then and only then should he be rewarded.

How to Handle Accidents

No matter how careful you are, occasionally inappropriate elimination happens. If your puppy has an accident do the following:

- Never correct the puppy after the fact. Do scold yourself by saying, "How could I have let that happen?"
- If you catch him in the act, startle him by saying "Ach" loudly or picking him up in midstream and carrying him outside to stop him.
- Clean up messes immediately. Remove debris and blot up any moisture, then use a cleaning solution, and finally treat the soiled area with an odor neutralizer.

Until your puppy is perfectly potty trained, remember:

1. Puppies who can hold it for long periods while they're in their cage or at night are not necessarily well on their way to being housebroken. Don't judge his capacity and trustworthiness by his behavior while crated. Metabolism slows down with inactivity, so even a totally untrained puppy may not soil for up to twelve hours when he's crated. Puppies aren't trained until they understand it's okay to move about, explore, and go potty outdoors, but must hold it as they move about and explore indoors.
2. Puppies enjoy playing, observing, and investigating, and often forget about going potty when they're left alone outdoors. Don't let your puppy out without supervision and assume that he did his business. Even if your puppy has just spent a lot of time outdoors, he may mess soon after he comes back inside.
3. Puppies often indicate when they want to go outdoors and play, instead of when they need to potty. Don't rely on or encourage him to tell you

he wants to go out. Many puppies will indicate frequently and always eliminate when taken to the potty area. This causes bladder and bowel capacity and control to be underdeveloped. So, if he's used to going out on demand to go potty, he may have to relieve himself immediately whether you're available or not.

Common Housetraining Problems

He Forgets to Go

On common problem is that your puppy will forget to relieve himself when he is outdoors, but will remember as soon as he is back in the house.

Leashing your puppy during potty breaks will enable you to keep your puppy moving and sniffing within the appropriate area, and thus speed the process of elimination. If you sense your puppy is about to become distracted from his duty of looking for a potty spot, use a light, quick jerk on the leash as you slowly move about the area yourself. If you don't get results within five minutes, take puppy back inside and put him in his crate for another ten minutes or so. Eventually he'll have to go, and then you can reward him for going outside in the designated spot.

He Takes Forever to Go

Only give your puppy a few minutes to potty. If you give him twenty minutes, he is likely to demand thirty the next time. After a couple minutes, put him back in his crate long enough to make him thankful for the next potty opportunity you give him. As stated earlier, have your puppy earn playtime by pottying first and playing afterward. Potty breaks will be much less time-consuming if your puppy learns to associate the initial act of walking outdoors with the act of going potty, not playing.

Cutting Back on Taking Your Puppy Out

Many owners make the mistake of continually taking a puppy out before he really needs to go. Although they do so hoping he won't soil the house, they are actually preventing him from developing the capacity to hold it. Since housetraining is a matter of teaching the puppy to control his bladder and bowels until he has access to the outdoors, taking the puppy out too frequently slows the housetraining process. When you think he doesn't need to go out but he does, try umbilical cording or crating him for a half-hour before taking a walk.

Regression

Plan on a year or more to complete the housetraining process. Although your puppy may be flawless for days, weeks, or months, under certain conditions any puppy can backslide. Seemingly benign events such as these can cause housetraining regression:

- Changes in diet can affect bowel and bladder control.
- Weather changes (too hot, cold, or wet, or noisy thunderstorms) can make outings unproductive potty times.
- New environments (vacation homes, new house, or friend's house) may be treated as an extension of his potty area rather than his living quarters.
- Some medications (like allergy medications) and certain conditions (like hormone changes associated with estrus) can cause more frequent elimination.

Submissive Urination

If your puppy wets when he greets people or is disciplined, he isn't having a housetraining problem. Uncontrollable and unconscious leaking of urine is common in puppies and certain breeds. If your pup has been given a clean bill of health by a veterinarian so that you know his problem isn't health-related, work on the problem by:

- Never yelling, striking, or showing anger toward him
- Making your entrances and greetings devoid of emotion
- Avoiding eye contact, talking, and touching during emotional states
- Withholding water if you're going out for a short period of time. Offer water every time you take him out to relieve himself.

Since living with this behavior can be exasperating, consider diapering your dog for the first thirty days so you don't have to continually clean up. To diaper your dog, simply pin a bandanna or towel around his privates and teach him not to remove it. Acclimate your puppy to wearing the diaper by umbilical cording him to you with the leash and distracting him if he even sniffs at the diaper by tugging on the leash. When he is totally uninterested in the diaper—usually after less than a week of umbilical cording—let him walk around the house unleashed as usual, without concern about dribbling.

Avoid vigorous petting, impassioned tones of voice, and strong eye contact. Only interact with a superficial, brief pat, calm word, or fleeting glimpse when his bladder is empty. When he consistently responds without tinkling, test his control after he's had water. Gradually try a warmer approach, but be ready to turn off the affection and issue a command if it pleases the pee out of him.

Papertraining can work for some dogs and some people, and might be a consideration for you. To work, though, it must be done properly and used consistently.

Paper Training—If You Must

Owning a small puppy offers lots of advantages. One of these is that if you don't want to walk him outdoors, you can teach him to eliminate on papers indoors. To start, get full-sized newspapers (not tabloids) and a sixteen-square-foot, wire-mesh exercise pen, available from puppy supply catalogs or by special order from a pet shop. Place the pen on an easy-to-clean floor and line the bottom with newspapers opened flat out. For one week, keep your puppy in the fully papered pen anytime you aren't supervising or exercising. Then, put a bed in the pen and gradually reduce the papered portion to one full-sized newspaper, overlapping five sheets to ensure proper absorption. Once he is pottying on the paper, open up the pen within a small room or hall. When he consistently soils on the paper, gradually give him access to the house, room by room, when you are able to supervise him. Shuttle him over to the papers if he attempts to go elsewhere. If he begins missing paper to any degree, follow the confinement and umbilical cording procedure described for outdoor training, except take puppy to the paper, rather than the outdoors, to eliminate.

Once trained, some paper-trained puppies only go on their papers; others prefer the outdoors but will use papers if necessary. You can paper-train a previously outdoor-trained puppy and vice versa, but you'll avoid extra work by deciding what you want up front.

CHAPTER 11

Socializing—
Raising a Friendly Dog

Puppies have so much potential, curiosity, and intelligence. That's why puppy training begins the moment your puppy comes into your house—whether you want it to or not. Soiling, biting, jumping, barking, and running are natural behaviors; as a new puppy parent, it is up to you to demonstrate where and when those behaviors are appropriate and, more importantly, where they are inappropriate. Begin teaching and socializing your puppy as early as eight weeks of age if he is properly vaccinated and his good health is confirmed by your veterinarian. Although the techniques in this chapter are best suited for puppies two to four months of age, you'll find the information valuable when training older puppies, too.

Why Socializing Is So Important

This chapter will detail why socialization is important for so many parts of your dog's life, but here's an example to help you understand. You bring home your pup on a long weekend so that you and your family can spend the first few days with him and really get your schedule off to a successful start. You have a dog walker lined up so that, when it's time to go back to work and school, your pup will continue to be well taken care of. When your real life of work, school, and other activities settles into a routine, you continue to walk your growing pup in the morning and evening, and your kids play with him in the afternoon, often with friends. He learns Sit, Down, Stay, Wait, and Off, and besides some accidents in the house, things seem to be going well. Your pup/dog is always happy to see you, sleeps in your room, plays nicely with the kids, and seems well adjusted.

Then you decide he can come along on a holiday weekend to your in-laws' house. They also have a dog, and you are excited to introduce your dog to theirs. You finally arrive at their house and everyone piles out of the car to excitedly say hello. You put your pup on a leash to introduce him, and your in-laws' dog comes bounding out of the house to greet everyone. He is a pleasant but large dog. When your puppy sees him, he wants to bolt. He doesn't know what to do. His fear causes the other dog to assume an aggressive stance, and your pup responds in either fear or aggression. There is a squabble and everyone is upset. As the weekend goes on, your dog has accidents in the house, especially when there are several people in the same room together. When strange kids want to pet him, he runs away or, worse, snaps at them. You are upset and reprimand, then punish, your pup, exacerbating rather than appeasing him. You return home wondering if getting a dog was such a good idea, and whether your dog will ever be able to go on trips with you.

Is it Your Puppy, or You?

While you're driving and wondering what's wrong with your dog, you should be looking in a mirror, because the problem is you. In the throes of work and a busy family schedule, you didn't take the time to expose your puppy to all different kinds of people, places, and experiences. Then you took him along and threw him into one of the craziest experiences any dog can have: a family holiday, with the common ingredients of extra people, extra noise, easily available trash and food, strange people, strange smells, strange animals, and many distractions.

Read on to discover how and why socialization can make a major difference in your life with your puppy.

Meeting People

Socialize your puppy to people, making sure he gets plenty of experiences with both genders and a variety of races and ages. Go to the park, a parade, the beach, outside of a shopping center, or an airport. Bring some of your puppy's kibble or some other tasty treats and have strangers ask your puppy to sit for a greeting and a treat. If you do this often enough, your puppy will start to think, "If I sit when I see someone coming I'll get a treat." Not a bad thought!

Allowing friendly puppies to interact with friendly children—even toddlers—is great for both of them when the experience is positive. To ensure success, keep a careful eye on the pup and the child. It can be pure magic.

Occasionally, leave your puppy in the care of a trustworthy, level-headed friend for a minute, an hour, or a day. Your objective is teach the pup to be self-assured in your absence; therefore, don't say goodbye or hello to the puppy. Treat the situation as a nonevent so your puppy is less likely to experience separation anxiety.

Think about items people carry and equipment they use. Expose your puppy to wheelchairs, canes, bicycles, lawn mowers, roller skates, vacuum cleaners, etc.

Getting to Know the World

Help your puppy to become a savvy traveler who is accustomed to elevators, stairways, manholes, and grates. Acclimate him to walking on a variety of surfaces such as gravel, wire, sand, cobblestone, linoleum, and brick. Because some puppies prefer to eliminate only in their own backyard, teach him to eliminate on command in different areas, so weekend trips and the like won't be a problem.

If you want to foster enjoyment of the water and your puppy isn't a natural pond-puppy, walk him on-leash along the shoreline. Once he is at ease with that, venture into the water. Gently tighten the leash as you go, forcing him to swim a couple feet before you let him return to the shoreline. Never throw any puppy into the water.

QUESTION?

Why is confidence so important when it comes to training and raising your puppy?
A confident dog allows guests in the house with little fanfare, but will always be alert should something go wrong. The confident dog does not shy away from people or act skittish. He is sure of himself, and can be depended upon for a steady temperament. He is not overly aggressive toward strangers or other dogs. A skittish dog, a dog that lacks confidence, is one who is unsure of people or other dogs. His behavior can be unpredictable.

Meeting Other Animals

Let him get to know other animals—cats, chickens, horses, goats, birds, guinea pigs, lizards, and of course, other puppies and dogs. Often upon meeting a new species a puppy is startled, then curious, and finally some become bold or aggressive. For his own protection and for the protection of the other animal, always keep him leashed so you can control his distance and stop unwanted behaviors by enforcing obedience commands.

Whatever you are socializing your puppy to—animals, objects, or people—approach the new thing in a relaxed manner and avoid any situation that would intimidate the average puppy, such as a group of grade schoolers rushing at him. Be prepared for three reactions: walking up to check it out and sniff, apprehensive barking with hackles raised, or running away.

No matter how well-socialized your pup may be, there will be situations where it would be unfair to trust him to ignore his instincts. For example, if your niece has a pet mouse and you have a Dachshund or a terrier, you can't expect that the mouse could safely play outside of its cage with your dog in the room. These dogs have been bred through time to hunt down such small animals.

No matter his response, remain silent. In the first (and, by the way, best) scenario he is thinking rationally and investigating his environment— don't draw attention to yourself by talking, praising, or petting. Allow him to explore uninterrupted. This good boy is entertaining himself and being educated at the same time. If your puppy lacks confidence or displays fear, don't console him because this will reinforce his fear. Use the leash to prevent him from running away. If he is still slightly uncomfortable, drop some tasty bits of food (like slivers of hot dog) on the ground. Most puppies will relax after a nibble or two because the uncomfortable situation has been positively associated with food.

If loud noises frighten your puppy, desensitize him by allowing him to create a racket. Offer him a big metal spoon with a little peanut butter on it. Give him an empty half-gallon or gallon milk jug with the cap removed and a bit of squeeze cheese in the rim to bat around. It won't be long before he is creating hubbub and loving it. Of course, if the clamoring drives you nuts, feel free to limit his playtime with these items. Also socialize your puppy to walking on leash, riding in the car, and being examined and groomed.

When introducing a new puppy to your current dog or cat, remember that your established pet considers your home its territory. If possible, try to introduce the animals in neutral territory, maybe in a friend's yard. It's very important to make sure neither of the animals becomes afraid of the other, or the other pet will quickly become a bully.

Riding in the Car

As soon as your puppy is large enough, teach him to enter and exit the car on command. Practice this by leashing him, walking him up to the car, and commanding him to go in as you give him a boost. Invite him out of the car by calling Come as you gently pull the leash. Practice several of these, several times a day until he goes in and out on command. Even before your puppy is ready for that lesson, decide where you'd like him to ride. Crating is the safest option. If it isn't the most convenient, try a puppy seatbelt, which is available at many pet shops or by mail order. Don't feed your puppy for hours prior to riding if he has any tendency toward carsickness. It is also prudent to keep the air temperature inside the car comfortably cool (if you roll down a window, choose one that your puppy cannot stick his head out of). Additionally, you'll reduce the chance of motion sickness by avoiding bumpy roads and abrupt stops or turns.

Leaving a dog in an unattended car in the summer is extremely danger-ous. Remember that just because it's cloudy now, doesn't mean the sun won't poke through any minute. Whenever you take your dog with you to run errands, be sure to have a place to tie your dog up outside, even cracking all the windows won't help much as the temperature in your car can climb well above 100 degrees quickly.

Socializing as Your Puppy Grows

Facing strange people and situations is going to be a part of life for you and your dog, so don't think socializing him has a beginning or ending time. It is always happening, and the more of it you continue to do, the better adjusted your pup will become. Remember, slow and steady wins the race, and it is life with all of its peculiarities that will really test your pup, not a made-up situation you create for him.

One of the best ways to continue socialization is through classes and activities you can do together. Because there are so many activities for dogs, there are lots of ways for you to get involved in something really interesting. If you have an energetic pup, consider fast-paced agility. If your pup is a love muffin, he may be the perfect dog for therapy situa-tions, whether they're with older people or kids. If you have a breed with a performance history, by all means get involved in that sport, whether it's herding, lure coursing, hunting, or water work. All these things will expose you to lots of people, dogs, travel, new places, new sights and sounds, and so on. They will also teach your dog that no matter where you go or what you do together, he is to take his cues from you. You're his trainer and his leader. This is very reassuring for him, and useful in any situation.

The Dos and Don'ts of Socializing

Perhaps your veterinarian advised you against exposing your puppy while his immune system is developing, but you fear the risks of neglect-ing his socialization during this critical period. Though you may not be able to walk him around the big city, you can start a socialization program at home:

- Desensitize him to noises by letting him play with an empty plastic half-gallon or gallon milk jug or big metal spoon.
- Accustom him to walking on a variety of surfaces such as bubble wrap, big plastic bags, and chicken wire. Put a treat in the middle so he gets rewarded for his bravery.
- If his experiences with meeting new people will be limited, you can get creative with costumes. Wear hats, masks, and capes, walk with a cane, or limp, skip, and hop.
- Handle him as described in the grooming and examination section.
- Take him for car rides with permission from your veterinarian.

CHAPTER 12

Exercising Your Puppy

You can love your puppy with all your heart and soul, wanting nothing more than to return or be home with him so that you can cuddle and coo over him. You can give him the best food, wonderful treats, toys galore, take him out to his potty spot regularly, and be sure he makes his regular appointments with the veterinarian. You can do all this and think there is nothing more a pup could want. But there is. And it's exercise.

Why Exercise Is So Important

It's a fact for puppies and people alike: exercise is just plain good for you all over. It keeps your weight in check; it helps maintain all vital organs, especially the heart and lungs; posture is supported by healthy muscles; endorphins stimulate a more positive attitude—it's a win-win endeavor.

Puppies who don't go out, who don't get to stretch their legs, use their noses, explore their world, play with others—who don't get to be puppies— literally go crazy and in turn drive their human companions crazy. These pups often resort to the problem behaviors described in Chapter 14—often because they have nothing else to do. A sad and avoidable plight.

Assessing Your Puppy's Energy Needs

When your puppy is still a baby, be careful not to overdo the exercise you give him. For very young puppies—ages ten to twenty weeks or so— sufficient exercise could be having plenty of time to play, wrestle, scamper, and bounce around the way puppies like to do. Any sustained or more intense forms of exercise could damage growing bones and muscles and possibly do more harm than good.

After a nap and the opportunity to relieve himself, a puppy is most energetic. Like small children, they move erratically and their attention spans are very short. You need to be engaging and spontaneous. Try getting down on the floor with your puppy and playing with one of his favorite toys. You can shake it at him gently so that he grabs on and plays a gentle game of tug. (If the game starts getting rough, completely stop playing on your end and, when he drops the tug toy, quietly and calmly take it away and remove it from his reach.) You can roll a ball or a stuffed sock along the floor so he can grab and carry it around. You can imitate the play of another dog and bring your hands down in front of you in a mock play bow, signaling to your puppy that you want to play and wrestle. Always, if the play gets too rough, simply stop all movements and end the game.

Playing is a good way to teach your pup some of the basic manners that are explained in Chapter 15. These include Drop it, Off, and Wait. Puppies tend to learn more when their reward comes in the form of play or food, so take advantage of your receptive audience to reinforce manners.

Outdoor exercise and play are some of the best things for your pup – and the stuff that memories (and great photo opportunities) are made of. This is a Bernese Mountain Dog.

Another regular part of an exercise program will be walks with your puppy. These essential outings provide your pup with the opportunity to relieve himself and stretch his legs and to explore his world. With their incredible sense of smell, dogs pick up all kinds of information in the scents they encounter on their walks. A particular post in your neighborhood may be the favorite "pee-mail" spot on the block, where all the dogs squat or lift their leg. Your pup will soon figure out where that place is on your walks and be eager to sniff it every day. Allow him that indulgence.

FACT

The Parsons Russell Terrier, the Border Collie, the Doberman Pinscher, and the Golden Retriever are known to be high-energy breeds. The intensity of their playtime is greater and it takes longer to wear them out.

As your pup grows, getting bigger and stronger, you can begin to take longer walks or spend more time outside exercising. Try to find a park near you that includes a dog run—a special area where dogs are allowed to play off leash (more on that later in the chapter). This is a great time to start expanding your puppy's world—and seeing more of your neighborhood yourself. If you live in or near a town that has a nice downtown area, take your pup for a walk there. It's a great place to socialize him to all kinds of people. Even without a downtown, you can learn more about your neighbors and your neighborhood by taking longer and longer walks. You'll be amazed by what you discover.

Don't judge your puppy's capacity by what any other puppy does. A littermate of his may be more energetic and need and/or be able to take a longer walk than your friend. Watch your pup's body language to determine when he's reached his limits. On the other hand, don't let your pup get lazy and shortchange your walks. If he seems lethargic, you may want to ask your veterinarian to evaluate him.

Ask your breeder about your pup's potential energy needs, or be sure to ask the previous owners of an older puppy you adopt how energetic that puppy was. At least this knowledge will help prepare you for making the adequate exercise needs of your puppy a priority. Whatever those may be, it is critical that you take your puppy out for walks at least twice a day. The walks may be short or long, but they are necessary. If you are fortunate enough to be around the house during the day, your puppy will benefit from a short walk or some outdoor play time at midday.

If you have a fenced yard and let your pup out in the morning and evening to do his business, it's very tempting to relegate that to exercise time. If you get lazy and do this, though, you'll start to get the ramifications of it pretty quickly. Boredom will set in for your pup, and with it, naughty and even nasty behaviors.

ALERT!

As you learned in Chapter 10, it's important to teach your puppy to eliminate at the start of the walk so the exercise becomes the reward. If your puppy figures out that you bring her in immediately after she goes even when she wants to stay out, she may hold it so that she gets to walk a while first.

Obeying Rules of Common Courtesy While Out and About

No matter where you live or walk your puppy, you are responsible for her actions. That is why there are leash laws, waste laws, nuisance laws, and so on. The things you need to be aware of include:

- **Clean up after your puppy.** You may think it's not that important, but what if everyone walking puppies felt the same way? Soon our streets and parks would be covered in you-know-what. Every scoop makes a difference. It may seem gross, but you get used to it fast. Use a plastic bag to cover your hand, pick up the offending matter, turn the bag inside out so the waste is securely inside it, tie up the bag and toss it in a trash can.
- **Keep your puppy on a leash.** This is necessary for people who live in cities and suburbs, and owners of country puppies should have a leash handy when walking their puppies. Even if your puppy is responsive and reliable off-leash, you never know what might happen. See the section below on Letting Your Puppy Off Lead for more on this subject.
- **Keep your puppy under control.** If you're walking with your puppy and see someone walking toward you who appears uncomfortable at the sight of your puppy, be kind and courteous, reel your puppy in, and hold her while the person passes. No one likes a puppy—even one on a leash—who approaches enthusiastically and tries to sniff or jump up on them.

- **Be mindful of trouble.** You are responsible for your puppy. Use common sense and only consider approaching strange puppies if they appear calm. When you're a safe distance away, ask the other owner if their puppy is okay with other puppies. Approach slowly and be ready to pull your puppy away if necessary. And if you know your puppy starts trouble with other puppies, don't let others approach him.
- **Be mindful of street signs and traffic patterns.** Be sure that oncoming traffic has a stop sign before you begin to cross. Pay attention to pedestrian signals in large cities.

Letting Your Puppy Off Lead

When you think about it, restricting a puppy's experience of the world to walks on a leash is tantamount to animal cruelty. Imagine if someone did that to you! Puppies need to run and play. They need to be able to go off and explore scents that waft over to them. Puppies who love the water should have the experience of swimming and fetching—it's what makes their hearts and souls sing.

FACT

For a list of puppy parks across the United States and in Canada, visit *www.dogparkusa.com*. There is other information on the site for finding places and ways for more off-leash time, and a resource for forming a puppy park in your area should you be interested in doing so.

Unfortunately, many conscientious and caring puppy owners live in places that make it difficult to allow this. Certainly someone living in the heart of a large city can't let their puppy off leash; even the parks in most suburbs have leash laws; and with countryside being gobbled up by developers everywhere, even rural puppy owners need to fear that a car could come barreling along even the most remote road at any time.

A romp outside with another puppy or dog is wonderful for all involved in every way.

Because of this, a movement started years ago to set aside special puppy parks and puppy runs that would provide safe, enclosed space for puppy owners to gather and let their puppies run free. There are now several such Puppy Parks in large cities like New York, Chicago, or San Francisco. Large parks in the suburbs often designate times that allow puppies to be off-leash (typically early mornings and evenings). Sometimes you can find playing fields or tennis courts that are fenced in. Even these provide some space for your puppy to cavort at will. Beaches also post signs alerting puppy owners as to when they are welcome.

Hide-and-Seek Games

There are all sorts of ways to play hide-and-seek, and they all make for fast-paced and exciting times that definitely give your puppy a physical and mental workout. The best way to lay the basics for all hide-and-seek games is with food. Using pieces of cereal or popcorn (things that are small, easy to chew, relatively healthy, and won't make a mess), show them to your puppy so she knows you have something good. Ask her to Sit and Stay (see Chapter

13). Watching her so she doesn't break, put a piece or two out of her sight but nearby; for example, behind a table or chair leg, or next to the sofa. Without making her wait too long, give her a break word (Okay), then say Find It, indicating that she can come and get the goodies. When she finds and eats a piece, tell her what a good girl she is.

Increase the difficulty and challenge of this game slowly and only playing a couple of times a day. As she's sitting and staying, put more pieces down and encourage her to find them all. Don't put so many that she doesn't have to sniff them out, and don't put them in places that are too difficult to reach or find, but slowly put pieces farther away from her and in places that may not be quite so obvious.

Another way to play hide-and-seek is with yourself and other family members. When you're first starting, have a piece of food with you so you can reward her when she finds you. Ask her to sit and stay in a room where you can hide not too far away. Tip-toe to your hiding spot, then shout, Okay, Find Me! You should hear her start to come looking for you. As soon as she finds you, tell her what a good puppy she is and give her the treat. Make finding you increasingly difficult by hiding in places that are trickier for her to discover, like in the tub behind the shower curtain instead of just behind the bathroom door. This is a silly game you can play every day and neither of you will tire of it.

Out with Other Dogs

Some people hook up together in the morning or evening to go for a power walk or even a jog to make the task more fun and keep them on track. You can do the same with a fellow dog owner, making plans to meet on a particular corner and walk your dogs together. This can be great for you—and great for the dogs.

A word of caution, however: Be sure the other dog(s) you walk with are friendly—and that yours is, too! Before plotting out the next several months with your friend, talking about the various parks you want to visit, introduce your dogs and make sure they get along.

The toughest thing about introductions between dogs on leashes is— the leashes! The leash is a conduit of your feelings about the other dog or person you're about to meet, and vice versa. If you sense your pup getting excited or nervous, you will hold the leash differently. If you restrain her, she may sense that you are nervous, too, and may think that she needs to protect you or be on guard. So while the leash may send the wrong message to your dog, it is also essential that you keep it on, because if you do need to yank your pup out of a situation, you have to have it.

ALERT!

Walks are great times to reinforce basic training, too. Carry treats with you, and as you're walking along, turn to your dog, get her attention, and ask her to Sit, or Heel, or simply focus on you for a moment. When she does, give her a treat. Being able to listen on a walk is important.

The best-case scenario is to spend some time with your friend's dog without your dog. If you're sure you can trust it, you have nothing to fear when making the introduction with your dog, and you won't need to choke up on the leash. When it's time, ask your friend and her dog to meet you in neutral territory for your dogs—not at either of your houses, where territorial feelings may surface.

While on your walks, keep an eye out for other dogs and try to read their body language or the body language of the people walking them. Avoid any that seem to be straining too much or are unusually distracted. When you approach another dog, always ask the person with it if the dog is friendly.

CHAPTER 13

Basic Training

Even though you may love your puppy or dog more than you ever thought possible and think of her as one of your "children," it's important to remember that a dog is not a person. Their genetic makeup dictates that they respond to things differently—after all, you wouldn't get to know your neighbors by sniffing around their toilets. But for a dog, the scents that are released from other dogs are key communicators about how they interact. This is one example of how dogs differ from humans. However, dogs are responsive to human signals and you can train them to behave in ways that are acceptable.

When you see your puppy in an attentive sit, you'll be so proud and happy. It is easy to teach and reinforce, and is the foundation of good manners.

Training for Good Manners

Chapters 15 and 16 explain how to take basic training to the next levels—more advanced training, and activities you can do together. They are for those of you who really get into training and want to challenge yourselves and your dogs to do things from walking nicely by your side to high-speed agility to amazing pet therapy.

This chapter is for the majority of dog owners who are interested in training for good household manners. What does that mean? It means having a dog who listens and responds to your requests. It means sharing your home with a dog who respects the house rules—just as your children or guests do. It includes teaching your dog what you expect from her, as it is unfair to think that because you love each other she will simply do what you want her to do.

F A C T

Dogs who end up in shelters are there not because they weren't loved by their owners, but because their behavior became uncontrollable. Don't let this happen to you! Training is easy and fun and so rewarding for both of you. Start early and keep it up to enjoy a great relationship with your dog for many years.

Good manners start with a thorough understanding of the basics: Sit, Stay, Down, and Come. They grow to include requests like Heel (walk nicely by my side) and household manners—requests like Off, Drop it, Quiet, and Wait. This chapter will guide you through the basics and give you examples of how to use the requests around your house to enforce (and reward) good manners (behavior).

What You'll Need to Get Started

There are some general rules for teaching Sit, Down, and Come commands: Use a buckle-type collar; give commands only when you can enforce them and never repeat them; praise your puppy before releasing her from duty with the Chin-Touch Okay (step forward as you gently touch her under jaw and say Okay as an invitation to move).

Since dogs thrive on consistency, ideally one person should be the trainer. But if the puppy is a family pet, she can adapt to a multiple-trainer system and feel a special connection to everyone who works with her. If family members aren't committed to learning the proper skills, agreeing on rules, and working with the puppy, the person with the most interest should take responsibility.

You'll need the right equipment to train your puppy or dog. This includes a well-fitted collar, a six-foot leather leash, and a fifteen-foot long line. Additionally, when working toward off-leash control, you'll need a tab (a short nylon rope) and a fifty-foot light line. All are described in some detail below.

Collars

When you begin training, use the collar your dog wears around the house. It should be well made and properly fitted. If it's not, or if she doesn't wear a collar, start with a snugly fit, flat buckle-type collar. Consider switching to a slip collar, a prong collar, or a head halter if you've used the procedures recommended in this book but, because of her size or strength, would like an extra measure of control.

- **Slip chain collars:** When using this type of collar, take advantage of the quick slide-and-release action of a slip chain with flat, small links. It should be only one-half to two inches larger than the thickest part of your dog's skull. Although collars this small can be difficult to slide on and off, snug collars deliver timelier corrections. This type also stays in place better when properly positioned—high on the neck, just behind the ears, with the rings just under the dog's right ear.

- **Nylon slip collars:** Nylon slip collars offer the slide-and-release action of a chain, and deliver stronger corrections than buckle collars. As with any collar, the nylon slip should only be tightened momentarily while correcting; constant tension means the dog isn't being told when she's doing well and when she's doing poorly.

- **Prong collars:** Strong or easily distractible dogs may benefit by use of a prong or pinch collar. The prongs come in an array of sizes from micro, to extra large. The length is adjustable by removing or adding prongs. Since some brands of these collars can fall off without warning, when you're working in open areas, consider fitting your dog with a buckle or slip collar in addition to the prong, and attach your leash to both.

Some people think prong collars look like instruments of torture. If you're turned off by the appearance of the prong collar, look for another tool to aid you. But if you are both apprehensive and curious about this collar, it's actually a very humane tool when properly used. Ironically, some harsh trainers abhor them and some soft trainers embrace them.

Leashes and Lines

To teach commands and mannerly walking and to umbilical cord your dog, use a six-foot leather, Beta, or Biothane leash (see examples at *www .tackatack.com*). Use a quarter-inch width for dogs up to fifteen pounds; use a half-inch width for dogs sixteen–forty-five pounds; use a three quarter-inch width for dogs forty-six–seventy-five pounds; and use a one-inch width for dogs over seventy-six pounds.

Many exercises, including sneakaway and advanced distance stays, are done on a fifteen-foot nylon cord called a long line. Since many pet stores don't carry them, just go to a hardware store and buy a swivel snap and 15 feet of nylon cord—quarter-inch diameter for a medium-sized dog, and one-eighth-inch smaller or larger for small or large dogs, respectively.

Then tie the snap on one end and make a loop for your thumb on the other. The tab is a piece of quarter-inch diameter nylon rope, approximately eighteen inches long. If your dog is tiny or giant, adjust the length and width. Tie the ends of the rope together, then slip the unknotted end through the ring of the collar and, finally, thread the knot through the loop. The knot will keep your hand from slipping off the tab as you enforce commands. But when you're not holding it, it will be dangling on your dog's chest, which means she may be thinking about mouthing it—in which case, you can't use it. So if she takes it in her mouth, tell her Drop It. If necessary, enforce your command by saturating the tab with a chewing deterrent spray.

The light line is a fifty-foot nylon cord. Use parachute cord for large dogs, Venetian blind cord for medium or small dogs, and nylon twine for tiny breeds. The light line is tied to the tab and used as you make the transition to off-lead work.

Finding a Trainer to Work With

This book makes every effort to explain training techniques in ways that help the reader learn and succeed. That said, there is nothing like working with a trainer to really get it—and for faster results (for both of you). Puppies are sponges, soaking up the world around them and, for the most part, trying to please the people who ask them to do things (while also taking care of their own needs). If you train with treats, you'll get your pup's attention because he loves treats, and you'll be amazed at what he'll do for you. If you work with a trainer who can clearly demonstrate how to optimize the use of treats so that your pup isn't just learning, but listening—well, you can understand the advantages.

So where does one find a trainer who will do wonders to make a well-mannered dog out of your precocious pup? You can ask trusted friends or dog professionals like veterinarians, groomers, and dog walkers. Or you can do an online search of the Association of Pet Dog Trainers (*www.apdt.com*), a national organization that certifies its trainers and insists on positive methodology. APDT trainers are all over the world, and it is easy to search for one near you. The International Association of Canine Professionals also has a valuable listing (*www.dogpro.org*). Call to talk to some nearby trainers and ask if you can visit a class. Get a feel for the trainer before committing to a class session. If you pick a good one, you'll be excited about classes; if you don't, you'll end up dropping out and feeling alone and frustrated by the behavior of your growing pup.

Using Treats to Train

Most trainers want their dogs to obey out of love rather than because they were beaten or bribed. But since most dogs love tasty treats, food has long been used as a training aid. There are basically three ways to use food: (1) as a lure to get the dog to perform a task, (2) as a reward for completing an already learned task, or (3) as reinforcement for behaviors offered by the dog (click and treat training).

Most people use treats and body language as a lure because it is the fastest way to entice the dog to perform a task. But beware: there is a huge gap between following a lure and obeying a command. To bridge that gap, learn how to enforce your commands with your hands, leash, and praise. This will also prove invaluable if your dog isn't interested in the treat because she's full or distracted.

In the classes taught at Amiable Dog Training (the school owned by coauthor Amy Ammen), beginners are shown how to communicate and control their dogs without the use of food. Amy feels that although there are many reliable training methods, after instructing 40,000 graduates over the course of thirty-some years, she favors this food-free approach. In her opinion, it stands the test of time for producing reliable dogs and satisfied students.

If you are reluctant to build your training foundation using a food-based approach or prefer not to use treats, don't. You, too, are likely to find it simplifies and improves your communication with your canine.

Clicker and Treat Training

Clickers were once used almost exclusively for training service and trick dogs to learn more complicated requests than is required of the average pet or even obedience-trained dog. However, today clicker training is much more mainstream, and trainers are applying it to everything from introductory dog training to complicated requests a rider makes of her horse.

How does it work? Simply put, when the dog does something desirable, she is given a signal (the click made by a plastic clicker) that the behavior is right, offered a food reward and, eventually, taught to do it on command, possibly without the food. For instance, if the objective is to teach a dog to sneeze, the trainer would wait for her to do that, click the clicker and offer a treat or other reward. Because of the power of association, soon the dog reacts to the sound of the clicker with as much delight as to the treat. Therefore, if the dog is working far away or retrieving and can't be given a treat, the clicker communicates that she is doing a great job. Of course, many people do the same thing with the word Good instead of the clicker. With animals who are unresponsive to verbal praise—such as rodents and farm animals—the clicker is an invaluable training tool, but a variety of methods are equally successful when teaching basic dog obedience.

The methods used in this book are those that have been developed through Amy Ammen's thirty-plus years of working with dogs of all breeds, sizes, ages, temperaments, backgrounds, and abilities. She is comfortable with them and has seen them work. If you prefer to learn more about clicker training, there are some outstanding books devoted to just that method. For a simple, effective and practical approach to clicker training for dogs, Amy recommends investigating the resources by Gary Wilkes (*www.clickandtreat.com*).

Training with Patience

Dog training is an adventure of sorts: never predictable, sometimes elating, and sometimes tedious. Be optimistic about your dog's potential, but expect progress occasionally to be slow or nonexistent. Don't, however, abandon your original goals and settle for meager results: Shoddy, half-learned obedience can cause annoying problems or allow them to fester. Many owners give up on training but later decide to give it another try—this time approaching it with far greater determination and achieving far better results.

ALERT!

Whether this is your first time around or your last-ditch effort, recognize that a degree of frustration is part of the learning process, and keep training. You may be five seconds from a learning breakthrough. Don't let your frustration or impatience get the better of you!

Finally, learning anything new—including how to train your dog—is challenging, so show yourself compassion. For example, Amy has been training dogs for over thirty years, and though she doesn't want to make mistakes when training, she admits that sometimes she does. Her philosophy is that if she attempts to train, she may make a mistake, but if she never tries, she'll never have the dog she really wants. Her goal: Decide what kind of behavior you want and pursue it with patience and kindness.

Twelve Ingredients to Teach Any Command

This is a great list to keep handy and review before and after you work with your dog.

1. Decide what you'd like your dog to do.
2. Decide what clear visual or auditory signal you will use to initiate the desired action.
3. Give verbal commands using the right tonality, inflection, and volume (don't plead, mumble, or shout; rather, use a more excited tone of voice, as you would to get the attention of a toddler).
4. Preface verbal commands with the dog's name. The name and command should sound like one word (Buster Heel, rather than Buster . . . Heel). Just one exception: Don't use her name in conjunction with the Stay command, since hearing her name implies she should be attentive and ready to go.
5. Say the command only once.
6. Make an association: While teaching, give the command as you make the dog do the action (for example, say Sit as you pull up on the collar and push down on the dog's rear).
7. Give commands only when you can enforce them—otherwise, you risk teaching disobedience.
8. Decide on reinforcement: How are you going to show the dog what to do? Unlike the other eleven steps, this will change depending on your dog's stage in training.
9. Show your appreciation with precisely timed praise—like fireworks: full, but brief.
10. End every command by releasing with the Chin-Touch Okay.
11. Test your dog's understanding by working her around distractions before progressing to the next level.
12. Don't take obedience for granted. Dogs forget, get lazy, become distracted, and inevitably fail to respond to familiar commands. Especially if she rarely makes a mistake, correct her so she understands the rules haven't changed and neither should her behavior.

Just as important as the cue you use to start an action is the one you will give to end it. Release your dog with words like Okay or All Done. Pair this with an outward stroke under the dog's chin—what is called the Chin-Touch Okay. Dogs who rely on a physical and verbal release cue are less inclined to "break" their commands. For the first three weeks, step forward when you deliver to make the dog move from her previous command on cue.

Basic Skills: Sneakaways

Use the sneakaway as the foundation for teaching commands and solving problems, and to teach your dog to walk nicely on lead. This mesmerizing exercise teaches your dog to be controlled and attentive despite distractions. Even without specifically addressing problem behaviors, you may find they magically disappear as your dog learns her sneakaway lessons. At the very least, you'll find sneakaways improve her general trainability and therefore greatly reduce your workload.

Walking Sneakaways

The sneakaway is simple: When your dog goes north, you go south. When she is thinking of things in the west, you head east.

To begin (Step 1), put your dog on the long line (the fifteen-foot nylon cord described earlier). Then take your dog to an obstruction-free area at least fifty feet square. Put your thumb through the loop of the line and your other hand under it. Plant both hands on your midsection to avoid moving them and jerking your dog. She may get jerked during this exercise, but it won't be because of your hand movement.

As you stroll with your dog, watch her closely but inconspicuously. If she becomes distracted or unaware of you, immediately turn and walk briskly in the opposite direction. The line will tighten abruptly if she isn't following as you move away.

After an hour of practice—split up any way you like over the next two days—your dog should be keeping her legs tangle-free, be aware of your movements, and be willing to be near you.

Remember these key points when practicing sneakaways:

- Keep your hands steady so you don't use arm movements to jerk your dog.
- Don't allow your dog to hear you move or stop, or see you with her peripheral vision. Avoid tricks like scuffing your feet, or inching, bowing, or arcing away; instead, always sneak directly away, with conviction, so your dog will learn to pay attention to you rather than your tricks.
- Move at a constant rate until your dog is following you, then stop dead.
- Use momentum to your advantage by heading away from your dog while there is still generous slack in the line. Calculate your departure so you'll be able to take two running steps before the line tightens.

Although most dogs will be strolling along cooperatively after an hour of sneakaway practice, a rare dog may continue to display odd resistance such as refusal to move or biting at the line. Although this is unusual, it, too, can be remedied by creating an umbilical cord for her by tying her leash to your belt. For two days, make her walk by your side as you perform your daily activities around the house and yard. After a few hours of umbilical cording, staying near you should be second nature. Now practice sneakaways again, using a slip chain or prong collar. If you do so for a total of three hours over the course of a week, she is likely to be following happily.

Running Sneakaways

In Step 2, instead of walking away, pivot and run when your dog's attention wanders from you. Once she's begun running after you, stop dead. Also, take inventory of your dog's personality, desires, and fascinations. These may include noises, smells, certain activities, food, toys, different areas, or other animals and people. From now on these things will be referred to as distractions. Each time you practice, run a little faster as you sneak away and use more challenging and irresistible distractions.

Leash Walking

Begin Step 3 once your dog is content to be near you no matter what distractions are around. This step teaches her to walk on a loose leash at your left side. Attach the six-foot leash to her collar and put your right thumb in the handle. Enclose your fingers around the straps of the handle below. Hold the midsection of the leash with the right hand, too, so your left hand is free. The leash should have just enough slack to touch the middle of your left thigh when your right hand is at your hip—unless you are really tall and your dog is short, or vice versa; the taller the handler and shorter the dog, the lower on your leg the leash will hang.

If your dog forges ahead, open and close your hand to release the slack, then grip the handle as you pivot and run away. Do this when her shoulder is only inches ahead of your leg, rather than waiting until she is tugging at the end of the leash or lunging frantically ahead. When your dog is running after you, pick up the slack in the leash again and stop dead.

If your dog runs right past you, pivot once again and sneak away before she bolts ahead. If your dog is a charger, watch her body language closely so it becomes easy to anticipate when to do multiple, direction-changing sneakaways. If, on the other hand, your dog attempts to lag, reduce the slack by tightening the leash a bit—about one to five inches—as you briskly walk forward. Use your left hand to pat your left thigh as you continue moving briskly. Praise by saying Good, Good, Good so your dog knows you're happy with her.

The dog may bump into the back of your legs for the next few steps, but that, along with the fact that the leash tightens against your left thigh with every step, will encourage her to return to your left side. Remember to keep your left hand off the leash so nothing interferes with your thigh pulling into the leash.

Priorities change when a dog becomes distracted. She might never think of disobeying—unless food is being prepared, leaves are blowing, people are laughing, or rabbits, cats, birds, or squirrels are present. Prevent distractions from rendering all your obedience training useless by making fascinating temptations a part of every training session.

Do sneakaways to get control, and then give commands to teach listening skills. Your dog's dignity will grow in proportion to her obedience, so he'll be more relaxed in those social settings even when he's not been commanded.

Sneakaways teach your dog to watch you in anticipation of your speedy departure. As a bonus, your dog will enjoy the sneakaway if she likes running with you. Being astute observers of human behavior, it's easy for your dog to avoid the correction by "catching you" before the line tightens. So sneakaways not only teach your dog to walk nicely—he'll also watch you, have fun, and never be the victim of an unjust correction.

Sneakaways teach your dog that when she is attached to a line that you're holding, she is expected to control herself even though she isn't under command. This lesson in self-control is the foundation that makes everything else in dog training—problem solving, command training, and off-lead control—easy.

Teaching Sit and Sit-Stay

To teach the Sit command, put your dog on your left side, hold her collar with your right hand, and put your left hand on her loin just in front of her hip bones and behind her rib cage. Ask her to sit as you pull upward on the collar and with authority rather than dominance, push downward on the loin in one fluid motion. It's important that you project confidence to your dog. Praise her, then release her with the Chin-Touch Okay.

Practice a few times, but don't overdo it—especially with a young puppy. You want her to come away from the experience having been praised for doing what you've asked, not with you upset about something she can't understand.

As your puppy learns what Sit means, begin teaching her to hold the position in a Sit-Stay. In a nutshell, teaching the Sit-Stay involves the Sit command, teaching Sit-Stay from one step away, then advancing to teaching the leash-length Sit-Stay.

Teaching Basic Sit-Stay

Talk, pet, and praise, but don't let your dog move. When necessary, smoothly and instantly reposition her by pushing her back into the sit as you tighten up on the collar. If she is rigid and won't budge, move her forward and walk her into the sit. After a few seconds, release with a Chin-Touch Okay.

After three days with no sign of resistance, command Sit and wait for a response. To reinforce your command, push downward on the loin and give a quick upward jerk on the lead as you praise. Release with the Chin-Touch Okay.

Here are some basic guidelines for teaching your dog to stay:

- Just before leaving your dog, use a hand signal along with your Stay command. (Using hand signals is explained in Chapter 15.)
- Use distractions—people, places, movements—to test your dog and confirm that she's learning.
- Be acutely attentive. Move in to correct the instant your dog begins leaving the stay position; otherwise, she'll wonder what the correction was for.
- Correct silently. If your dog didn't listen the first time, repeating yourself will only cause further confusion or disobedience. Use the leash, your hands, and praise to guide her into the appropriate response.
- Leave instantly after the correction. Avoid lingering next to or slowly moving away from your dog after correcting her; instead, immediately return to where you were at the time the dog made the mistake.
- Adjust the strength of your correction to your dog's size, level of training, why she moved, and how excited or distracted she is.
- Finish all stays by returning to your dog's right side, giving lavish praise, then using the Chin-Touch Okay.

Teaching the Sit-Stay One Step Away

Before you begin, your dog should be able to sit on command and wait to be released with a Chin-Touch Okay.

To practice, hold the leash taut over the dog's head. Command Stay, then step in front of her and act busy while producing distractions—use many distractions, return to praise frequently and, finally, release with Chin-Touch Okay. Moving the head and wagging the tail is acceptable, but you should curtail attempts to scoot forward, rotate, or stand with a light, snappy upward jerk and praise.

If your dog tries to lie down, tighten the leash enough to prevent her from lowering comfortably into the down position and praise warmly as she realizes she doesn't have enough slack to lie down. Loosen the lead and prepare to repeat this sequence many times during the next week of training if your dog is one who is inclined to recline.

Teaching the Leash-Length Sit-Stay

To practice, command Stay and walk out to the end of the leash, holding its handle. Use distractions such as stepping side to side, bending down, pulling forward lightly on the leash, or dropping food or toys in front of your dog. This teaches her that no matter what your preoccupation or what activities surround her, she stays put. Frequently tell her she is a good girl. Stop movement immediately by (1) sliding your free hand down almost to the snap of the leash as you step into your dog, (2) quickly maneuvering your dog back into place without saying a word, (3) jerking upward, and then (4) moving back to the end of the leash.

Enforce Sit-Stays while you (1) address a postcard, (2) read the headlines, (3) pop in a video, (4) empty the garbage, (5) download your iTunes, (6) tie your shoes, (7) wrap a gift, (8) get stuck on hold, (9) weed a flowerbed. When you no longer need to allow spare time for corrections, your dog has mastered the Sit-Stay.

Teaching Down

Start with your puppy or dog in the Sit position. Then, to teach Down, follow the same procedure as described for Sit, except as you command Down, gently pull downward on the collar as you use the palm of your left hand to push down on her shoulders or neck. When she lowers her body to the ground, pet her tummy. If she rolls on her side or back, continue rubbing her belly, then release her with the Chin-Touch Okay.

If your dog braces and won't lower her front end to the ground, lift the paw that is bearing most of her weight as you push downward on her shoulder blades. If her fanny stays up as her front end lowers, simply keep your palm on her shoulder blades and praise her until she relaxes her rear legs and lies down so you can give her a tummy rub. If you still simply can't get her down, discontinue work on the Down and concentrate on perfecting the Sit command around distractions; rare is the dog who resists the Down after becoming completely cooperative on the Sit.

To practice with a jerk-and-push combination, which teaches your dog to lie down without the two-finger push, first enforce Down by simultaneously using a two-finger push and a bouncy and light jerk. Jerk diagonally toward your dog's right rear foot by holding the leash close to the snap while you stand facing the dog's right side.

Exceptional dogs may learn the verbal Down command in a week. With an average of twenty repetitions per day, most dogs will Down 50 percent of the time after one month.

Test whether your dog really understands what you're asking by trying these things:

- Eliminate body language by putting your hands in your pockets and evaluating yourself in front of a mirror. Your mouth is the only part of your anatomy that should move when commanding Down.
- Whisper the Down command.
- Turn your back and look over your shoulder at your dog to give the command.
- Stand in the shower (without running the water), sit in your car, and lie on a bed, stairs, or sofa. See if your command still has authority.

Working on Down-Stay

Use this request to ask your dog to lie down and stay for grooming and examinations, during meals, or as guests arrive, or simply to calm your dog.

To practice, ask your dog to Down and then command Stay. Examine her ears, eyes, teeth, and paws. Correct inappropriate movements such as crawling, rolling, or ascension. Praise her frequently when she cooperates, and return to her right side to praise and then release her with the Chin-Touch Okay.

Teaching Come

Simply put, to teach this, leash your dog and wait for her to get distracted. Call (dog's name) Come and reel in the lead as you back up and say Good, Good, Good! Kneel down to celebrate her arrival and release her with the Chin-Touch Okay.

A great way to teach your pup that it's rewarding to come when she's called is to play a game called Pass the Puppy. Get your family to join the program by leashing the pup when at least one other member is present. Have one person hold the leash while the other holds the pup. When the person holding the leash calls (dog's name), Come, the other lets go so the pup can be reeled in as the person with the leash backs up slightly until the pup gets to him or her. After praising and petting the pup, that person then holds the pup and gives the lead to the next person. This exercise can be practiced daily for up to fifteen minutes; if you all habitually use the same, consistent training techniques, the puppy will learn to respond to everyone in the family.

Here are some basic guidelines for teaching the Come command:

- Don't put your authority at risk by calling Come when your dog may not obey and you know you can't enforce.
- Standardize your voice, always using the same enthusiastic tone which suggests urgency to say (dog's name), Come!
- Appeal to your dog's chase instinct and help ensure a faster recall by moving away after calling Come.

- Praise enthusiastically while she approaches. If you wait until she arrives, your lack of commitment will reduce her commitment to the process, too.
- Squat to acknowledge her final approach and arrival.

Perfecting the command so that your dog will listen to you while you're walking or otherwise distracted demands more work. First, leash your dog and take her for a walk. If she begins sniffing something, gazing around, or meandering off, call (dog's name), Come! Immediately back up quickly as you reel the leash, praising enthusiastically. Kneel down when your dog arrives, using verbal praise only. Release with a Chin-Touch Okay and continue practicing the sequence.

After doing this about twenty times, your dog is probably running toward you faster than you can reel. Now see if she'll leave distractions when you stand still and call Come. If she doesn't respond promptly, use a light piston-type horizontal jerk toward you as you praise and back up. If she does respond to your command, praise and back up.

Practicing the Come Command from a Distance

When your dog responds to your command around strong distractions 80 percent of the time, you can start working on asking her to come from a distance.

Arm yourself with a glove and a long, lightweight line to do this (the glove will prevent the line from hurting your hand should it get pulled). Attach the line to your dog's collar. When she's distracted, position yourself over the line and call her. Praise her during the entire recall, from the time she begins taking her first step toward you until you release her. As she arrives, squat down and release with the Chin-Touch Okay.

If the dog ignores your command, correct her by grabbing the line and using "wrap, run, and praise"—wrap the line around your hand twice just above where your thumb attaches to your hand, make a fist around the line, and anchor your hand on your waist as you run away from your dog, praising all the way. Release with the Chin-Touch Okay when she arrives.

CHAPTER 14

Common Problems

So, you thought puppyhood would be full of Kodak moments—the kids happily playing ball with the puppy, puppy curled up asleep in Dad's lap, a smiling, happy ball of fur scampering beside you—and instead you've got a miniature terrorist on your hands. Does it seem like all your puppy does is get into or cause trouble? Is he playing too rough with your kids, barking or crying too often, roughly jumping onto people and making a speedway out of your home? Welcome to the chapter that's going to help you get perspective and solve those puppy problems.

A Puppy Is a Puppy Is a Puppy

The first thing to remember is that a puppy is a puppy. Does that mean you just have to grin and bear this trying time? Of course not. But it does mean you need to understand your puppy for what he is: a baby learning about the world. Like human babies, puppies explore with their mouths, their paws (hands), and all their senses. They are soaking up everything about their environment, including how their littermates and the "adults" in their world respond to it. If something's exciting to others in their pack, it'll be exciting to your puppy; if something smells, tastes, or feels good, he wants a part of it.

So what are you going to do about it? Like any responsible parent, your job is to teach your puppy the rules. Not by yelling, hitting, choking, or hurting your puppy—which only makes him afraid of you—but by truly teaching. Knowing what you want your puppy to do is the first step. Then set up small but achievable goals that you and your puppy can celebrate together. Review the basic training methods described in Chapter 13, because if your puppy learns to listen when you ask him to sit, lie down, come, and so on, he'll be responsive to your teaching when it comes to solving problem behaviors.

ALERT!

To teach your puppy good manners, which should minimize problems, remember the following: Teach fairly and wisely, be the role model for your puppy, and ask yourself how you're contributing to the problem. Remember, it's only a problem if you think it's a problem; your puppy doesn't think digging in the yard is a problem, he thinks it's great fun.

Typically, attempts to solve problems with a single tactic or object usually fail. For example, using odor remover on your carpeting won't abolish house-soiling, and using a no-pull harness won't teach your dog to heel. On the other hand, multifaceted solutions are recommended and highly successful—such as removing carpet odor *and* using the housebreaking advice in this book.

Looking at the Whole Picture

Chapter 11 described how not socializing your puppy could lead to significant behavior problems. An example showed that a caretaker's typical response to a problem is to wonder what's wrong with the puppy. This is natural and definitely worth considering. The other side of the coin is to look at what is causing the puppy to behave in a particular way. Contributing factors could include: a move, a noisy environment, poor diet, insufficient exercise, overly rough play with children, isolation, and so on.

Problems are frustrating and challenging, like puzzles. To solve them, you need to look at them from all angles and consider all the possibilities. As this chapter discusses techniques for remedying certain behaviors and you begin to apply them, you may want to keep a journal about a particular problem and note things like the time of day it occurs most frequently, any extenuating circumstances (like a visit from someone), whether your pup is taking medication, and so on. If you notice a pattern, you can do something about the circumstance as well as the behavior, effecting greater change all around.

A puppy is a puppy is a puppy, and just like a young child, he will act in ways you find undesirable or inappropriate. It's up to you to be his teacher so he can learn how to behave in your world. Take heart in moments like these when your pup is catching up on his sleep and appears perfectly angelic.

Naughty Problems

These are defined as the things your puppy does because he almost can't help himself. They're extensions of normal puppy (and dog) behavior—such as barking—that become problems because they're done in ways that are unacceptable in your household (or to your neighbors). The bad news is you can't completely rid your pup of these behaviors because they are part of being a dog; the good news is that you can curb or redirect them so that they are done in a place or at a time that is satisfactory for "your" world.

Naughty problems are:

- Mouthing and nipping
- Chewing
- Barking, crying, and whining
- Digging
- Jumping up
- Begging

Many people think their puppies are so cute. And as such, when their puppies do something mischievous, they tend to sometimes laugh. Now, you shouldn't be a curmudgeon, but don't indulge your dog in things as a puppy that you would not want them to do as dogs. What puppies can get away with becomes tiresome and annoying when they become dogs.

Mouthing and Nipping

Even if you've only had your puppy one day you've learned that he explores things with his mouth. This is completely natural; he can't help it! If your puppy came from a sizable litter, he learned to roughhouse and play with his littermates using his mouth, body, and paws. So his mouth is his direct access to everything pleasurable, and his method of saying, "Enough" or "Back Off."

Here's how to discourage your puppy using his mouth to "maul" you or anyone with the sharpness of his teeth or the strength of his jaws.

If your puppy chomps down too hard on your finger, hand, wrist, ankle—any body part—immediately cry out in pain. Say OUCH, and make it sound like you just got your entire limb bitten off by a shark. Don't raise your voice in anger. Don't strike out at your puppy. Don't shake your limb or pull it away from your puppy's mouth. Just let out a big YELP. That should surprise him enough so that he stops pressing down and looks up at you.

As soon as your puppy releases you, change your tone completely and warmly (not excitedly) praise your puppy. Hopefully you have a toy available nearby. Give that to him and tell him what a good puppy he is to take the toy. Instructed this way, most puppies quickly learn bite inhibition.

The biggest problem with a mouthy puppy and a family is that while it might be easy for you to control yourself and respond correctly when puppy gets you with those razor-sharp puppy teeth, it's usually not the way children respond. Their natural tendency is to pull away from the puppy or flail at the puppy—both behaviors that may incite the puppy to increase his attempts to nip because he thinks this is rough play.

Teach your children how to react to this situation by staging it with your puppy and demonstrating to them the response you want. Your puppy and your children will learn at the same time.

If you suspect that your puppy is acting inappropriately even when you've tried to teach him right, don't let him continue to mouth and nip so that he's harming anyone. Ask your veterinarian to refer you to a trainer or behavior specialist who can assess and diagnose your puppy—before it's too late.

Barking

Out of respect for other household members, neighbors, tenants, and anyone with a low tolerance for barking, correct this problem—otherwise, you may be forced to get rid of your dog or face eviction. Don't worry that your dog will stop barking all together. Teaching barking inhibition increases his value as a watchdog because when he barks, you'll know it's for a valid reason.

To correct barking, even if it is only a problem in your absence, teach the dog to be "Quiet" or "Shush" on command when he's standing next to you. Leash your puppy and create situations that may cause your dog to bark. For example, ask a neighbor or family member to walk past the window or walk in the front door, or take him to the park in the early morning when squirrels are active, or drive him to a busy shopping center where customers will be walking past the car. When he barks unnecessarily, calmly close his mouth by gently encircling his muzzle with one hand while giving the collar several quick jerks as you say Quiet. If possible, enforce a Sit, Down, and Come command in quick succession to put him in a more compliant state of mind.

For more determined barkers, substitute the muzzle closure with a spritz of Bitter Apple spray. When he barks, reach for his collar so you can quickly place the nozzle at the corner of his mouth. That way he'll get a taste of the Bitter Apple without you wasting valuable time trying to open his mouth.

If your dog will obey your Quiet command without raising your voice or repeating yourself, no matter what the distractions, barking in your absence will usually subside. If it doesn't, you may be unintentionally reinforcing excessive barking by attempting to silence a dog by petting him or giving him a toy or by allowing him to be vocal without repercussion.

If your puppy respects the Quiet command and you never tolerate barking or try to appease him but he continues to vocalize in your absence, find out exactly when and why he is barking. Record him with a tape recorder when you leave, ask a neighbor about his habits and spy on him. If he is not barking at outside noises, separation anxiety is probably the problem. Read about handling separation anxiety later in this chapter.

Crying and Whining

Believe it or not, these two behaviors can bother you even more than barking. Why? Because it's so hard for your puppy to understand what you want him to stop doing when he's crying or whining. The best remedy is to completely ignore your complaining pup when he's doing either of these things. It will be very difficult for you. After all, a crying pup is like a crying baby—your instinct tells you to go and do what you can to relieve the discomfort.

Remember the old adage that dogs do things to get what they want. If your dog has been adequately fed, exercised, and loved, the only other thing he could want is more attention, more food, or more exercise. But he's not the one who should be dictating that, because next thing you know he may decide he wants to stroll the block at 3 A.M. No, your puppy gets the things he needs because you oversee his environment responsibly enough so his needs are taken care of. Therefore, crying and whining become behaviors whose sole purpose is to get your attention. Don't become a slave to them!

If your puppy is crying or whining for no apparent reason other than to get you to pay attention to him, try turning on a radio or television to block out the sound of his protestations. As hard as it will be, ignore your puppy's cries. However, the second he stops crying (eventually he has to stop), go to him and reward him with attention, exercise, or food. If you're trying to break a habitual cry or whine, you'll need to increase the time between when your dog stops and when you go to him so that he truly associates that he's being praised for being quiet. Another solution to crying or whining is to startle the puppy. This doesn't have to be a physical force correction; instead, it's intended solely to break the offensive action and try to redirect the behavior.

Chewing

The table. The chairs. The rug. The sofa. The car seats. The kids' toys. The garden hose. The swimming pool cover. The remote control. A cell phone. You name it and a dog has chewed it to bits. Is there a worse feeling than coming home and seeing your beloved sound asleep amid a cyclone of destruction? After all, you feed him, exercise him, buy him great toys, comfy beds, keep him up on his shots, and love him to pieces. And this is what you get in return?

You're not going to want to hear this, but 99 percent of the time the destruction is your fault. You allowed the puppy too much freedom while alone in the house. You didn't provide any puppy-friendly chew toys. You left the puppy alone too long. You left one of your favorite things (cell phone, remote, handbag, shoes, pillow, etc.) within reach of your inquisitive puppy—and don't underestimate the reach of a bored puppy. Next thing you know, your stuff's history.

What do you do when this happens? Yell at your puppy? Spank or shove your puppy? Isolate your puppy (to "show him")? No. For your sake and your puppy's. The first thing to do is take your puppy outside. He will probably need to relieve himself after all the fun he's had and the stuff he's eaten. If possible, leave him outside in a fenced area while you go back in to survey the damage. Make sure immediately that your puppy hasn't eaten anything that could be poisonous (prescription drugs, household cleaners, some houseplants) or damaging to sensitive body organs (pins, splintered bones, large buttons). If you find any remnants of anything dangerous in the debris, call your veterinarian immediately and ask if you need to bring your puppy in for an examination.

If the damage is just, well, damage, bring your puppy inside and put him in his crate. While you're cleaning up, it's okay to cry or curse but don't direct it at your puppy. He'll sense you're upset, and if he thinks he's the cause, he may worry that you will always react this way to him. Then you have a puppy who hasn't learned anything except that Mommy or Daddy is very scary when they come home, which will make the puppy more anxious and lead to more destructive chewing.

After you've cleaned up, assess how your puppy was able to get to what he got into. Did you leave the garbage can where he could tip it over? Did you think it was safe to confine him to the kitchen and the den now that he's older? Lesson learned: don't do it again.

FACT

Puppies need and love to chew, and it's up to you to give them the kinds of chew toys that will satisfy—or they'll invent their own! Getting your puppy into a chew toy habit now will save you thousands of dollars in destroyed belongings. Choose a durable rubber toy that can be filled with something yummy. There are lots of these toys on the market now.

Your pup will find things to chew on to relieve herself from boredom or the physical need and desire to chew. Providing appropriate toys will keep her from selecting furniture, shoes, and other inappropriate items.

What you want to do is make sure that your puppy has chew toys he's really interested in. Smear peanut butter in a rubber Kong. That'll keep him busy. Add different sizes of treats and kibble so they fall out gradually over the course of a few hours or the day. (Remember to subtract this amount of food from his regular meals.) Supply him with nonedible Nylabones and sterilized bones into which you can stuff goodies. Get a cube or round toy that you can put treats into and that puppy needs to bat around to get the treats out. Puppies are most prone to get into trouble just after you leave and just before you come home. They miss you when you go and get excited to see you later. This time can seem like an eternity. But you can have your puppy loving to see you leave and well-behaved when you come home by getting him hooked on safe chews that earn tasty rewards.

Don't think your puppy will want to chew less if he's by himself outside or in his crate. He'll get bored just as quickly in these spots as he will the well-appointed living room if he doesn't have something to chew on to take his mind off things.

Digging

Digging is practically the only problem that cannot be prevented, lessened, or solved with obedience training (although sometimes training, because it relieves boredom, indirectly reduces the behavior). Dogs don't dig because they are dominant, belligerent, unaware of authority, or out of control—they do it instinctually to make a cool or warm place to lie down or to make a nest-like den for their puppies. And, yes, interesting smells in the soil, the wonderful feeling of vigorous burrowing, and dirt in their toes are hard for any dog to resist. Therefore, monitoring your dog and correcting digging attempts is an ongoing process—you aren't fighting your dog, you are fighting nature. The best thing to do is recognize and accept your dog's need to dig, and anytime he is in an area with digging potential, be watchful. Stop him with a quick jerk of the lead followed by praise, calling him to come and sit, and more praise. If he is off leash, substitute the jerk with a startling noise, then praise him and call him to come as you run away.

Another option is to exercise him vigorously and regularly so he doesn't seek aerobic activity from digging.

Jumping Up

Some puppies have no desire to jump up. They are content to let you bend down to pet them. Others jump up either because they are very bold and sociable or because they have been rewarded for doing so with petting and attention.

If you don't want your puppy to get into a bad jumping-up habit, or if you want to teach him not to jump up now, here's what to do. When guests or family members enter your house and shower the dog with affection, they teach the dog to jump up and act crazy. For good-sized, healthy adults, this can even be fun. But for elderly, frail people, young children, and finely attired guests or strangers, not only is it not fun, it can be very dangerous. This doesn't mean your dog can never jump up on someone to play. It means that he can do so only when asked, and always well after anyone has entered the house. Though play, fun, and enthusiasm are an important part of a well-balanced, bonded relationship, they should never be associated with people coming and going.

Encourage visitors and members of your household to show self-control. Practice calm arrivals by making it a habit to busy yourself doing other things, oblivious to your dog's prancing, barking, jumping, or panting. As you walk in the door, if your puppy starts leaping on you, simply ignore him. Don't even make eye contact or say anything to him. Walk away. Listen to your phone messages, sort through your mail. Totally ignore him until he settles down. Then calmly say "Good puppy," and gently pet and praise him. Ask him to sit, and give him extra petting when he does. Insist that guests and family members do the same. Within two weeks of practicing uneventful arrivals, usually jumping up entirely subsides.

If your pup can't be dissuaded from jumping up on a particular piece of furniture, you may find that compromise is your best option. Put an old sheet or throw over your pup's preferred piece of furniture. That way, when you're not there, he won't stain or shed all over the furniture. As often as you want, remove the sheet and throw it in the wash. This works for sofas, chairs, and beds.

Begging

It often takes only one tidbit for your clever puppy to be convinced that your meals are better than his and that you're willing to share if he begs. If you've fostered this bad habit, it can be broken, but you probably can't be cured. You have to stop feeding him *any* human food any time around mealtime. Why? The answer is: Be aware of the repercussions. Don't expect your puppy to differentiate from the times you eat a pizza in front of the tube and gladly share it with him and the time you have your daughter's soccer team over for pizza and you don't want him underfoot or being fed by every member of the team, then getting sick.

Differentiate your mealtimes and his by confining him in his crate or a separate room where he can't watch you while you eat. Give him a favorite toy so he's distracted and doesn't whine, cry, drool, or stare you down. Stay strong!

Nasty Behaviors

These are the ones that go a bit beyond naughty in that they can cause serious damage or can lead to more aggressive behavior. These are more serious for everyone who's involved with them, and the best thing to do if you can't manage them with any consistency is to call in a professional. It could be the difference between life and death for your puppy, whether it's because he bites someone in your family, or his aggressive behavior labels him unadoptable from a shelter.

Nasty behaviors include: playing too rough, rowdiness, and stealing food, clothing, or other objects.

Playing Too Rough

Many owners say their dog's favorite game is tug of war. And for many owners it's pretty fun, too—until your once fifteen-pound fluff ball is seventy pounds of adolescent muscle and will do anything to win. Or until he starts to growl whenever you come near any of his toys. This doesn't mean you can't play tug of war. It just means that, like everything else, you have to call the shots. You determine when the game begins and when it ends. This is where Drop It comes in handy again. If tug-of-war is turning into war, say Drop It and stop pulling. If he doesn't let go right away, don't pull again. Say Drop It again. If he doesn't, get up and walk away. It's you he wants to play with. Don't turn his resilience into a contest of wills. When he has dropped it, without saying anything, go get the tug toy and put it away where he can't reach or find it by himself.

QUESTION?

How do you know if you're playing too rough with your puppy?
Never work him into a frenzy; instead, learn how to make games fun and low key. You should be able to stop the game and give a command or walk away at any time. Never use games to frighten your puppy or hurt him. Your puppy is going to get stronger and bolder as he ages. If your puppy doesn't develop an appropriate level of control, you run the risk of your puppy injuring someone.

If you keep tug games short and in control from the very beginning, you and your dog will be able to enjoy them within appropriate limits. Make sure the rest of your family understands these tug game rules, too.

The same goes for any kind of rough-housing, whether you're doing it with a toy, your hands, rolling on the floor, whatever. Start with fun, short sessions, and when you've had enough, say "That's all," and calmly stop whatever you're doing.

Playing Rough with Other Puppies

Rough play among puppies is usually harmless amusement for humans and canines. If generally friendly and tolerant of one another, puppies rarely inflict injury. They will get noisy and animated: growling, barking, squealing, tumbling, and dragging one another by convenient body parts (like ears and limbs) is common. Break them up only if one is being endangered or if the play occurs in a formal living room or while people desire quiet. Don't raise your voice to break them up. Instead, leash one or both puppies and give a few commands in very quick succession to stop the behavior, then enticingly lure your puppy away from the action and reward him for following you by giving him a treat and telling him what a good boy he is.

Stealing and Scavenging

If you were all alone in someone else's house, what would you do when you got bored? Would the thought of looking at their stuff or even rummaging through cabinets, closets, or the refrigerator tempt you?

Now you know how a dog feels. He is trapped and bored and has plenty of senses yearning to be indulged. When given too much freedom too soon, he will quickly discover the joys of hunting for household treasures too often left easily accessible by negligent humans.

Many dogs steal for amusement when you're home. They know the only guaranteed way to rouse you from the recliner is to show off the valuables that have been confiscated. Police your canine kleptomaniac by:

- **Incarceration**—crating
- **Chain gang**—umbilical cording
- **Surveillance**—keeping your eyes glued to him

Don't be a victim, keep the garbage out of reach, close cabinets and closets and put laundry away, teach the Drop It or Leave It command, and dispense justice fairly. Only correct crimes in progress, never correct stealing after the fact. Upon discovering the infraction, leash your dog, invite him to make the same mistake, and correct it by redirecting his attention to something he needs to do to get a reward, such as praise and/or treats.

Perplexing Problems

Some problems are simply vexing or perplexing because they are more complicated and therefore harder to figure out. These problems need to be worked at from several angles at once for best results. They include:

- Separation anxiety
- Submissive urination
- Stool eating

Separation Anxiety

Having to leave a dog alone is worrisome if he gets frantically frustrated when he's separated from his owner. Overly dependant dogs commonly respond to separations by continually barking, whining, and howling, destroying his living space, and attempting to escape by chewing, digging, and jumping over fences and out of windows. In addition to causing expensive damage, many dogs injure themselves. When panicked, they are oblivious to the physical discomforts of laryngitis, bloody-raw gums and paws, broken teeth, self-mutilation caused by chewing and licking, and even broken limbs as a result of jumping out of windows.

How are you supposed to live with a puppy who practically holds you hostage by not being able to be left alone? First, avoid both after-the-fact corrections, which increase anxiety, and consoling tones or gentle petting, which reinforce the neurosis. Instead:

- Exercise your puppy vigorously and regularly.
- Improve his ability to handle all sources of stress by teaching reliable obedience.
- As you come and go, remain relaxed and refrain from addressing your dog.

To directly increase his tolerance of separations, practice these three exercises:

1. **Random time outs:** Insist that he remain quiet when you leave. Take your dog to indoor and outdoor areas, familiar and unfamiliar, filled with or absent of distractions. Silently tie his leash short to a stationary object and walk away for a few minutes. Sometimes remain in sight and other times walk out of sight. Ignore noise making; wait for puppy to settle down or become otherwise distracted by giving your attention back to him by approaching him. When you do return to him, calmly untie his leash without acknowledgment. Concentrate on the areas that make your dog most uncomfortable. Practice every other day for a half hour until he'll be silent regardless of where you leave him, where you go and how long you're gone.

2. **Out-of-sight Sit-Stay and Down-Stay.** This is the same principle as the previous exercise, except you're commanding your puppy to remain in a Sit or Down position as you leave. Don't expect a puppy younger than six months old to sit and stay for longer than a couple minutes. As your puppy gets older, increase the lengths of time you ask your puppy to stay seated or remain down.

3. **Whirling dervish departures:** Dash from room to room grabbing your keys, brief case, jacket, lunch box, etc. Rush out the door and to your car then back out of the driveway, motor around the block, pull back in the garage and saunter into the house. As you put your keys, jacket, and paraphernalia away, completely ignore your puppy. After relaxing for a few minutes, repeat the frenzied departure and relaxed arrival over and over for an hour. To thoroughly desensitize your dog to comings and goings, repeat this pattern three times the first week, then once a week for a month.

To reinforce your training, make it a habit to periodically confine your puppy while you're at home. Sequester him in a quiet area and place your recently worn sweatshirt or bathrobe on the floor on the other side of the closed door. If your smell permeates his room, he may not even realize it when you finally do leave. Give him his favorite toy only when you confine him. Reduce the agitating sounds of neighbors or delivery people by creating "white" noise with a motorized fan to soothe your dog. This is a better solution than subjecting your dog to TV and radio stations with their unsettling cacophony (bells, whistles, applause, sobbing, screeching, and laughter). Then, when you do actually leave, follow the same routine.

Since separation problems can periodically return despite these precautions, reinstate these recommendations as needed.

Many people leave the radio or TV for their puppies while they're gone from the house. With a radio or TV, however, your puppy may become a victim of unsettling and noisy programming and advertisements. Replace that cacophony with white noise; the gentle whir of a fan puts puppies at ease (so long as it's not blowing cold air on them), or you could try an indoor fountain (one your puppy couldn't reach or get to), or a white noise machine.

Submissive Urination

If your dog wets when he greets people or is disciplined, he isn't having a housebreaking problem. Uncontrollable and unconscious leaking of urine is common in puppies and certain breeds. If your dog has been given a clean bill of health by a veterinarian, extinguish this tendency by practicing the following:

- Teach commands so you can give orders that force your dog to focus on his responsibilities instead of his emotions.
- Keep your dog leashed to enable unemotional, silent correction of misbehaviors.
- Avoid eye contact, talking, and touching during emotional states.

- Make your entrances and greetings devoid of emotion.
- Never yell, strike, or show anger toward him.

Since living with this behavior can be exasperating, consider diapering your dog for the first month so you don't have to continually clean up. To diaper your dog, simply pin a bandanna or towel around his privates and teach him not to remove it. Acclimate your dog to wearing the diaper by umbilical cording and jerking the leash if he even sniffs at it. When he is totally uninterested in the diaper—usually after less than a week of umbilical cording—let him walk around the house unleashed as usual, without concern about dribbling.

Avoid vigorous petting, impassioned tones of voice, and strong eye contact. Only interact with a superficial, brief pat, calm word, or fleeting glimpses when his bladder is empty. When he consistently responds without tinkling, test his control after he's had water. Gradually try a warmer approach, but be ready to turn off the affection and issue a command if urination begins.

Stool Eating

So your dog has a thing for poop. Don't be embarrassed. This tendency is so common that virtually every dog training book devotes a section to it. Nutritional deficiency can be the cause for this behavior, so you should first consult a veterinarian. As a rule however, coprophagia is simply a behavioral problem.

Preventative measures are the best solution. Accompany your dog outdoors on-leash and command him to go potty so you'll be able to clean up immediately and stop the habit before it starts. If he prefers to eat other dog or animal poop, the leash will allow you to pull him away from that, too.

Products such as Forbid can be added to your dog's diet to make the resulting poop less palatable, and therefore may dissuade your dog from sampling it. However, many dogs will instantly resume the behavior once they are no longer fed the supplement. Supervision and attention to cleanliness are the best remedies.

Problem Prevention

Giving an untrained puppy freedom in your house can be deadly. Natural curiosity and boredom cause them to chew electrical cords, ingest toxic substances, and destroy valuables. When given freedom too soon, puppies who don't accidentally execute themselves often become homeless because of damage the owner is angry about but could have and should have prevented. Puppies are opportunists. This doesn't mean they are bad; it just means we are foolish if we walk out of the room leaving goodies on the coffee table and truly believe our puppies would never even think about touching them.

If you don't know where your puppy is, he is probably into something he shouldn't be. Save your valuables, your sanity, and your puppy by watching his every move, umbilical cording him, or confining him to a safe, destruction-proof area.

CHAPTER 15

Advanced Training

Once you've gotten a taste of how simple and rewarding basic training can be, you'll want to have access to ways to teach your puppy other things. This will expand your vocabulary with your pup as he grows, and with that, it will improve your relationship.

All sorts of things fall under the umbrella of advanced training, from an everyday instruction like Heel (walk nicely by my side), to improving household manners, to getting started in more organized activities like the extremely popular sport of agility or the more formal work of obedience training.

Teaching Heel (or Walk Nicely by My Side)

Like the skill and art of dancing, the benefits of heeling stretch well beyond the exercise itself. Dancing is a wonderful form of recreation on the dance floor, but the posture, alignment, controlled energy, balance, and poise practiced in dance movements spill over into everyday tasks.

Similarly, the heel command teaches the dog to walk at your left side, regardless of your pace or direction, and to sit when you stop. Gone are the days of her pulling ahead or dragging behind, weaving from side to side, or getting underfoot during walks. As she learns to heel and you learn how to teach her to move precisely, a deeper learning takes place for both of you. To remain in position, the dog's awareness, watchfulness, and willingness must grow. Since you need to watch your dog very intently during the process, you'll develop a sense of what the dog is going to do before she does it—otherwise known as reading your dog. Trust and respect develop as you and your canine partner master the art of heeling. This bond will help you channel the dog's energy more efficiently.

Done properly and consistently, mastering the heel takes time. The precision and attention a solid heel demand are beyond the capabilities of a young puppy, and even a young but immature dog. If you get too demanding with this one, it can backfire on you, leaving you and your dog frustrated and confused. Keep it simple for your puppy.

If you are using a slip collar, make sure the active ring (the one the leash attaches to) comes across the top of the right side of your dog's neck. This is to ensure that the collar will loosen after corrections.

When you begin to practice heeling, hold the leash in your right hand with your right thumb through the loop and four fingers holding the slack just as you did during leash-length sneakaways. Command (Dog's name) Heel as you begin walking. Prepare to stop by grabbing the collar with your right hand and using your left to place her rear end into a sitting position so her right front foot is alongside your left ankle.

As you walk along preparing to halt, control your dog's position using the fold-over maneuver. Grab the leash with your left hand and hold it taut over dog's head, then use your right to grip the braiding or stitching of the leash just above the snap. Next, take your left hand off the leash and use it to place dog in a sit in perfect heel position as you halt.

If your pup forges ahead, do a leash-length sneakaway. Drop the slack of the leash, grip the handle, hold your hands at your waistline, and run away. As the dog returns to your side, return to the original leash grip, holding the slack, as you continue walking.

If your pup lags behind, say Good Dog! as you spring ahead by taking a puddle jump with your left leg first. As you do this your left thigh will pull the leash, and your pup, back to heel position. The jump ahead will also prevent her from crossing behind to the right side.

Enforcing Household Obedience

Maybe your pup responds well to you in the backyard and at class or in the park, but won't listen in the house. That is your cue to leave the leash dragging from her collar in the house so you can stop misbehavior and enforce commands. If she does well until the leash comes off, try this intermediate step: Replace the leash with a tab and a five- to ten-foot piece of light line, and then follow this training routine.

FACT

Remember, obedience isn't supposed to be treasured like a fine crystal vase you admire and display but don't use. Anything you teach your dog should be used constantly and consistently. Wear and tear may not enhance crystal, but the more you utilize obedience, the more positively ingrained in your dog it becomes.

A great way to reinforce basic training is to work in different locations—in your kitchen, in your yard, while out on a walk, and so on. This teaches your pup to pay attention to you in all kinds of environments.

Attach the light line to your dog's tab and give her commands periodically. Tell her to sit in odd places where she is allowed but has never been expected to obey—on the stair landing, or a sofa, or in the bathtub, for instance. Give commands while you wash dishes, fold laundry, wrap a gift, open mail, put on your jacket, or attach a collar and leash (have an additional collar and leash attached so you can enforce). When she is interested in what other household members are doing, or who is in the yard, at the door, or pulling into the driveway or garage, give commands. In all these situations Sit is practical, but also utilize Down, Come, Front, Stay, and Heel for variety.

Manners: Wait, Off, Quiet, and Drop It

It's really helpful if you can teach your puppy to understand some variations on the basics of Sit, Stay, Down, Come, and Heel. For example, when it's time to go for a walk you can call your dog to the place where her leash is hanging and ask her to Sit and Stay while you put it on. Most dogs are so excited about this part of their day that it's hard for them to stay still. Asking an excited puppy to sit still while you put on your coat, get your poop-scoop bags, put on your shoes, and check for your cell phone may result in your having to reposition her as she moves from the Sit/Stay several times. Instead, you can ask her to Wait, which means to remain in a specified area rather than in an exact position.

Another useful request is Drop It. Dogs typically learn this request when it's time to give up the tennis ball during a game of fetch. Once they understand it, though, you can use it to ask her to let go of a child's toy or anything you don't want her to have in her mouth.

Here are some of the particularly useful requests for well-mannered dogs and the ways to teach them.

Wait

As discussed, the Stay command means freeze in the Sit, Down, or Stand position, and therefore is very restrictive. The Wait command, though, allows your dog to move about, but only within certain areas. You can use it to keep your dog in the car or out of the kitchen. The only thing Wait has in common with Stay is that both last until the next direction is given.

Teach the Wait command at doorways first. Choose a lightweight door and estimate how wide your dog's front end is. Open the door about two inches more than that as you say Wait. Stand with your hand on the knob of the partially open door, ready to bump the dog's nose with it should she attempt to pass through the opening. Be sure never to shut the door while correcting. Instead, leave the door open with your hand on the door handle, ready to stop attempted departures with an abrupt and silent bump of the door.

ALERT!

Work with your dog on a leash so that, if your attempts to deter her fail and she successfully skips across the border, you can step on the leash and prevent her escape. Practice with lightweight doors until you feel confident that the timing and strength of the tap is appropriate to deter your dog. Then apply the technique at heavy or sliding doors.

Work with your dog at familiar and unfamiliar doors as a helper tries to coerce your dog to leave. Your helper can talk to the dog and drop food, but your helper shouldn't call your dog. As your helper remains on the opposite side of the door, engage in lively conversation to teach your dog that even when you are preoccupied, the Wait command is enforced. When that lesson has been learned, you'll no longer need the leash.

Off

Here's a request that can be confusing for you and your puppy. You're sitting on the sofa reading a magazine when your dog comes in and jumps up next to you. Your instinct is to say Down, while directing her off the furniture. Think about it, though: What should Down mean to your dog? It should mean "assume a position of lying down until I ask you to do something else." So when you say Down and push her away, you're sending a very mixed signal. That's when you need to remember to use the word Off instead. Off should mean "remove yourself from what you're on" or "get off of whatever you're jumping on." To enforce the Off command pull her off her target with the collar or leash and praise her the instant her feet hit the ground.

Quiet

It's nice when your dog barks at the door to alert you that someone is there. It's not nice when she won't stop barking, especially if your baby is asleep or you're talking on the phone. Fortunately, teaching her to shush is simple. There are three ingredients to teaching your dog to be quiet on command.

First, if you've been trying to silence your dog by petting her or giving her a toy, stop. You may not even realize you've been inadvertently encouraging her excessive barking, so the habit can be tough to break.

Second, leash your dog and enforce the quiet. Be on the lookout for opportunities to enforce, such as when she barks at your neighbor, a distant noise, or because she's bored.

Third, when you are confident of your ability to quiet your dog at will, introduce the command. If you start saying Quiet before developing a strategy, you're likely to get hoarse long before she tires of barking.

Should I say Quiet every time my dog barks?
No, in fact, feel free to praise and encourage your dog for appropriate barking, such as when an intruder is near. There is nothing wrong with a dog barking if you can silence her easily when necessary. But barking isn't necessary for a dog's well-being, so if you find virtually all barking disturbing or unacceptable, correct it.

Drop It

Use the Drop It command to teach your dog to release objects from her mouth or not to pick something up. Some dogs, and virtually all puppies, like to chew, carry, and mouth anything they can—hands, clothing, the leash, gravel, cigarette butts, landscaping timbers, tissue. Your first reaction may be to pry her jaws open to remove it, but if you do, he'll soon be prowling for another item to grab. Teaching Drop It will reduce her scavenging tendency.

When you notice her eyeballing a taboo item, give your command. Accompany the Drop It command with a prompt jerk of the leash, as you quickly back away and offer to play with an acceptable object. If that doesn't work, carry Bitter Apple so you can give a spritz along with your command.

Using Hand Signals or Whistle Commands

Using something other than a verbal request to ask your dog to do something can come in very handy. For example, a snap of your fingers followed by a point to the ground could mean lie down—and wouldn't that help when you want your dog to settle while you're brushing your teeth?

Teaching hand signals is easy. Always give your hand signal in a distinct way so the dog doesn't assume you are just scratching your nose or grabbing for something. Formal obedience trial regulations allow the handler to use a single motion of the entire arm and hand but penalize any body motion—something to think about! It's imperative to use clear, concise, and consistent commands if you want your dog to understand and comply.

The hand signals that will be most useful are those that communicate the frequent requests like Sit, Down, Stay, and Come.

Whistles are commonly used to train hunting dogs or dogs who need to work at a distance from their handlers. That's because the sound travels so well and serves as the clear, concise form of communication that's necessary for this kind of work. Initially, though, the dog must be trained close to the handler to understand the association between behaviors and whistles. Using the leash, guide the dog in the desired movement following your whistle. As you move your dog into position, she should associate the movement with your verbal command, and because she has felt and seen the same movements, she should understand and follow the guidance eagerly. Generally, one toot of the whistle means sit and stay, and multiple toots mean come into the heel position sitting by the handler's side.

Tricks as Fun Ways to Train

Teaching your puppy a few tricks gives you both a break from the routine of the common requests—and it's a great way to impress your family and friends. Some simple ones are Jump and Shake. With a very young puppy you can try very short versions of these; expand on them as your pup grows and gets stronger and more mature. So long as you keep training sessions short and fun, your pup will be happy to play along.

Jump

Teaching a controlled jump is a fantastic way to burn off your pup's excess energy while bringing a smile to your face (and probably to her). Teaching the jump is easy if you have a hungry dog, a leash, and tasty but tiny treats.

Begin by positioning your dog in a sit, parallel to a barrier like a wall or a couch. Kneel next to your dog at a right angle. The first step is achieving a very low leg jump by extending your leg and putting your foot against the barrier and the floor so your dog has no option except to jump over it. Show her the treat in your far hand, and use it to lure her over your leg. Reward her for her success by giving her a treat. Reverse the process, luring her back over your leg with the other hand. (You may need to put the non-luring hand behind your back or by your side so she won't be distracted by it, since it was the source of the preceding treat.) Once she's mastered this low hurdle, raise your leg in two- or three-inch increments until she's actually leaping over it.

Here are a few success-building tips:

- Try to anticipate when your dog is likely to go off course. Use the food lures or leash to keep her on track.
- Don't jerk the leash. Instead, pull it—and praise her lavishly when she responds properly.
- Keep the jumps low until she's responding to the Over command. Then raise them gradually to build her confidence bit by bit.

As she gains confidence and is performing successfully, begin directing her over your calf, and then over an arm. Again, maintain the barrier but raise the height of the jump incrementally. Next, go back to the beginning and repeat the entire process—this time without the barrier. Once she's mastered these component jumps, take your show on the road, practicing in new locations and in the presence of increasingly tempting distractions. (Keep a line on her to maintain control.) Soon you can start mixing it up, combining various leg and arm leaps into a mini canine ballet.

Shake

A pup who knows Shake is an instant crowd pleaser—and it's easy to teach. Sit your dog facing you, kneel in front of her and reach for her pastern (which is the equivalent of your wrist). Especially if your dog is touch sensitive or easily spooked, do this calmly and gently. Tell her how good she is as you hold her paw in both hands and move it gently up and down. Release her paw and repeat the pattern several times. Do it prior to walks or feeding so she looks forward to the routine.

After a handful of experiences, add the simple command, Shake, or get creative and say something like Howdy Doody or What's Up as you look at her paw and reach for it. Become more animated in your praise and shaking her paw so she knows that's what you want.

The next step is to look distinctly at her front leg and give your command as you begin reaching toward it. Hesitate for a few seconds before touching her paw. Ideally, she'll surprise you by lifting her leg and offering her paw. If not, continue practicing, and when she finally does offer her paw, let's hope you have a juicy tidbit waiting in her bowl to acknowledge her greatness!

CHAPTER 16

Taking It to the Next Level

With a puppy in the house, anything is possible. After all, this is just the start of your dog's hopefully long and full life. While growing up to be a companion is a wonderful thing for your pup and for your family, it is possible for your pup to be so much more—and in the process for you to develop a much deeper bond together. This chapter gives you an overview of activities so you can get a sense of what you and your puppy might enjoy. By taking your pup to the next level, you'll be taking your relationship with him or her to the next level—and that's a great thing.

Dog Shows

So, you're a consummate stage mother? Maybe you bought your pup because he came from championship lines and you wanted to try your hand at showing. Maybe you've been to a dog show and it looks like fun. Or maybe it's just something you want to try once. Believe me, you're not alone. Dog shows are held all across the country on just about every weekend of the year, and hundreds of thousands of people and their dogs compete in them—at all levels, from beginners to lifers.

A word of caution: Dog showing is very competitive. You are not the first who went out and bought a puppy and thought, "Gee, wouldn't it be fun to show Rover?" Dog show people can seem haughty; many are very dedicated to their "sport," and don't take dabblers very seriously. Some will ask you if you bred the dog yourself, or from whom you bought it. Many people who "compete" are breeders whose livelihood—or at least some part of it—comes from dogs. You're just one more obstacle for them to overcome.

FACT

There are many different people involved with showing: The Breeder—The person or people who bred the dog (which involves selecting just the right parents). The Owner—Not necessarily the breeder, this is the person to whom the dog belongs at the time of the show. The Handler—Person in the ring with the dog. Many handlers are professional handlers whose job it is to show a dog, though many owner-handlers compete, too.

That said, there are also many lovely people in the sport, and the camaraderie and competition are lots of fun. It's also fun because you'll be meeting people who have dogs just like yours, and you'll trade all kinds of information. Let's take a look at how shows work, and how the show world works.

Dog shows are not run by the AKC; rather, they are sponsored by a specific organization (usually a breed club) that runs the show based on the AKC's rules and regulations. At a dog show, there are different kinds of classes: Puppy; Novice; Bred by Exhibitor; American Bred; and Open.

Puppies and dogs entered in those classes are judged on how they conform to the written standard for their breed. Standards are "blueprints" for their breeds, detailing physical makeup and temperament.

A dog's appearance includes all parts of its body—head, neck, forequarters, hindquarters, coat, color, and gait. Dogs are also judged on their temperament according to the standard. For example, a Golden Retriever is supposed to be "eager to please" according to its standard. A beautiful Golden Retriever who moped around and slinked away from the judge could not be considered a true representative of the breed because that behavior doesn't match the standard—any more than prick ears would on a Golden.

You may think your dog matches up beautifully against the standard for the breed, and you may even get a few others to agree with you. But when you step into a ring with a dog, you have to be ready to really show off the dog to the judge so that he or she really pays attention. This means your dog needs to be in the best physical shape possible for his breed, that he must be groomed to perfection, and that he moves masterfully in the ring so that he is in the best position for the judge's examination both standing and in motion. To accomplish this takes training and dedication.

The dogs are not judged one against another to determine which is the prettiest or soundest or the nicest. The dogs are judged individually by a person well-versed in the breed, who decides if the dog is the best possible representation of what the ideal dog of the breed should look like.

Dogs that compete at the highest level—at the annual Westminster Kennel Club show, for example—are seasoned professionals that have often crossed the country to be at the show. They are all champion-titled dogs who have sometimes competed at hundreds of shows. It can be a fun, companionable world, but it can also be tough. If it sounds challenging to you, take a closer look. Visit a nearby dog show and start talking to people to learn more. If your pup has potential, you will want to start working with him right away.

You can start competing in Match Shows with your puppy to see if showing your dog is something you might be interested in.

Competing in Obedience

The idea of obedience is to help meld you and your dog into a working team. This should be fun for both you and your dog, and will make him a better pet and you a better owner in the process. Because it demands precision, your dog must be fully tuned into you when he's working. People who really enjoy teaching their pups and dogs how to listen and respond to them will do well in obedience. Of course, your pup or dog will have to want to listen and respond, or yours will be a challenging journey.

You will discover how well you and your puppy can work as a team when you start taking basic training classes, which teach you how to communicate with your dog. In formal obedience, the idea is to be able to train your dog so that he can eventually comprehend and act on commands regardless of distance or interference. There are three levels that increase with difficulty: Novice, Open, and Utility. Each has its own requirements. In any trial, the dog must score 170 or more of the possible 200 points to earn a title. Novice exercises include standing for examination, heeling on lead, and a long sit off the lead (and more). In Open, your dog will need to do a marked retrieve, go down in the middle of being asked to come to you (a drop on recall), and sit for a long time off lead with you out of sight, among other things. At the highest level, Utility, your dog has to discriminate scents on objects, clear hurdles away from you while you direct him with hand signals, and other challenging exercises designed to truly test his competency.

You can learn so much about your dog and yourself through competitive obedience, and it is a very popular sport. You and your dog will truly become a team while you work through the demands of advancing to greater and greater challenges.

Fast-Paced Agility

If you've never seen dogs doing agility before, you're in for a treat. If you have, you know how exciting it can be for the dogs—and for people. Agility is the sport of maneuvering your dog through an obstacle course while you race against the clock. Point deductions are assessed if your dog knocks down or misses any part of the obstacles while racing through the course. He is also timed. The dog with the highest score and the fastest time wins.

Some dogs get so excited to compete in agility that they bark and bark not just before their turn but sometimes while they're on the course. It is hard to contain your enthusiasm whether you're a handler or spectator of this fast and fun activity.

FACT

Because agility demands a certain athleticism, you don't want to start your puppy too young. The running and jumping could be tough on his growing bones. You can train him to go over small jumps for fun, or to run through a toy tunnel, but so that he can enjoy the sport with you for many years, hold off on doing too much with him until your veterinarian and your trainer think he can handle it.

Getting started is easy—all you need is a basic training class so you and your dog know how to work together, and then you can sign up for a class where you'll learn how to train your dog to handle and work the obstacles individually and as a course. In competitions, to be fair, the sizes of the obstacles are determined by the sizes of the dogs. Larger dogs compete against each other and smaller dogs compete in another group. As in Obedience, there are levels at which to compete, and they increase in challenge and difficulty. In Agility, these are: Novice Agility, Open Agility, Agility Excellent, and Master Agility Excellent.

Becoming a Canine Good Citizen®

The American Kennel Club introduced its Canine Good Citizen program in 1989 in response to ever-increasing restrictions on where dogs could be taken or kept. The idea behind the program was that if dogs could demonstrate that they were well-mannered in response to everyday situations, then they should be given the distinction of being called good citizens in the same way that people are. To earn their Canine Good Citizen certificate, dogs must pass a series of ten tests to demonstrate manners in various situations. Since 1989, hundreds of thousands of dogs have been certified.

Puppies are great candidates for CGC certificates, as the tests are not physically challenging but involve the kinds of behaviors you would like your pup to demonstrate throughout his life. Young puppies won't have the attention span to complete the entire test, but it is certainly worth working toward in small ways. Then, when your pup is mature enough to be put to the test, he'll be ready.

The ten parts of the Canine Good Citizen Test are:

1. Accepting a friendly stranger. This shows that your dog will willingly accept the friendly advances of a stranger.
2. Sitting politely for petting. In a controlled sit, your dog should allow a friendly stranger to pet him.
3. Appearance and grooming. Your dog needs to be well groomed, and should welcome being gently groomed and examined by a friendly stranger.
4. Out for a walk (walking on a loose lead). This shows that you can walk your dog under control without him pulling at or lunging on the leash, and that he is attentive to your presence as his handler.

5. Walking through a crowd. Your dog should be able to pass by several strangers without displaying any inappropriate behavior.
6. Sit and Down on command and Staying in place. With this test your dog will demonstrate that he understands these basic commands.
7. Coming when called (from about ten feet away).
8. Reaction to another dog. This shows your dog can behave politely around other dogs as a handler approaches with his dog and engages in casual conversation with you.
9. Reaction to distraction. When presented with a couple of common distractions—such as a dropped chair or cane, or a person jogging by—your dog should show interest but not panic or aggression.
10. Supervised separation. The objective of this test is to see if your dog can be left on his own with a trusted person. With you out of his sight, your dog should remain calm until your return.

If you intend on making your dog a significant part of your life (especially if you live in an urban or suburban area), then taking advantage of Canine Good Citizen testing is an excellent idea. It's fun to do, and it's valuable to be able to trust your dog and how he interacts with others. Earning a CGC certificate is another way of letting the world know that your dog truly is a well-mannered and adaptable companion.

Therapy Work

Is there anything more adorable or huggable than a puppy? Anything that brings a bigger smile to the faces of young and old alike? If puppies can help normal people feel so good, imagine what they can do for those who are elderly or sick. Though it would seem that bringing a puppy to visit a nursing home would be a wonderful thing, in reality life is more complicated. You, your puppy, and the facility you want to visit must be prepared for things that could go wrong. That's why there are organizations that train volunteers and their dogs to prepare for visits to hospitals, nursing homes, and schools.

Only puppies and dogs who demonstrate that they can be calm and nondisruptive in the day-to-day world of strange smells, unfamiliar equipment, and human behavior typical of such facilities earn the privilege to be therapy dogs. It's not impossible for a pup to make it, but it would take a very mature pup—and owner, too.

If this kind of work is something you feel you would enjoy doing, you can expose yourself and your pup to it early so that you know what to expect and can work toward earning a therapy dog position. Volunteering and helping others might be a way to start, as is doing basic training with your pup and starting the Canine Good Citizen program.

The organizations that oversee the majority of therapy dog programs in the United States are the Delta Society and Therapy Dogs International.

Other Activities

Your puppy may be one of the many breeds that can become involved in sports that mimic the original jobs they had. For example, a herding breed like a German Shepherd, Border Collie, Shetland Sheepdog, or Corgi can do herding tests and trials. Terriers have earthdog events where their going-to-ground instincts are tested. Scenthounds do trail-hunting work, while sighthounds dash across fields after "prey" in lure coursing. The retrievers, pointers, setters, and spaniels can all test their birdiness in hunting tests and field trials.

For a Particular Breed

Breed- and Group-specific activities are sanctioned by the American Kennel Club and other purebred registry organizations and are conducted by clubs on local and national levels. Whether or not you want to get involved, there is no denying the amazement you'll feel when you see dogs doing what it is they were bred to do.

If you have a Lab, for example, you should find out where a hunting test or field trial for retrievers is being held near you. Even if it means going on an overnight trip, make a weekend out of it and plan to go. (Leave your dog behind when you go to the event, as only entered dogs are permitted on the grounds.) When you arrive, be respectful of what's going on around you, as the participants and their dogs will be very focused. Find out where the best place is to watch, and join others who are doing the same. When you see the Labs at the test or trial watching the fields or waters to see where a duck drops and then waiting to be sent by their handlers—and pursuing the game with such intense enthusiasm—you will understand why your Lab is the way he is about tennis balls, stuffed animals, or anything else he likes to retrieve. The other thing you'll see is how "alive" the dogs are when they're working.

If you want to better understand your purebred dog's heritage, then you will want to at least see, if not participate in, these activities. Learn more about them at the website of the American Kennel Club (*www.akc.org*).

For All Breeds

Yes, there are even more things you can do with your dog than have already been described! These include tracking, flyball, rally, Frisbee, dancing with your dog (canine freestyle), weight pulling, and Schutzhund. For all of these activities there are clubs or groups that participate regularly and with whom you can discover worlds of fun—and even competitions.

Canine freestyle—dancing with dogs—developed out of the natural instinct and desire for greater expression in the otherwise fairly stiff and routine world of obedience. How much more interesting and fun the routines might be if they were first set to music, and then improvised upon. Now freestyle has taken on a life of its own, with handlers and dogs wearing matching costumes, performing to all kinds of music, and incorporating all kinds of moves. You can find examples of freestyle routines on YouTube, or research the sport online through the World Canine Freestyle Organization (*www.worldcaninefreestyle.org*), Canine Freestyle Federation (*www.canine-freestyle.org*), and Musical Dog Sport Association (*www.musicaldogsport.org*).

CHAPTER 17

Your Puppy's Health

Your puppy can't tell you what's wrong with him, so it is up to you, as his caretaker, to notice when he seems to be ill or in some kind of pain. That's why regular grooming sessions are so important. Spending an hour or so brushing, petting, and checking your puppy all over his body gives you the opportunity to find anything that might seem odd. This chapter will review the common health concerns of puppies and dogs based on certain parts of the body or body systems. Should you notice something unusual on your pup, you can reference it here, and then decide whether it's worth bringing to your veterinarian's attention.

Basic Preventive Care

As described above, simply paying attention to and noting anything unusual with your puppy is an excellent preventive care strategy. When you find a suspicious lump, for example, and it either grows or changes in some way over time, you'll want to let your veterinarian know about it. If you catch things in their early stages, you can mitigate the potential damage.

Preventive care means more than just paying attention to trouble. It means caring for your puppy in a way that keeps him healthy to begin with. That includes proper diet, plenty of exercise, socialization and training, mental stimulation, grooming, and rest. When you care for a puppy or dog properly, you really shouldn't have too many health concerns to worry about. Along with the assistance of a trusted veterinarian, your canine companion should live to a ripe old age.

Let's take a look at common conditions so you understand how your puppy's body works.

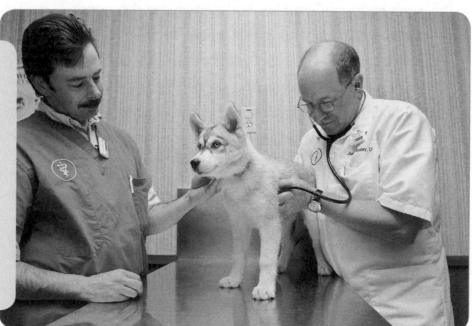

Regular veterinary examinations are important, but it is up to you to practice the best preventive care you can for your pup at home so that his visits to the vet are just routine checkups. This Husky pup is happy to have the attention of the veterinarians.

Problems of the Skin

The puppy's skin is a dynamic and vital organ. No matter if your puppy is short- or long-haired, his skin is always shedding dead cells and replacing them with new ones. The skin is made of two layers: the epidermis, or outer layer of skin cells, and the dermis, or second layer. A puppy's skin is prone to many problems that can affect either or both layers of skin, most notably itching, hair loss, swelling and inflammation, and flaking. Because skin problems are often the most visible and pronounced of ailments afflicting dogs, it's not surprising that they represent a large percentage of the overall cases referred to veterinarians.

Scratching and Itching

While all animals occasionally scratch themselves, excessive or constant scratching or itching is the sign of a problem. The most common causes are fleas, hypersensitivity (an immunologic or allergic reaction), and pyoderma (a bacterial infection). If the underlying cause isn't determined, the condition can grow increasingly worse.

At the first signs of itching, check your puppy for fleas. You can do this by moving the fur backward and looking for fleas themselves, or "flea dirt"—the digested blood fleas excrete that indicate their presence. If your dog has fleas, you will need to remove them from his body and from the environment.

Some puppies and dogs are so sensitive to flea bites that they develop Flea Allergy Dermatitis. The dog develops an immunologic hypersensitive reaction to the saliva injected by the flea when it feeds on the dog. By constantly licking, scratching, and chewing at his skin, the dog develops areas of hair loss, which can further progress to open sores that lead to infection. The areas most affected seem to be the base of the tail and lower back.

Flea Allergy Dermatitis typically develops when a dog is three to five years old, and it can be extremely tough to reverse, even if your dog is flea-free. The sooner your veterinarian can diagnose the condition, the sooner you can begin treatment and hope to alleviate the symptoms. Treatment will involve being vigilant about keeping your dog and home flea-free, the use of special shampoos, dips or ointments to prevent itching, and possibly prescribing anti-inflammatory drugs.

Dogs can also develop immunologic hypersensitivities to foods—anything from beef to wheat to dairy. This is why so many premium diets feature ingredients like lamb, rice, or turkey.

Allergies and Hot Spots

A hypersensitive reaction to things in the environment like certain fabrics, detergents, molds, or fungi, can mean the dog is allergic to that thing. Symptoms usually develop when the dog is one to three years old and begin to show in the spring or fall. Areas of the body most affected include the face, stomach, paws and, oddly enough, the creases of the elbows. If your dog is constantly rubbing his face, licking and scratching his paws, or scratching his tummy or elbows, you should suspect an allergic hypersensitivity. Left untreated, the itching will lead to areas of broken, exposed skin that are ripe for infections. Often paw licking will develop into a behavioral habit, perpetuating the condition.

Because of the enormity of potential allergens in the dog's environment, your veterinarian will need to evaluate your dog's symptoms carefully and perform blood and skin tests to try to determine the allergen. Once pinpointed, elimination of the source is necessary, and you will probably need to use special shampoos and ointments to alleviate itching.

Hot spots are quarter-sized areas of red, moist, swollen sores, typically found on longhaired puppies during warm, humid weather. They can be caused by the puppy's licking itself in response to some other problem like a parasitic infection, or general hypersensitivity. Often the cause goes undiscovered. Treatment involves applying antibiotic ointment to the wound and using an Elizabethan collar on the puppy so he cannot reach the spot to continue licking or chewing at it.

Seborrhea

When there is an imbalance of new cell growth to replace dying cells, the result is a thickening of the skin with noticeable shedding of the dead cells. This is called seborrhea. Symptoms include extreme flakiness; an overall greasiness to the skin and coat; an unpleasant and persistent odor to the coat; itchiness and bald patches of thick skin. The causes of seborrhea include hormonal imbalance, parasitic infection, excessive bathing or grooming, and nutritional disorders—all factors that contribute to the skin's not being able to properly regulate itself. Diagnosis is fairly simple, but treatment can be quite involved and may necessitate antibiotics, special shampoos, and anti-inflammatory medications.

Problems of the Eyes, Ears, Nose, and Mouth

You are probably most familiar with these parts of your puppy because—admit it—you spend a lot of time looking at and petting his adorable face. Your puppy also does a lot activities face-first, exposing these sensitive areas to things that can lead to tearing, sneezing, coughing, itching, and so on.

Eyes and Ears

Eyes and their surrounding tissues are susceptible to a number of problems. Dogs have three eyelids: top and bottom, and a third eyelid called the nictitating membrane, an extra layer of protection against the elements. The eyelids and the nictitating membrane all produce tears to lubricate the eye.

If one or both of your puppy's eyes is tearing excessively, suspect a problem. It could be that a speck of dust or dirt or a grass seed has lodged between the eyelid and the eyeball. If you can see the particle, you can try to remove it with blunt tweezers or a moistened paper towel or cotton ball. To help the eye heal, apply some antibiotic ophthalmic ointment such as Neosporin just inside the lower lid.

Likewise, if an eye appears red or swollen, the dog may have an infection caused by a foreign body. It is best to consult your veterinarian if such a condition exists.

Sometimes eye irritation in puppies or dog is caused by the eyelashes rubbing against the eye. If the eyelid rolls inward, causing the eyelashes to aggravate the eye, the condition is called entropion. When the eyelid rolls outward the condition is known as ectropion. Dogs with ectropion have exposed eyelid tissue that's particularly prone to damage and infection. Entropion and ectropion are both common congenital defects that may require surgical repair.

The membrane that lines the inner sides of the eyeball up to the cornea is called the conjunctiva. If it becomes infected, you'll notice a discharge from the corner of the dog's eye. The discharge may be clear and watery or opaque and thick. Typically this is the result of a bacterial infection. Your veterinarian can give you the best diagnosis.

Puppies' ears come in all shapes and sizes, from small and erect to long and pendulous. The most common problems they're susceptible to are cuts, hematomas, and infections. Many breeds' ears are cropped to both enhance appearance and to reduce the incidence of ear infection.

The skin of a healthy inner ear should be pink with some waxy light-brown secretion in the ear canal. If you notice your puppy scratching at his ears, excessively rubbing the side of his face against the floor or other surfaces, or whining with discomfort when you stroke around his ears, suspect an infection or other problem. The skin that lines the ear canal is the perfect host to bacteria, which thrive in warm, moist environments. Puppies who swim regularly, who live in humid environments, who have long, hairy ears, or whose ears are not regularly inspected for excessive dirty wax build-up can easily develop an infection. Your veterinarian will diagnose it and give you instructions for treatment.

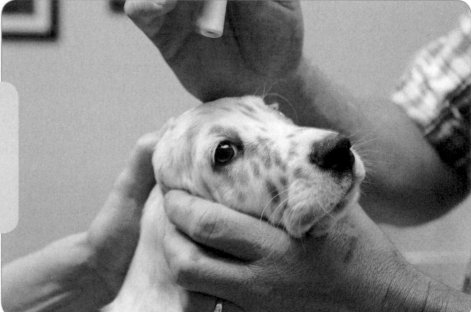

A veterinarian is examining the eyes of an English Setter to make sure no problems are present or developing.

Ear mites can be another source of itchy, inflamed inner ears. These microscopic parasites also like warm, moist environments, where they feed on skin flakes. A scraping at the vet's office will confirm this diagnosis.

Ear flaps are most prone to cuts, bites, and hematomas. Often dogs involved in a fight will get their ears bitten. If the bite is deep, take the dog to the veterinarian; otherwise, wash it thoroughly, apply antibiotic ointment, and monitor it for infection.

Hematomas are the result of a pooling of blood in the ear flap. This can happen after a dog shakes his ears violently, scratches them excessively, or knocks them against a sharp object. Consult your veterinarian about the best way to deal with a hematoma.

Nose and Mouth

First of all, forget the folk remedy that says a puppy with a warm, dry nose is sick. Yes, a puppy's nose should typically be cool and moist, and if it's not the puppy may have a fever. But some sick puppies will have cool, runny noses. Regardless, the nose is an all-important organ to the puppy. Smell is his most acute sense; through it he learns the most about his environment and the other creatures in it.

Because the nose itself doesn't have any sweat glands, when a puppy is excited or sick, the nasal mucous membrane will secrete water. Only secretions that persist for several hours indicate a problem.

This indicates an irritation to the front of the nasal cavity (coughing or gagging means the irritation is further back). It could be the inhalation of dust or dirt, which would cause the dog to sneeze several times and then stop, or it could indicate a fever or infection if it persists. If the sneezing is accompanied by discharge from the nose and/or eyes, see your veterinarian.

The dog's mouth is made up of the lips, teeth, gums, and tongue, and is the passageway to the esophagus. While the lips and tongue can be injured by cuts or burns, injury and disease most commonly affect the teeth and gums, and it is on these that we will concentrate.

The average adult dog has forty-two teeth in his mouth (this can vary by breed, with shorter-faced breeds having fewer teeth). With improper oral hygiene, the teeth can become encrusted with plaque and tartar, leading to smelly (dog) breath, inflamed or infected gums, tooth loss, and general deterioration of the mouth.

Because of the high incidence of dogs suffering from periodontal disease, veterinarians and others in the pet industry have gone out of their way to educate owners and provide them with materials that make taking care of their dog's teeth easy.

QUESTION?

How do I take my puppy's temperature?
Use a rectal thermometer that has a string tied to the end so you can't lose it. Dab petroleum jelly on the end and coat the tip so that insertion will be smooth. While the puppy is standing, hold the tail up with one hand, while with the other you insert the thermometer by gently twisting as your press in. Hold the puppy in place for approximately three minutes or so. This should be sufficient for taking the puppy's temperature. A normal temperature is between 101 and 102º Fahrenheit.

Healthy puppies and young dogs have bright white teeth and pink gums. It is possible to keep your dog's teeth looking almost as good as they did when he was a pup. This requires regular brushing, proper feeding and chew toys, and inspection for problems.

Get your puppy used to having his mouth handled by regularly lifting his lips and gently opening his mouth. Look at his teeth and gums. Is the gum line red or swollen? Are the teeth white all the way to the gums? Do you see any chipped teeth? Brushing your pup's teeth regularly will keep you abreast of what's happening in his mouth.

During your annual checkups at the veterinarian's office, the doctor can advise you whether your puppy's teeth need to be surgically scraped to have any lingering or stubborn tartar removed. Since this procedure requires anesthesia, discuss it with your vet at length before subjecting your puppy to it.

As previously stated, healthy gums are pink and should be firm. Red, swollen, painful gums are a sign of gingivitis and require immediate attention. Your veterinarian will probably need to scrape your dog's teeth to remove offending tartar, after which you'll need to aggressively brush and inspect your dog's teeth. Severe gingivitis can lead to infection and tooth decay.

Problems of the Digestive System

This system is made up of the esophagus, stomach, small intestine, liver, gall bladder, spleen, colon, rectum, and anus. The problems most typically associated with this system are:

- Vomiting
- Bloat
- Diarrhea
- Constipation
- Flatulence
- Anal sac disorders

Every dog will experience upsets of the digestive system in the course of his life; most problems are easily treated and symptoms resolve within hours or days.

Vomiting

If your puppy is vomiting, there is definitely something wrong with him. Determining what that something is, however, is trickier than you might think. You'll need to take special note of what and how he vomits to figure out what's wrong.

The most common cause of vomiting is simply overeating or eating so quickly the food is gulped down and then comes back up again. Puppies and adult dogs will also commonly vomit after eating grass, and some dogs get carsick and vomit in the car. If your dog vomits what's obviously partly digested food or chewed grass and only vomits once or twice, or is distressed by the car, don't worry about it. If you notice blood in the vomit, or if the vomiting is severe and frequent, make an appointment to see the veterinarian. These are signs that your puppy is truly not well. Make an appointment with your veterinarian immediately.

Bloat

This condition is also called gastric dilatation, which is exactly what it is: a swelling up of the stomach due to gas, fluid, or a combination. When the stomach fills up this way, it is prone to twisting, which quickly leads to shock and death. Puppies and adult dogs can develop bloat by eating too much dry kibble; exercising vigorously after eating; or gulping their food or their water. Some breeds seem prone to it, and it appears to run in some breed lines. Dogs experiencing bloat become restless, drool heavily, try to vomit or defecate unsuccessfully, and cry in pain when their stomachs are palpated. It is imperative to get your puppy to the veterinarian as soon as possible if you suspect bloat.

Diarrhea or Constipation

Like vomiting, the type and consistency of diarrhea vary depending on what's wrong. When all is normal, the puppy eats and drinks and his digestive system absorbs nutrients from the food and water and passes along undigested materials in the stool, which should be firm and consistent in color. Any irritation to the intestines or the bowel will trigger diarrhea. These irritations can vary from a change in food or water; over excitement; eating something that can't be digested or is toxic; or something that produces an allergic response. The color, consistency, odor, and frequency of the diarrhea can help you and your veterinarian determine the underlying cause and set about providing the proper treatment.

If you notice your puppy straining to defecate, or even whimpering or whining while doing so, with the result being no passing of stool, your puppy is constipated. Most cases of constipation are caused by inappropriate diet, which causes stools to form improperly and either block the colon or become painful to pass. Try giving your puppy one-half to two tablespoons of a gentle laxative like Milk of Magnesia. Take the puppy out often so you don't risk an accident in the house. If you don't get results in twelve to twenty-four hours, consult your veterinarian.

Flatulence

Having an overly flatulent dog is no fun! Through no fault of his own, a dog who passes gas can clear an entire room in no time. Chalk your dog's flatulence up to inappropriate diet yet again. A diet high in meats, fermentable foods like onions, beans, or even some grains, or dairy products can lead to excess gas. Review your dog's diet carefully, including the ingredient list of his dog food, and slowly integrate a diet change. If this doesn't yield results, your veterinarian can help.

Anal Sac Disorders

Dogs have two anal sacs, one on each side of the rectum at about five and seven o'clock, commonly called "scent sacs." They secrete a distinctive odor that leaves the dog's scent when he defecates. If the sacs become blocked, they can become sore and infected and will need to be expressed. If your dog frequently scoots across the floor dragging his bottom or wants to lick the area often, suspect an anal sac problem and ask the vet to show you how to handle expressing them to relieve the build-up.

Problems of the Respiratory System

Dogs breathe through a series of airways that comprise the nasal passages, throat, windpipe, and bronchial tubes that lead to the lungs. Any of the following symptoms indicate a problem in the system:

- Rapid breathing
- Noisy breathing
- Coughing

Dogs will breathe heavily and rapidly in a number of circumstances, such as after strenuous exercise, in excessive heat, or if they're excited or stressed. If your puppy is breathing rapidly while at rest and you can't attribute any of these other factors to his condition, consult your veterinarian.

Noisy breathing includes wheezing, sneezing, labored breathing, hoarseness, and any odd sound the dog makes while trying to breathe. Owners of some short-faced breeds live with this problem. Their dogs have shorter airways and will regularly snort, snore, or breathe heavily. For other dogs, noisy breathing is generally due to an obstruction, though it can also indicate a lung disease or heart failure. It's best to have your veterinarian listen and look.

Coughing results from the effort to extricate an obstruction in the airways, whether it's a bone chip, a collapsed windpipe, or a fluid build-up in the lungs caused by a respiratory disease like kennel cough. Kennel cough is highly contagious between dogs and can spread rapidly at a dog show or in a kennel. There is a vaccine to help prevent kennel cough, and if caught early treatment is successful.

FACT

Many veterinarians have suggested aspirin for arthritis in older dogs. When puppies have hurt themselves, have a fever, or are not feeling well, you can give them an aspirin. For puppies up to eighteen months of age, you will want to give them children's aspirin. Give them half of a tablet (small to medium dog) to one whole tablet (medium to large). For dogs older than eighteen months, you can give them half to one whole regular aspirin, using the same guide.

Problems of the Circulatory and Nervous Systems

At the center of the circulatory system is the all-important heart, a muscle that pumps blood to the rest of the body. Diseases that affect the canine heart include birth defects, aging, infectious disease, and heartworm. Heartworm is a condition that can be deadly but is easily avoided by giving regular preventive heartworm medication, as discussed in Chapter 18.

All activity in the nervous system generates from the brain, the spinal cord, and the peripheral nerves. Spinal cord diseases, seizures, head injuries, and paralysis are some of the problems that can result from injury or disease of this system.

A seizure is caused by a sudden burst of electrical activity in the brain, affecting the entire body by causing uncontrolled convulsions: foaming at the mouth, jerking of the limbs, snapping of the jaws, or rolling of the eyes. Depending on the severity, the dog may collapse and slip into unconsciousness. Seizures can be caused by trauma to the brain or the healing associated with it, or by a hereditary condition.

Epilepsy is a state of recurrent and similar seizures that typically happen in three phases: sudden restlessness accompanied by champing or foaming at the mouth; falling to the ground with head thrown back and pupils dilated, slobbering and drooling; and a recovery phase in which the dog is disoriented. The more violent phases, one and two, happen in just a few minutes; the recovery phase may last hours. You must consult with your veterinarian and your puppy's breeder if your puppy has epilepsy.

Complete paralysis is the result of permanent damage to the spinal cord. But a dog can experience partial paralysis due to a spinal cord disease or infection. Lyme disease is a form of tick paralysis in which the effects of the tick bite come on slowly, impairing movement to the point of paralysis. A speedy diagnosis is key to recovery. Normally the paralysis resolves with treatment by antibiotics.

Problems of the Musculoskeletal System

Bones and muscles support the body and protect the internal organs. All dogs, regardless of size, have an average of 319 different bones in their bodies. The bones are connected by ligaments and surrounded by muscles.

If your puppy is limping or is favoring a particular leg (lame), chances are he's got a bone or joint disease, a strained muscle or tendon, or possibly a broken bone. The causes range from something as severe as a congenital disorder like hip or elbow dysplasia, to something as ordinary as a strained muscle or age-related as arthritis. Your veterinarian should give you a professional diagnosis.

Canine hip dysplasia (often referred to as CHD or just HD) is a disorder of the hip socket. In a healthy hip, the head of the thigh bone (femur) should fit snugly in the hip socket (acetabulum). If the ligaments around the socket are loose, the head of the femur will start to slip from the socket. This causes gradual hind end lameness and pain. Treatment varies depending on the age of the dog, the severity of the condition, and the options available to dog and owner. Rapid advances are being made in the treatment of hip dysplasia.

While a specific cause of CHD has not been identified, it is suspected to be an inherited disorder, and breeders are encouraged to x-ray their dogs before breeding and to only breed dogs that have been certified free of the disease. It has happened, however, that CHD-free parents have produced pups that develop hip dysplasia. Weight, nutrition, and environment have all been implicated in the possible exaggeration or development of CHD, which normally manifests at an age of rapid growth.

Another common occurrence in dogs—particularly larger, active dogs—is a rupture of the cruciate ligament. These ligaments support the knee, where the femur, tibia, and patella connect. A sudden movement or a trauma to the area can result in tearing, or rupturing, of one of these critical ligaments. Obesity can also contribute to injury to these ligaments. An ACL injury is one to the anterior cruciate ligament in the front of the knee; a PCL is one to the posterior cruciate ligament behind the knee. A dog with a CL injury will pull up lame, usually unable to put weight on the foot of the affected leg. An immediate trip to the veterinarian is in order, and from there, if the diagnosis is ACL or PCL, treatment is typically surgery.

Problems of the Urinary and Reproductive Systems

The components of the urinary system are the bladder, prostate, and urethra, as well as the kidneys and uterus. The system works together. The two kidneys siphon excess waste created by ordinary metabolism, yet regulate water and minerals. Wastes are deposited into the ureter, which empties into the bladder. Urine passes from the bladder to outside the body via the urethra (in the male, the urethra also transports semen).

If all is functioning well, your puppy will urinate regularly (not frequently), and his urine will be clear and yellow in color. A problem of the kidneys, bladder, urethra, or prostate will be evident as straining to urinate, blood-tinged or cloudy urine, excessive drinking accompanied by excessive urination, or pain upon urination. The problem could be something as minor as dehydration or as complicated as renal failure. You must consult your veterinarian for a diagnosis.

The reproductive system of the female (bitch) includes two ovaries, a uterus, and fallopian tubes. A spayed female will have all of these removed. Intact females will experience regular heats and are prone to false pregnancies and infection of the uterus called pyometra.

You and your female dog will be happier and healthier if she is spayed. Some believe that a spayed bitch is prone to obesity. While it is true that she will not be under the same hormonal influence that keeps an intact bitch in form, with regular exercise and the proper diet, a spayed bitch can be kept in top shape.

The male dog's reproductive system includes the testicles, penis, and prostate gland. Intact males are prone to damage or injury of the penis or scrotum, cancer of the testes, and inflammation, enlargement, or cancer of the prostate. Once again, you and your dog will live happier, healthier lives if the dog is neutered. Neutering is the surgical removal of the testicles. The empty scrotum eventually shrinks and leaves no scar.

Neutering not only guarantees the male won't develop testicular cancer or prostate problems, it also lessens a male's territoriality, making him (with proper care and training) a friendlier pet. Neutering does not significantly change a dog's temperament, however; if you have an aggressive male or one with housebreaking issues, neutering will not solve the problem, but combined with training, it can certainly help.

First Aid and Emergencies

Emergencies elicit two states that don't help matters any—shock and/or fear in the dog, and panic in the owner. When dealing with an emergency, keep reminding yourself to stay calm and focused on what you can do for your dog. The first thing to do is call your veterinarian or the emergency clinic and let them know that you are on your way and why. Ideally, you should have someone drive you to the clinic while you manage your dog. Then follow these steps:

1. Evaluate the dog's condition and deliver any first-aid procedures, such as reducing bleeding, putting on a muzzle so the dog doesn't bite you or someone else, applying any ointment, or wrapping a wound.
2. Keep your dog still and warm by reassuring him while down and keeping a blanket on him.
3. Make preparations to transport him so he experiences as little turbulence and commotion as possible. Be very careful when lifting him. Use

a large sheet as a kind of hammock in which to contain him, or lift him onto a board that will keep his body flat and somewhat immobilized.

Common First Aid

A first aid kit is simple to put together yourself, and if you do you'll know it has what you need in it when you need it. Use a container that can be securely closed and conveniently stored. A large, plastic pencil holder or a shoebox can do the job. Once you have the container picked out, be sure it is clearly marked First Aid For Dog. The supplies you'll need include:

- Gauze pads
- Antibiotic ointment
- Nonstick adhesive tape
- Cotton balls and swabs
- A roll of stretch bandage
- Tweezers or hemostat
- Styptic pencil
- Rectal thermometer
- Long strip of fabric or old pair of nylon hose for use as a temporary muzzle
- Thin plastic gloves for treating wounds and heavier gloves for possible bite protection

Other supplies you should have on hand for your dog's (or your family's) general care include hydrogen peroxide 3 percent for cleaning and disinfecting; Pepto-Bismol or Maalox for minor gastrointestinal upset; syrup of ipecac to induce vomiting; a topical anti-inflammatory; and plain aspirin for pain.

CHAPTER 18

Coping with Shots and Bugs

Even if your dog is a model of good health, she will still need vaccinations, and protection from internal and external parasites. There is a lot to understand about these more routine aspects of overall well-being, so let's get started.

Why Your Puppy Needs Shots

Vaccines are given so that pets and people can be protected from potentially fatal diseases. Unfortunately, some pets (and people) are sensitive to a particular vaccine or a combination vaccine, and their sensitivity can lead to becoming sick from the vaccine itself.

Because of this, and because the formulations and types of vaccines are always evolving, it's important to understand why your dog should receive vaccines and whether they should be given individually, in combination, annually, for particular diseases, and so on.

Though there is a lot of debate around which vaccines to give and how often, no one will argue that vaccinating puppies is absolutely necessary. It wasn't that long ago that puppies and dogs routinely died from diseases like distemper and rabies. Now only unvaccinated dogs are at risk of developing a life-threatening case of either, especially since a rabies vaccine is required by law in most states.

FACT

The American Animal Hospital Association (AAHA) issued Canine Vaccination Guidelines for the General Veterinary Practice in 2006. You can access them through the website at *www.aahanet.org*.

In sum, vaccines have been categorized as "core" and "noncore" to assist veterinarians and owners in determining which are absolutely necessary, and which are recommended and why. The AAHA guidelines also give specifics about what age puppies and dogs should be when they receive the vaccinations.

Core and Noncore Vaccines

The core vaccines are those that are absolutely necessary. They are given to protect against the highly infectious diseases of parvovirus, distemper, adenovirus (hepatitis), and rabies.

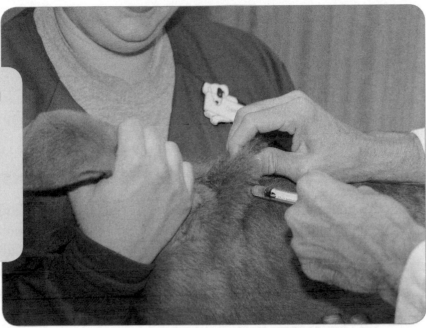

A vaccination protocol is essential to the overall health of your puppy. A veterinarian gives this Lab pup a shot to protect him against potentially deadly diseases.

The noncore vaccines are those that have been determined to be advantageous in certain situations (for example, in kennels where many dogs live together) or that provide temporary relief in some cases. The vaccines listed as noncore in the AAHA guidelines are the distemper-measles vaccine, parainfluenza virus, bordetella, leptospirosis, and Lyme (Borrelia burgdorferi). It's important to note that the connotation of noncore doesn't necessarily mean your dog shouldn't receive it; rather, its use should be considered as relevant to the individual circumstances of the dog (for example, dogs living in areas of high Lyme disease exposure will benefit from the vaccine).

ALERT!

A puppy vaccination schedule should begin around the age of six weeks and continue through the age of sixteen weeks. Your veterinarian will provide you with the complete schedule so your pup can receive all his shots at the right times.

A vaccine is intended to work with the immune system to fight against invasive infections of bacteria and viruses. The injection contains a harmless amount of the organism the body may someday need to fight off. This "jump-starts" the immune system to respond to that organism again if it enters the body. Without vaccines, dogs are far more susceptible to contracting infectious diseases from other dogs and other animals.

The Diseases Vaccines Protect Against

It's important to know about all the diseases for which there are vaccinations available. As mentioned earlier, some of them are considered core and should absolutely be vaccinated against. Others, however, can be more specific to a living condition (such as a Lyme disease vaccine for those who live in areas of high infestation), and may not be necessary for your dog. Understanding the diseases will help you discuss the necessity of the vaccination with your veterinarian.

Adenovirus (Canine Hepatitis)

Another viral disease, hepatitis attacks body tissue, particularly the kidneys and liver, and most often strikes dogs under one year of age. Symptoms include increased thirst, loss of appetite, abdominal discomfort, high fever, and lack of energy. Eyes may appear to have a blue tint. The disease is spread through contact with an infected dog or his urine or feces. It is a core disease against which to be vaccinated.

FACT

Especially for those who spend a lot of time at the local dog run, letting their dogs socialize with others, kennel cough is almost a certainty. Make sure your puppy and mature dog are always up-to-date on their vaccinations. Socialization is very important, so make sure you do it.

Distemper

This is a viral disease that attacks a dog's nervous system and progresses to affect every tissue in the body. It is an airborne disease that can strike at any age, but is most deadly if acquired young, which is why it's one of the first shots a pup receives. A dog with distemper will secrete a thick, yellowish discharge from his nose and eyes. He'll run a fever and he will not want to eat. The pneumonia, encephalitis, and dehydration that can result can be deadly. This is a core disease against which to be vaccinated.

Parvovirus

This viral infection manifests itself as an inflammation of the intestinal lining, causing sudden vomiting, bloody diarrhea, a high fever, and rapid weight loss. It is transmitted through the feces and can survive outside a dog's body for three to six months. The disease is extremely debilitating and rapidly lethal; treatment is intensive and often unsuccessful. It is a core disease against which to be vaccinated.

Rabies

The rabies virus attacks the central nervous system, causing unpredictable and often aggressive behavior. This erratic behavior is what, in turn, can cause the virus to spread, because it is through the bite of an infected animal that another animal is infected. Rabies can be transmitted from species to species, too, making it a health hazard to domesticated animals and people. This is why it is a core disease, and in fact all states require that dogs and cats be vaccinated against rabies. Rabies is common in the northeastern United States, where there are large populations of skunks, raccoons, foxes, bats, and groundhogs. If you observe erratic behavior in any of these animals, call your local animal warden immediately.

QUESTION?

What happens if my pet is bitten by a wild animal?
First, contact your veterinarian immediately. Any animal bitten or scratched by either a wild, carnivorous mammal or a bat that is not available for testing should be regarded as having been exposed to rabies. Dogs and cats that are currently vaccinated are kept under observation for forty-five days.

Bordetella (Kennel Cough)

Kennel cough is the common name given to the respiratory condition that results in a harsh, dry cough in a dog that sounds like a case of bronchitis in a person. It is caused by the bacteria *Bordetella bronchiseptica,* though the bacteria doesn't always act alone. Dogs who live in kennels, or who will be boarded with other strange dogs, or who visit strange dogs frequently should be vaccinated against the disease. It's highly contagious, though it can be treated with antibiotics, rest, and the proper environment. Affected dogs must be isolated from other dogs, and especially from puppies, who are more severely stricken than older dogs.

FACT

Kennel cough is the most common sickness passed on from dog to dog at dog runs and dog parks. It is the equivalent of a cold passed from one first grader to another. It is annoying, but if properly treated, it disappears in ten days to two weeks. And then it's like chicken pox—luckily, dogs tend to only get it once.

Leptospirosis

Lepto strikes the liver and also the kidneys, but this disease is caused by bacteria. Severe infections cause shock and death, but if it's caught early, aggressive treatment with antibiotics can fight it off. Symptoms include vomiting, excessive thirst with decreased urination and dehydration, and abdominal pain. Lepto is highly contagious, and an infected dog can also pass the bacteria through his urine for some time, even after treatment. Dogs who spend a great deal of time outdoors seem most affected. The disease is also contagious to people. It is a noncore disease against which a vaccine should be given if the dog or his environment is susceptible.

Lyme Disease

Lyme disease is a tick-borne viral disease that causes often debilitating joint pain. While once a disease predominantly of the eastern United

States, it is now documented in the northern Midwest and Pacific Coast areas of the United States. It is a noncore disease, but dogs living in areas of high possible infestation should be vaccinated.

QUESTION?

What is Lyme disease?
Lyme disease is caused by the bacterium Borrelia burgdorferi, and is transmitted to humans by the bite of infected blacklegged ticks. Typical symptoms include fever, headache, fatigue, and a characteristic skin rash called erythema migrans. If left untreated, infection can spread to joints, the heart, and the nervous system. Most cases of Lyme disease can be treated successfully with a few weeks of antibiotics. Preventive measures should be followed when spending any time in potentially tick-infested areas.

Other Vaccines

Some potentially life-threatening conditions for which vaccines currently exist are periodontal disease and rattlesnake venom. Both are fairly new to the market and are still being clinically evaluated for their overall benefits. If you worry about the potential for your dog to be bitten by a rattlesnake, or if you are concerned that poor dental health will affect your dog's teeth, gums, and other body systems, discuss these with your veterinarian.

Vaccinating as Your Dog Gets Older

It was once standard practice that the veterinarian needed to see your dog once a year after he was given his full range of vaccines. This was to administer booster shots as well as to give an overall evaluation so your dog's condition could be monitored as he aged. Now, it is understood that vaccines can continue to protect a dog for longer than one year, and that to over-vaccinate is potentially harmful. Does this mean that if your dog is looking and acting healthy he may not need his annual veterinary visit? No!

Is a combination vaccine safe for my puppy or dog?
Now that leptospirosis is considered a noncore disease that not all dogs may need to be vaccinated against, fewer puppies and dogs are given what was once a standard combination vaccine: DHLPP (distemper, hepatitis, leptospirosis, parainfluenza virus—a contributor to kennel cough—and parvovirus). Ask your veterinarian if any of the shots your puppy or dog is scheduled to receive is a combination vaccine and what the advantages or disadvantages might be.

At his yearly checkup, the vet will examine your dog from head to tail, including his eyes, ears, mouth, feet, limbs, chest, back, and anus. He will ask you about any lumps or bumps he might detect, or any swellings or tender spots. He'll let you know if your dog's teeth need a scraping, and he'll advise you about your dog's weight and overall condition.

If you live in an area with a high susceptibility to a particular kind of disease, or if you plan to board or travel extensively with your dog, your veterinarian may recommend a vaccine to protect your dog. He or she can also perform a blood test to assess the level of antibody concentration in the blood (a titer). This test is helpful if you're concerned about something like Lyme disease or kennel cough in your area because it will show whether your dog is adequately protected or needs a booster shot.

Bad Bugs—External and Internal

The nasty bugs that can make your puppy really miserable have another name, and it evokes an image of what they really are: parasites. Common parasites that plague puppies and dogs are fleas, ticks, and worms.

Parasites are organisms that are dependent on a host for part of their life cycle. You'll learn how your puppy is the perfect host for these horrible things as you read on. While fleas and ticks are generally more of a nuisance than an immediate threat to your puppy's health, all parasites can be a general threat to the host animal's wellbeing and can spread serious illnesses. The bubonic plague was spread primarily through flea bites. You probably need not worry about catching the plague from your puppy, but parasites are a definite nuisance and legitimate danger to keep under control.

Fleas and Ticks

Fleas have been annoying humankind and animals for centuries, and they're almost as tough to control today as they were in the days of ancient Rome. The flea's exoskeleton is amazingly resilient, and fleas can jump several feet to land on an unsuspecting host. Despite what many dog owners believe, fleas do not spend most of their lives on their pets. In fact, fleas only stay on dogs to feed and breed. They feed by biting the dog and sucking its blood. Because fleas often harbor tapeworm larvae in their systems, besides aggravating dogs with their bites, fleas can transmit tapeworm disease to the animal via the bloodstream or by being eaten by a dog trying to chew the fleas off himself.

When fleas mate, the females lay hundreds of eggs. These drop off the dog and into the environment. Larvae hatch from the eggs in two to three weeks, and these feed on environmental debris like human or animal dandruff, mold, and other protein and vegetable matter. From the larval stage, the flea develops a cocoon shell in which it matures. In the cocoon stage, the flea can live with no nutrients for almost a year. Then all it takes is the slight vibration of an animal's passing for the cocoon to release the adult, which jumps onto its host and begins the life cycle all over again.

FACT

Your puppy can pick up fleas almost anywhere—outdoors, in a neighbor's house, even from another dog. Chances are, by the time you spot adult fleas on your puppy, you can be sure you have a potential infestation in your home and/or yard.

You'll know you and your puppy are in trouble when you see him scratching or licking himself suddenly and with real purpose. To confirm your suspicions, part your puppy's hair to the skin or brush it backward and see if you notice any black specks. The specks can be dense around the dog's groin area, in the hair at the base of the tail, and around the ears and neck. With a moist paper towel, wipe the specks. If they turn red, it is flea dirt—particles of digested blood the flea has excreted.

If you know your puppy has fleas, you will have to be diligent about removing them from the pup and the environment. If you only remove the fleas from your dog without eliminating the flea eggs, larvae, and cocoons from the environment, you are guaranteed a continuing problem.

Puppy owners are fortunate to have a whole slew of flea-fighting products to choose from, ones that are safer than ever for dogs and the environment. Consult with your veterinarian before waging a war on the fleas that have infiltrated your happy home; you'll want to be sure that the products you select for use on your puppy and your home are appropriate for your dog's age, weight, and skin type, and that the ingredients don't clash with a product you choose for your home and yard.

The active ingredient in many of the topical flea products on the market these days is pyrethrum, a natural compound toxic to fleas but not harmful to pets or people. There are also formulations that stop flea eggs from developing, interrupt the reproductive cycle, and break down the tough skeleton of fleas.

Fleas in Your Home

Once you've selected the flea-fighters you'll need, plan a systematic approach to ridding your dog, home, and yard of all stages of the flea life cycle. Take every step seriously if you want to completely eliminate the problem. You'll need to vacuum thoroughly, using several vacuum cleaner bags and disposing of them all in airtight plastic bags. You'll need to wash all the dog's bedding in very hot water. This may include your family's bedding, too, if the dog shares anyone's bed. Any place that your dog passes through or sleeps in can be considered a flea hot spot, and potentially infested. Concentrate your efforts here.

To remove fleas on your puppy, wash with a flea-killing shampoo, then comb thoroughly with a fine-toothed flea comb. Dip the comb in a large glass of soapy water to drown any fleas that survived the bath. Dry your puppy thoroughly, and don't let him roll in his favorite hole in the yard or lie down in his usual spot on the porch—these are possible hot spots, too, and need to be treated with an outdoor insecticide.

Preventive Measures

Once you've treated the puppy, house, and yard, you'll never want to repeat the process, so you'll need to step up your preventive measures.

Figuring your puppy can get fleas any time he steps out of your home and into a well-populated area, you should check him regularly before coming inside. Run a flea comb through his fur. This will snag any free-loaders before they start breeding. Kill them on the comb by crushing them with your fingernail or immersing the comb in a glass of soapy water. During the warm months, when fleas are at their worst, bathe your puppy regularly with a flea-preventive shampoo, and ask your veterinarian about other products designed to keep fleas from settling on your pet. Vacuum your home frequently, and make sure to keep your pet's bedding fresh and clean.

Many puppies and adult dogs are allergic to the saliva that fleas inject into their skin when they bite them, or are particularly sensitive to fleas living on them. These dogs can develop serious skin ailments from their allergies and sensitivities, which often linger even after the flea problem has been eradicated. The excessive scratching, licking, and fur-biting they indulge in to get at the fleas leaves their skin damaged, causing further itching and, often, infection. The infection can leave the skin swollen or patchy, and can lead to permanent hair loss. Besides being unsightly, a flea allergy or sensitivity is extremely irritating to your dog. Your veterinarian will advise you on how best to treat this problem.

Ticks

There are many types of ticks throughout the United States, the most common being the brown tick, the wood tick, and the deer tick. All adult ticks seek out dogs and other animals as hosts for feeding and breeding. The brown tick is typically the size of a match head or small pea when engorged. The wood tick is a larger tick that, when full, swells to the size of a kernel of corn. The deer tick is a tiny tick that even when engorged is no larger than a speck. The brown tick is known to transmit Rocky

Mountain spotted fever, while the deer tick is the carrier of Lyme disease, both of which can be deadly.

The sooner you spot a tick or ticks on your puppy, the better. You need to remove the tick(s) immediately, then monitor the spot from which you removed the tick. To take a tick off your puppy, first wet a cotton ball with alcohol or a dab of petroleum jelly. Apply this to the tick to suffocate or numb it, then, with tweezers or with gloves on your hands, pull the tick gently off the pup. Deposit the tick in a jar filled with alcohol or nail polish remover. If your puppy comes out of a trip to the woods loaded with ticks, you may want to get a tick dip from your veterinarian to help remove them all at once.

Tick bites rarely become infected, but you'll want to keep an eye on your puppy's skin in the area from which the tick was pulled off, especially if it was a deer tick. Often a red, circular rash will develop around the bite—an early indicator of Lyme disease. If you notice any redness or swelling in the area of a tick bite, make an appointment to have it checked by the veterinarian.

Unfortunately, it's almost impossible to keep ticks off your puppy if you spend any time outdoors with him. Your best bet, yet again, is preventive care: bathing your puppy with a flea and tick shampoo formulated for his needs; taking your veterinarian's advice about what products work best to keep ticks off your dog; and always checking your dog thoroughly when you return from an outdoors adventure.

What to Do about Worms

Like the infectious diseases that are avoided by proper vaccinations, worms (intestinal parasites) are another potentially deadly enemy of your puppy's health easily prevented by proper care, hygiene, and attention.

Several types of worms infect dogs; tapeworms, whipworms, roundworms, hookworms, and heartworms are the most common.

Puppies and adult dogs become infected by worms by contact with contaminated soil; raw, contaminated meat (like a dead animal in the woods); or ingestion of an infected host (like a flea). That's why it's so important to clean up after your dog in the yard and around the house, and to have fecal exams performed by the veterinarian regularly (microscopic examination is often the only way to detect the presence of internal parasites).

You might suspect your puppy or dog has worms if his appetite decreases, he has an upset stomach, he loses weight, and you see blood or mucus in his stools. These symptoms are characteristic of an advanced state of parasitic infection; a dog can have a slight infection and appear normal until your veterinarian detects worms in his feces. For common infestations, safe, effective, and fast-acting worming medications are available.

Heartworm

The heartworm is a particularly deadly parasite because it infests and grows in the canine heart. Left untreated, heartworms literally strangle the heart, causing it to fail and the dog to die.

Heartworm is transmitted by infected mosquitoes. When they land on a dog to bite, heartworm larvae are deposited on the skin. The larvae burrow their way through the dog's skin, growing into small worms as they go. When they finally reach a blood vein, the worms travel to the heart, where they mature. Heartworms can grow four to twelve inches long, and a dog can be infected for years before symptoms are noticeable. A dog diagnosed with heartworm is in trouble either way. Treatment is intense and can even cause the inevitable death it seeks to avoid.

Today's dog owners are extremely fortunate to have heartworm preventive medication readily available. In some parts of the country veterinarians suggest giving dogs the preventive daily or monthly (depending on the type) only in seasons in which the mosquito is most active; in other parts of the country, veterinarians keep dogs on the preventive all year round as a safety precaution. Ask your veterinarian what's best for your dog and stick with the program. If you take your dog off preventive medicine for more than several months, he must be tested for the presence of heartworm before being allowed to go back on it.

CHAPTER 19

Alternative Health Care

Something you are probably well aware of is how you must be proactive about your own health and that of the people—and animals—you share your life with. While you should feel great about the veterinarian or veterinary team that takes care of your puppy, and you should seek their advice when you have any questions, it's still important to know that there are many different ways to approach a health problem.

Is it Right for Your Puppy?

Your veterinarian may already be incorporating some less traditional, or alternative, methods into the way he or she treats your puppy. If you're not really sure how these could or should benefit your pup, it's easy to find out. Through all his life stages, the more you know about all the approaches to health care, the greater your perspective when it comes time to treating your puppy for a disease.

FACT

Alternative care is also referred to as holistic, integrative, or complementary, as well as nontraditional. These are all ways to differentiate it from traditional or conventional care.

It seems everyone has their own interpretation of what "alternative" or "holistic" means relative to health care. Here's how the American Holistic Veterinary Medical Association defines it:

Holistic medicine, by its very nature, is humane to the core. The wholeness of its scope will set up a lifestyle for the animal that is most appropriate. The techniques used in holistic medicine are gentle, minimally invasive, and incorporate patient well-being and stress reduction. Holistic thinking is centered on love, empathy and respect.

This mixture of healing arts and skills is as natural as life itself. At the core of this issue lies the very essence of the word "(w)holistic." It means taking in the whole picture of the patient—the environment, the disease pattern, the relationship of pet with owner—and developing a treatment protocol using a wide range of therapies for healing the patient.

In a way, it's quite commonsensical, and rather than be perplexing, alternative care can be easily incorporated into what you do with and how you treat your puppy daily.

This chapter will explore some of the more common alternative therapies available, and you can certainly do your own research. One place to start is with the American Holistic Veterinary Medical Association (AHVMA) at *www.ahvma.org*. Founded in 1982, the AHVMA helps veterinarians and pet owners expand their understanding of treatment options.

How Does It Work?

When a veterinarian takes a holistic approach, he or she not only works from a complete physical examination, but also examines the influences of nutrition, behavior, past medical history, stress, and any other contributing factors. Like a conventional veterinarian, a holistic practitioner will start with blood work to gauge your puppy's overall health. A urine or feces sample may be necessary, as well. The veterinarian will go on to ask you about the nuances of your puppy's lifestyle and schedule at home. Maybe you moved recently, and your pup started itching more out of stress or an allergic reaction to a new carpet or floor finish. Maybe you switched detergents and when you washed his bed the new soap became an irritant. Maybe the sound of a garbage truck has spooked your puppy into soiling a particular area in the house.

While getting to the root of the problem may take longer this way, the "cure" is a real one, and not just a medication that might mask the real problem. Of course, medication may be just what your puppy needs, or medication in combination with a small but important environmental change.

Nutrition and Behavior

Readers of this book who have young children understand completely the cause-and-effect of what a child eats on his or her behavior. Some believe that too much sugar causes young children to become excited, jittery, and active—and then crash. A dose of junk food will do the same thing. It makes sense, then, that with their high metabolisms and rates of growth, puppies would be affected by what they eat, too.

The principles of sound nutrition are discussed in Chapter 8, which explains what's in dog foods and what to consider when choosing a food for your puppy. The thing about most commercially available kibble is that the nutrients have been cooked right out of them because they are processed at such high temperatures. When you consider that most dogs do not eat a varied diet, and what they do eat may be lacking in elemental nutrients, is it any wonder that so many have skin conditions, or gastrointestinal conditions, behavior issues, or develop illnesses at younger and younger ages?

Dogs can be pretty good self-medicators. If your puppy seems to want to eat dirt or grass frequently, suspect a nutritional imbalance. If she's chewing at her feet, she may be having an allergic reaction to an ingredient in her food. If she gets the "crazies" more often than you think is normal (and remember, at times puppies will madly dash around the house or act silly or out of control), there may be something in the food that's contributing to this behavior.

Ask your veterinarian to run a complete blood test on your pup if she's behaving in a way that seems particularly unusual. Even if you will need to work with a trainer to modify the behavior, it will be worth knowing what's going on inside the body so that it can be addressed, too. This is the holisitic approach in action: body, mind, spirit, environment, and relationships all come into play.

Massage and TTouch

If you enjoy petting and grooming your puppy, it will feel natural to take that tactile attention to the next level and touch her so that she is being massaged instead. This kind of touch has additional health benefits—from reduced stress and nervousness to weight loss.

The intention of massage is to knead, rub, or pat the body in order to stimulate circulation. Increased circulation means better blood flow, which leads to the release of stress, improved breathing, and a general feeling of well-being. Massage therapy has been known to reduce anxiety levels of students taking exams, assist cancer patients with the effects of their treatments, lessen depression in those who are grief-stricken, promote weight gain in malnourished infants, and much more. For athletes, the benefits of increased circulation translate to better functioning joints and muscles and improved performance.

Massage can benefit dogs in as many ways. It can reduce fear and anxiety, help the body to fight off disease, improve physical performance,

Puppies (and dogs) just beg to be petted! Turn petting into an even greater health benefit by learning simple massage techniques to increase circulation and reduce anxiety.

and enhance bonding. There are many books and even some DVDs that can teach you about massage techniques that benefit dogs in both general and very specific ways, and they're worth taking a look at.

Massage to the Next Level

Instrumental in bringing these practices to many people is Linda Tellington-Jones, a horse trainer who was curious about how touch could affect her horses' behavior. Basing her work on techniques developed by Moshe Feldnekrais for humans, Tellington-Jones started using circular touching motions to actually interrupt unacceptable behaviors so that the desired behavior patterns could emerge. Her system has become known around the world as TTouch, and it has essentially revolutionized how people could directly contribute to both improving their relationships with their companion animals, resolve behavior problems, and even assist in healing physical problems.

ALERT!

Tellington-Jones's TTouch method is beneficial for dogs with problems ranging from barking and chewing to pulling on the leash, jumping up, resistance to grooming, car sickness, and the effects of aging. Learn more at *www.ttouch.com*.

TTouch can help a puppy feel better about having his paws held and looked at (and his nails clipped), can help him feel less stress around the human members of his pack (family), and can keep his circulatory and nervous systems (and other systems by default) in their best possible shape. Both of you will benefit from the deeper bond between you.

Chiropractic and Acupuncture

Taking the work of touch to the next level, the use of chiropractic techniques and acupuncture on dogs (and other animals) are also becoming more widely used.

The term chiropractic comes from two Greek words—*cheira* and *praktikos*—and means "done by hand." It is the practice of assessing mechanical abnormalities of the spine and musculoskeletal system to effect relief through the nervous system. The premise is that pain is the result of an impaired nervous system as influenced by the position of the spine. Once adjustments are made to the spine and the surrounding musculature, the pain is relieved. Treatment depends on the condition being addressed.

Chiropractic is more and more commonly practiced on horses and companion animals—particularly those involved in competitive sports such as show jumping, dressage, and eventing for horses, and agility and other physically demanding sports for dogs. It's not always easy to find a canine chiropractor near you. Practitioners need to be trained just as human chiropractors do, but as success stories emerge, demand grows. The American Veterinary Chiropractic Association (AVCA) provides, "public educational, social, credentialing, and professional services to the animal chiropractic community and the community at large." Through its website, the association lists referrals as well as other information. Find them at *www.animalchiropractic.org*.

The ancient practice of acupuncture takes stimulation to yet another level: through needles applied directly to "meridians" in the body that correspond to the area(s) that need(s) relief. Acupuncture can benefit circulation, respiration, urinary problems, joint pain, and much more. It is an ancient healing procedure that dates back some 7,000 years but is only now becoming more mainstream. In fact, it wasn't until 1998 that the American Veterinary Medical Association (AVMA) finally gave the nod to acupuncture, stating in its Guidelines for Complementary and Alternative Medicine that acupuncture and acutherapy were integral parts of veterinary medicine. It's doubtful your young puppy would need these kinds of treatments, but it's nice to know there are more and more veterinary acupuncturists in the United States.

Aromatherapy

It's impossible for us to appreciate how powerful a dog's sense of smell is. With about four times the number of scent receptors lining their nasal passages, though, dogs can detect infinitely smaller amounts of a scent than we can—and smells are much more important to them than they are to us. It is through scent that dogs learn much about what is around them or even the condition of people and other animals. Of course, smell also helps them find food, and being the ultimate scavengers, this is very important to dogs. Don't think that just because you've put something tasty out of sight of your pup that she won't be able to sniff it down—even if it's wrapped in flavor-sealing plastic.

There are many ways that we need to keep smells from bringing out inappropriate behavior in our pups and dogs—making sure trash cans are secured behind latches, dousing accidents on the floor or carpet with enzyme cleaners so that all traces of smell are removed, putting fresh-baked foods in another room to cool—and there are also ways that we can work *with* smells to bring out better behavior.

The scents of flowers, roots, and trees can promote healing and wellness when used properly. With their exquisite sense of smell, for dogs, a little goes an extra-long way. Aromatherapy should be approached cautiously, especially with a puppy, as an overbearing smell can cause more harm than good.

Aromatherapy is done with essential oils. These are produced by steaming or otherwise extracting the scents from their sources—flowers, herbs, trees, etc. The oils are bottled and sold in pharmacies, health food stores, and even some grocery stores. They can be used in many ways, including diffused through a source of heat; combined with other ingredients to make things such as soaps, insect repellents, and so on; or, if they will be applied to the skin, diluted in a base solution (typically an oil, such as sunflower or grapeseed oil).

Which essential oil should I try with my dog?
Understanding which oils do what is critical to getting started. There are lots of books you can learn from, and of course many websites, as well. To get started, check out *www.aromaweb.com*—it's an excellent resource.

Once you've targeted some oils that are suggested for the ailment you're working with, it is extremely important that the proper dilution is made with the essential oil before exposing it to a dog because of their sensitivity. As you learn more about how to use the oils, you'll find advice on dilution concentrations, too. The next step is to start working with the oils and your dog. Aromatherapy practitioners who work with animals say that this is the beginning of an amazing journey of discovery for you and your dog.

Using Flower Essences

Because smell is such a strong sense for dogs, you don't want to overwhelm them. Puppies are even more sensitive, so you need to be especially careful. Another way to experience the benefit of plants on your puppy is to work with flower essences. These are formulas that contain intense concentrations of a single plant or flower essence or a combination of them. They work by being ingested in small quantities, and their effect is on the overall being of the puppy or dog.

Sharon Callahan, the founder and formulator of flower essences for Anaflora in Mt. Shasta, California, explains, "There are many single flower essences and combinations of essences that greatly benefit the beginning stages of the life of a healthy puppy. Such essences assist with weaning, bonding with the new family, adjustment to other animals, and the delicate development of a puppy's nervous system. Flower essences," she continues, "can also help lay the groundwork for a calm, steady, yet alert emotional and mental presence which will continue through the life of the puppy."

Sharon recommends the following single essences as beneficial. These include:

- **Heart's Ease**—eases the discomfort of separation from littermates and mother
- **BeGone**—balances the parasite/host relationship
- **Catalpa**—offers a feeling of protection and peace in a new environment
- **Mt. Shasta Lily**—offers nurturance during weaning and early stages of separation from the mother
- **Mountain Ash**—provides physical vitality for the growing body and psyche
- **Pear**—facilitates adjustment to new surroundings and routines
- **Star Jasmine**—helps animals adjust to indoor life

Animal Communicators

Wouldn't it be wonderful to be like Dr. Doolittle and be able to talk to the animals? Anyone who has a bond with an animal—whether it's their puppy or a snake—is curious about what their companion is thinking and feeling. When an animal is sick and can't speak with you about where the pain is coming from or what might have caused it, you wish even more that your friend could talk to you.

It turns out that there are Dr. Doolittles among us—people who can interpret and share the thoughts and feelings of animals. They are called animal communicators, and as skepticism about what they do diminishes, they are becoming more and more popular.

The objective of this book isn't to sell you on animal communicators any more than it is to get you to use flower essences, aromatherapy, or acupuncture. One of its goals, though, is to present it as something that could be helpful—especially if you are at your wit's end about how to handle a particular problem with your puppy or dog. You may have consulted a veterinarian, worked with a trainer, sought out a specialist, applied aromatherapy—almost everything—and come to the last option of seeming hope, asking an animal communicator to find out from the dog what's going on for him so that you can help remedy the situation.

How do I find an effective animal communicator?
It takes a leap of faith to consult with an animal communicator, as most work over the phone having never met your puppy before. If you don't know someone who can give you a personal recommendation, then you will need to research any leads you have. Check out the communicator's website, ask the communicator for references (and call them), and trust your own instincts.

Marta Williams, author of the books *Learning Their Language* and *Beyond Words* describes animal communication as an intuitive exchange of thoughts, images, and emotions. This is something animals do among themselves and other species (including humans) all the time. Intuitive communication can happen in four ways: through feelings (clairsentience); through mental telepathy (clairaudience); through visual images (clairvoyance); and through a feeling/knowledge that something is absolutely true even if you didn't know it before.

How does a session with an animal communicator work? Once an appointment is scheduled, all you have to do is get your questions ready. At the appointed time, either you call the communicator or he or she calls you. The communicator will ask you some basic questions—whether you want to talk to one or more pets in your home, an identifying physical feature, the dog's name, etc. From there, you can pose the questions you want the communicator to ask your dog. Once asked, there will be some silence as he or she contacts your dog. And then get ready for some revelations!

During a session, your puppy or dog will most likely be fast asleep by your side, sometimes in a seemingly very deep sleep. Don't disturb your dog; instead, focus on what you want to learn from your dog.

CHAPTER 20

Traveling with Your Puppy

It wasn't too long ago that when people went on vacations or even away for the weekend, they had to board their canine family member. Thankfully, the situation for those wanting to travel with their dogs is much improved, with many lodging establishments from hotel chains to exclusive resorts accepting dogs as guests. It is not unusual to see people exercising their dogs at rest stops along the highways, or to meet a new person and dog in your park only to find out they're traveling.

20

The Go-Everywhere Puppy

Traveling is a great form of socialization for dogs, and you should try to take your pup with you wherever you go. If he enjoys traveling in the car, he will soon expect that if you're going somewhere, he's going with you. Short rides, long rides, overnighters, visits to friends and family far away—for travel-happy dogs, it's not the length of the adventure, it's the adventure itself. Just as every time you come home is a cause for celebration for your dog, so is seeing you give her the invitation to join you when you pick up the keys and head for the door.

While it's wonderful to have your dog along, it's not so great to arrive somewhere and discover that you don't have what you need to be able to safely walk him or care for him. If you will be doing any traveling, be prepared and pack a bag for your puppy. It's something you can keep in the car so you won't have to scramble to find his things every time you want to go somewhere. What should be in your puppy's traveling case?

Seat Belt Security

Allowing your dog to be loose in the car is an accident waiting to happen. You may have done this without incidence for years and with many different dogs, but consider yourself lucky. Today, the roads are more crowded, people tend to drive faster, there are more distractions (cell phones, navigational systems, stereo systems, kids, etc.), and it's simply not possible to think that traveling without a seat belt is wise for any passenger in a vehicle—including your dog. All it takes is one innocent occurrence—dropping a French fry on the floor by your feet and having your puppy dive after it—to cause you to take your eyes and attention off the road, with potentially deadly results. It's fun and "free" for your pup to cruise around unfettered in your car, but it's simply not smart.

What if you were in an accident and were unable to move from your vehicle but your frightened dog got out and bolted away? He may be unharmed, but he may be lost forever. Better to know he's belted or crated and with you than lost in a strange place.

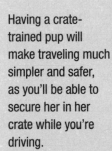

Having a crate-trained pup will make traveling much simpler and safer, as you'll be able to secure her in her crate while you're driving.

Today's canine passengers can be outfitted in many kinds of car safety contraptions to make traveling safe for them. These include specially made seat belts that pair with human seat belts, to booster seats with safety harnesses for small dogs, to tried-and-true crates, which keep your dog confined. You may even want to use different systems for different trips.

Blankets or Towels

These are indispensable. Use one to cover the car's cushion where your dog will be sitting. It is easier to remove it or wash it than it is to try getting every dog hair off the seat before someone else sits in that spot. It is also comfier for your dog, since car seat surfaces can be slippery or scratchy. Having a second old towel or blanket is handy for absorbing or wiping off mud, sand, or water after trips to the park or beach. If your pup travels in a crate, use a towel or blanket to keep it soft and cozy. You may want to keep the towels in a laundry bag to make transporting them easier.

Water and a Bowl

It can be surprisingly difficult to find water while you're on the road. Trying to get the water from a bottle into your pup's mouth in any way that doesn't waste the water and/or get both of you soaked can be a challenge. And water is the one thing your pup will definitely need at any stop you make, whether it's hot outside or not.

The best thing to do is buy a gallon jug of filtered water and put it in a cooler with some ice packs. You can put the drinks you'll want for the trip in there, too. When you've gone through the filtered water, replace it with water from your own tap so you can reuse the jug. The water should always be cool and fresh.

It's best to be able to have a supply of the water your dog is used to drinking to prevent any gastric upset. When you're at a rest stop, after a hike, or whenever you need to, fill your dog's bowl with water from this container. Keep it as cold as possible by keeping it in the shade while you're parked or near the air conditioning while traveling.

The best kind of bowl to have on the road is a collapsible bowl. It pops up and holds plenty of water when you need it, then crushes down for easy packing when you don't. These are available through pet supply catalogs or in some pet supply stores.

Poop Picker-Uppers

It is your responsibility and obligation to clean up after your dog wherever you travel with him. Make it a habit to keep a stash of plastic bags in your dog's travel case or in your car and have one with you when you bring her out of the car to exercise. Even if you don't do this at home, you must do it while on the road. It's a distasteful (but mandatory) chore that is easily accomplished by scooping with a plastic bag and disposing of the waste in a public trash receptacle. Imagine if all dog owners left their dogs' waste when they traveled. The areas would soon be littered with feces (and often are—don't contribute to the problem!).

Records

No, not the old vinyl LPs, copies of your dog's health records. These should be secured in a plastic bag so they don't get dripped on or ripped, and can come in handy in case of emergency. If your pup gets sick on the road, you'll be upset enough. Having her records available for the strange veterinarian who will be examining her can put both of you at ease. You'll want a copy of your pup's immunization records to show what shots she's had and when (rabies is especially important), as well as information about any medications she may be on, your veterinarian's phone number, and an emergency back-up number of someone to call should something happen to you.

A First Aid Kit

Better safe than sorry, right? This doesn't need to be excessive, but should include some basics: gauze bandages, vet wrap (to secure a bandage), tweezers, antibiotic ointment, premoistened antiseptic wipes, a supply of your pet's regular mediation, buffered aspirin, Mylanta, a pair of pantyhose for a make-shift muzzle, and anything else you think you might need. Label it as your dog's kit and stash it somewhere safe.

Extra Collar, Leash, and I.D. Tag

This may seem like a silly thing to have to pack, but you will be so thankful you did if something happens and you need it. For example, you may have had a wonderful visit with someone, asked your dog to jump in the car, and driven off without her leash. It could easily happen. As for a collar and I.D. tag, there should always be a tag on any collar your dog wears. If you change collars after your dog has gone for a swim, for example, you will be happy to have the spare.

Treats and Toys

One of the pleasures of being on the road is indulging in new and unusual foods. If you're doing this for yourself, why not for your puppy, too? Feel good about the kinds of treats you're giving her and avoid the potential for gastric upset by having a stash of puppy-appropriate snacks in the car. These can include small pieces of string cheese, freeze-dried liver, hot dogs, or itty-bitty dog biscuits. For longer rides where she may enjoy chewing on something, an appropriate chew toy can keep her occupied. If she has a favorite toy from home, like a pillow or stuffed animal, bring that along so she can snuggle with it.

A Supply of Food

Last but certainly not least, if you will be staying overnight or longer while on the road, be sure to bring enough of your dog's regular food to last the trip. Changing foods—especially while traveling—can upset your pup's stomach or keep her from eating. Even with a supply of the food she's used to, pups (and dogs) can get excited while traveling and often won't eat normally. This doesn't mean you should spoil her and start giving her your restaurant leftovers; it's too risky. Mixing some healthy scraps, like lean cooked meats or plain rice, into her normal food is fine and may encourage her to eat if she's fussing, but don't overindulge.

Unhappy Campers

Unfortunately, for many dogs a car ride is not a happy occasion. Many simply can't stomach the motion and become nauseous while traveling. Many become so worried that unless they can weave back and forth during the trip (not a safe or practical way to travel), they whine and howl until they are "freed" from the moving vehicle.

Some foam at the mouth, vomit, become extremely nervous, and can even become destructive (to the car, other passengers, or themselves). Because there are times when it's necessary for a dog to travel in a vehicle to another destination (such as the veterinarian), if this describes your dog, you need to help her get over her fears.

Not traveling well is the result of either not being properly exposed to a car from puppy hood or having a bad experience in the vehicle. Either way, it's your job to reverse the negative associations to positive ones. This takes time and patience and can be frustrating.

ALERT!

If you are frustrated by your pup's inability to ride in the car without incident, consult a professional trainer. It will help you and your puppy to have someone who can approach the situation unemotionally, and who can coach you through the process while targeting the things that may be upsetting your pup.

Before a dog can relax in the car, she needs to feel comfortable near the car. Using treats, reward her for not just approaching but being able to stay near the car. Leave the car door open so she can look into it, but don't in any way force her into the vehicle. Every day, for just a few minutes a day, make being near and getting into the car rewarding and safe for your dog.

Once she's in the car, secure her with a seat belt, close the door, and get in the driver's seat. Don't go anywhere, just pet her and give her a treat or two for just being in the car. Slowly, slowly, work up to starting the car and making very short, then progressively longer trips, always ending on a pleasant note.

If your dog is fine getting into the car but only gets carsick or upset as the trip goes on, you will need to adjust your strategy. You will need to make some trips that end at the first signs of upset. So for example, get in the car with your dog as usual and begin to drive. As soon as you notice your dog looking "off," pull over, take her by the leash and collar, and get her out of the car. The fresh air and new smells should divert and calm her so she won't be sick. After a few minutes, and with your reassurance, put her back in the car and start driving again. Drive in the direction of home, and if she makes it all the way, give air, act subdued, and go into the house. Working this way, your dog can learn that not all car rides end badly.

On the Road

You'll be so much happier when it's time to go on vacation knowing that you don't have to drop your dog at a kennel or worry about a boarding situation or dog sitter. Your pup will be in your care, sharing your experiences, and what could be better than that?

Part of proper planning is having a case or various bags with everything your pup will need, per the list earlier in this chapter. Before setting out, think about where you will be staying overnight, and make arrangements *before* you arrive. While it's true that more and more places accept dogs—whether your accommodation of choice is a tent over a sleeping bag or a suite at a five-star hotel—you don't want to arrive and be surprised by a change in policy or a "no vacancy" sign.

Finding Dog-Friendly Lodgings

While there are lots of great places to stay with your dog, don't presume that any place you want to stay will be one that's pet-friendly. The particulars of being pet-friendly change from place to place, too: Some places that allow small dogs won't accept larger dogs, or multiple dogs, or multiple pets, and so on. Always research where to stay ahead of time, call the lodging, and talk to them about their pet policy. Tell them about your puppy—they don't need a surprise from you, either, and if they feel they know your pup before you arrive, chances are they will look forward to meeting both of you.

Always make a reservation. This gives you the security you need when traveling with your dog. You don't want to arrive and find the place is booked solid even though it's their slow time of year. You can also request a certain type of room—you may want a first-floor room with immediate outside access, for example.

There are helpful guidebooks that list pet-friendly lodgings across the United States. But searching on the World Wide Web is a great way to see what's out there, too. One of the most trusted is Petswelcome at *www.petswelcome.com*. It has over 25,000 listings for hotels, B&Bs, campgrounds, resorts, and beaches, many with user reviews. There is even an Info X-Change area where people can share information about all aspects of traveling with their pets. Double-check all listings as the pet policies at hotels and motels can change frequently.

At Your Destination

When you arrive at a hotel, motel, inn, or bed-and-breakfast with your dog, the first thing you want to do is let her out so she can relieve herself. Be discreet, and take her to a somewhat out-of-the-way location if possible. Other arriving guests may not appreciate watching your beloved urinate on the flowers lining the walkway to the front door.

With her immediate needs taken care of and her waste properly disposed of, put your dog back in the car while you check in. Until you get the feel for the establishment, don't assume that everyone staying there will think your dog is the cutest and best-behaved they've ever met. In fact, assume the opposite. People checking into hotels have luggage, kids, agendas, business meetings they need to get to—you name it—and often the last thing they want to deal with is your dog wanting to say hello. Give them the benefit of the doubt and keep things as calm as possible for everyone concerned.

Always bring along an extra blanket, sheet, and towels. They come in handy for cleaning up after your pup and for impromptu snuggling.

At the front desk, remind the staff that when you made the reservation you asked about your puppy, and let them know that she is with you. They will probably have a note about it. Once you've found your room and are satisfied with it, *then* get your dog and bring her (and her stuff) to join you.

Settling In

Another thing hotels don't look too kindly on is damage to their rooms by unruly pets. Soiling, chewing, excessive shedding, towels that look like they've been used to bathe the dog—all of these are reasons hotels won't allow dogs. Be considerate and conscientious during your stay. Put one of the old towels or blankets you keep with you in the car on the bed if your dog is going to sleep on it—but only if it's clean! All the more reason to have spares when you travel.

Once you've put your stuff in the room, take your puppy out for a longer walk so she can release some pent-up energy. This will be helpful for her sanity and health, as she will get to sniff and familiarize herself with her surroundings, and it will be good for you. After a long drive, it is important to stretch one's legs, and a leisurely walk with your pup is an excellent way to do it.

When it's time for her meal, feed her in the bathroom or on a non-carpeted part of the room so any spills will be easy to clean up. At night—especially the first night you arrive in a strange place—consider ordering room service or bringing in a pizza or a sandwich so you won't have to leave her alone while you get something to eat.

The strange smells and sounds of new environments make dogs anxious. They need to explore to become more familiar with everything before settling down. Don't think you can check in, drop your dog with your luggage in the room, and take off again. For even well-mannered dogs this can be torturous.

Going Out Alone

If you travel often, or if you've done basic training with her, your puppy should be well-adjusted enough that you can trust her to stay alone in the room for a few hours. Make sure she has been sufficiently exercised, that she's relieved herself, that she's had something to eat and drink, and that there is nothing in the room that could harm her while you're out.

Close the door to the bathroom, put anything she might chew in a closed drawer or closet, leave a light on, and leave the TV on for background noise (not too loud). Be sure to put the Do Not Disturb sign on your door so the staff won't come in.

FACT

The safe and secure way of leaving your dog in your room while you go out is to put her in her crate (another great reason to crate-train your dog). Her familiar crate will help her feel at ease. Knowing she's secured in it means you won't have to worry about her getting into anything dangerous, making a mess of the room, or accidentally escaping should the staff enter your room even with the Do Not Disturb sign up.

When you return, release her from the crate and take her out immediately to stretch her legs and do her thing. Be careful walking your dog after dark. Stay on lighted walkways and pay attention to landmarks so you don't get lost. Consider that you may come across local wildlife like skunks or deer, or other people's dogs or cats. If your puppy can't be trusted to handle these encounters appropriately, only walk her where it seems safest.

Airline and Other Travel

Is it safe to fly with your dog? As safe as it is for you—though certainly not as comfortable. That means that there are no guarantees, but airlines do try to make travel for animals as safe as possible.

Unless you have a very small dog that can be brought into the cabin in an approved carrier, your dog will need to be crated and put in the baggage compartment. Before you even consider doing this, you need to do extensive research. Most major airlines have policies in place to make it as safe as possible to transport pets. You should read and compare them, plus try to talk to people with experience. Owners of champion show dogs often travel by air to get to the biggest shows around the world.

The airlines' policies also detail their strict requirements for the kind of carrier your dog can be transported in, what can be included inside it, how it should be labeled, and so on. Even a dog who loves her crate at home may find the experience stressful, but a dog who is not crate-trained is in for a very unpleasant experience.

ALERT!

You may think you can help your puppy by sedating her for a flight, but it's not true! High altitudes and sedatives are a deadly mix and should not even be considered. Study the guidelines provided by the carrier and be sure your dog is healthy before taking to the skies with her. If you have serious concerns, consult with your veterinarian.

Trains, Buses, and Boats

As of this writing, if you want to travel by train with your puppy, he must be a registered service dog. In fact, Amtrak specifies that service animals are to be accompanying people with disabilities, so even if your dog is trained as such, if you aren't the one for whom he is a service dog, you may not be allowed on board. Best to ask before taking any chances.

Some regional rail lines permit dogs, and if you want to leave the big city and head for the 'burbs for the weekend with your puppy, it's worth checking into. Of course, you should not expect other passengers to put up with anything but a well-behaved puppy, and that's your responsibility!

The Greyhound bus line has the noble sighthound as its logo, but you might have more luck getting your dog up Mt. Everest than on a bus unless you are disabled and your pup's a service dog. If you have a toy dog who travels nicely in a carrier, you can call your local office and see what can be done.

Cruises are more and more popular, but by their very nature of being "get-away-from-it-all" vacations, on most cruise lines your pup is not considered a legitimate passenger. Again, it is the legitimate service dog who can receive passage, and this must be disclosed at the time of a ticket's booking.

Just as it was once unusual to stay at a hotel with a dog, perhaps the policies of trains, buses, and boats will change to be more accommodating as well. It is all contingent on how well the dogs behave—nother reason to enroll your travel-happy puppy in a training class that preps for the Canine Good Citizen test. CGC-certified pups can be trusted just about anywhere.

CHAPTER 21

Raising a Green Puppy

There's so much talk now about "going green," that there can't be a book on raising a healthy puppy without exploring this topic, too. All of us need to reevaluate what we use, buy, eat, are exposed to, and give off every day so that we can live cleaner and healthier lives. The same goes for our puppies.

Does Your Puppy Have a Carbon Paw Print?

It's helpful to know what it means to have a carbon "footprint" as a person before you can think about how this might apply to your puppy. Essentially, a carbon footprint is the impact each of us has on the environment and climate, based on our daily consumption of fossil fuels or fossil fuel-related products. An individual carbon footprint takes into account a multitude of sources, including consumption of electricity, home heating (fuel oil, gas, or coal), transportation (cars, buses, trains, and planes), and food (mass-produced food requires a lot of energy to produce, for example).

ALERT!

A really easy way to measure your own carbon footprint is to go to a website that can calculate it for you. One of these is TerraPass at *www.terrapass.com.* When you understand your own footprint, you can begin to understand how your puppy has one, too.

Think about all the fuel-related activities your puppy participates in: car rides, being comfortable in the home with air conditioning or heating, having a radio or TV on while you're away for "white noise" to keep him company, keeping lights on so that as night falls he isn't in total darkness, and of course, the energy needed to create his food. It's easy to see that your puppy does, indeed, have a carbon paw print—and so do all dogs that are kept as companions in the home. That's some 70 million dogs in the United States alone.

Green Feeding

This sounds like adding a lot of vegetables to your puppy's food—and that is actually part of it, so it's easy to remember. But greening the feeding of your puppy involves more than that.

Chapter 8 covered all the elemental aspects of feeding your puppy from a very young age into adulthood and his golden years. The information in that chapter is solid and can certainly form the basis of any decisions you need to make about feeding your puppy. What the chapter didn't go into that you may want to consider is how commercial dog food is made, how it gets to the store, and how it may not be the best choice if you're concerned about that process's contribution to global warming.

Food production is, by its very nature, a major source of fuel consumption around the world. If this isn't something you've considered before, it's interesting to ponder. There's the energy needed to prepare the ground for the food source, whether it be animal or vegetable. There's the energy needed to raise the food source—everything from the chemicals used on fruits and vegetables to the equipment used to keep animals clean and so much more. Harvesting requires more machinery; the harvesting of animals is the process of butchering and preparing them. Then there's packaging and shipping. It's easy to understand that food production is energy-intensive when you look at its various components.

What feeding green boils down to is being conscious of what's in your puppy's food, where it comes from, and how it's produced. Chapter 8 explained the key nutrients puppies and dogs need to thrive, and dog food companies strive to provide those. It's the balance of the nutrients that's important, too. Dogs need different levels of proteins, carbs, fats, and so on as they grow, with puppies, active adults, and breeding animals needing the highest concentrations of nutrients. Those nutrients come from different sources (aha—that's the source of the food). For example, many foods for puppies and dogs contain beef, chicken, lamb, or turkey. Often, these are parts that have been cast off after the "human grade" meat is set aside for people. Sometimes these meats are cooked and processed, then added back to a food as "meal."

That's why it's so important to look at the ingredient panel. What is the source of the protein? Is it the meat, listed simply as "beef," or is it beef stock or beef meal? Subtle but important differences. Also, more and more dog food companies are now sourcing higher quality meats, which they'll list as human-grade or organic.

Remember that whatever is brought in to make your puppy's food, commercially prepared food is processed. Typically it is processed at such high temperatures that the nutrients are cooked out, and often the foods are supplemented with vitamins and even flavor additives to restore what's lost in the processing. Where is this processing done? At the factories owned and operated by the food companies. How does the food get from the factories to your store? How far does it travel? If you're interested in a greener approach to feeding, you'll need to do a lot of research to find out as much as you can about your puppy's food.

The Locavore Movement

Most people are familiar with the words carnivore (meat eater), herbivore (plant eater), and omnivore (meat and plant eater). Puppies (and dogs) are omnivores, just like humans. They can also be locavores, a word that came into common usage around 2005. Locavores limit their diets to foods that are grown and harvested locally, typically within 100 miles of where they live.

Depending on what part of the United States or the world that you live in, being a true locavore can be quite challenging. It may be too cold in your area for citrus fruits or bananas, for example, or it may be too hot for asparagus or maple syrup. Americans have become accustomed to having so many different kinds of foods available that it can be surprising to discover how far away many of them come from.

If you want your puppy or dog to be a locavore, you will need to research what is necessary for a proper diet for her, and then you'll have to see how many of those components you're able to acquire locally. This may be easier in some seasons than others—spring, summer and fall can mean lots of local vegetables, including root vegetables like potatoes, squash, and beets—and maybe there's someone in your area raising cows, pigs, turkeys, or sheep, or even hunting deer for venison meat. If you were even able to revert to this kind of diet for part of the year, you could significantly cut down on your puppy's carbon paw print.

Green Grooming

If your head is still reeling from the considerations relative to providing a greener diet for your puppy, you'll be glad to know that making greener grooming decisions is a bit less complicated.

Think about the grooming supplies you may need for your puppy, then think about the green motto of reduce, reuse, and recycle. There are the essentials: brushes, combs, toenail clippers, and a toothbrush and tooth-paste (and possibly other items depending on the kind of dog you have). Because you must have these and you will use them frequently, be mind-ful of needing to replace them, which is wasteful and "un-green." It may cost more initially, but buy quality tools that will last.

There are many other products you can use for grooming—shampoo, conditioner, hair accessories like bows, ointments, and solu-tions for cleaning eyes and ears, etc. So that you're not wasting these, think quality. Choose products that are first and foremost effective so you don't need to use as much of them, and then consider the source of the ingredients in the products you choose. Look for shampoos that are bio-degradable and free of dyes, alcohol, and petroleum products. While we enjoy scented products, dogs don't, and these are neither necessary nor healthy for your dog—especially "perfume" sprays.

If you prefer to have a professional groomer take care of your dog on a regular basis, ask to see what kinds of products they use. You can ask them to use what you'd like so long as you provide it.

Green Health Care

Green health care for your puppy is actually quite simple in concept, requir-ing only that you provide sound preventive care: proper diet, regular groom-ing, plenty of exercise, regular veterinary checkups, and the attention that a social animal like a dog needs. When these elemental aspects of care are provided for, you'll reap the benefits in many savings, including going through less food because it will be fully utilized by your dog; needing fewer medications (including over-the-counter drugs) because your pup will be healthy all over; spending less on problem-solving behaviors, because your pup will be getting regular exercise and attention.

In Chapter 17, you'll learn the intricacies of preventive care, as well as the common problems that puppies and dogs are prone to. The more you know about what to look out for, the better you'll be able to recognize potential problems before they become major issues. For example, if you pay attention to your puppy's eating and drinking habits, you'll notice immediately he's off his food or possibly drinking more than usual—both are signs that something is wrong.

Your partner in all of this is your veterinarian. There isn't a veterinarian out there who would be unhappy to see a puppy grow up healthy and well-adjusted, requiring only regular checkups. But veterinarians approach achieving this level of health from many different angles. As you explore the varied opinions and protocols of veterinarians and other dog health professionals, it's important to work with a veterinarian who has an open mind and is willing to explore these areas with you. It is his or her advice you may turn to in the end, but it is your puppy whose condition is at stake. If it's a greener perspective you're after, talk to your pup's vet about suggestions he or she has for providing the best diet, environment, vaccination protocol, and so on.

Care Product Choices

Some of the most common problems facing puppy and dog owners are invasions of parasites—such as fleas, ticks, worms, and mites. A huge assortment of over-the-counter preventives are available to help keep them at bay, from collars infused with chemicals to liquids that are applied on the dog's back to supplements that work from the inside out. Sure you want to keep those nasty bugs off and away from your puppy, but be careful that what you're buying and using isn't potentially undermining some other aspect of your pup's health. Puppies, like babies, are especially sensitive to harsh chemicals. Read the labels and ask your veterinarian about the safety of these common pest potions.

One of the greenest things you can do for your puppy is to have him or her neutered or spayed. Pet overpopulation is a huge issue, and it is awful to learn that millions of companion animals are euthanized every year. It is staggering to consider the drain on natural resources that this vicious cycle perpetuates. Spaying and neutering are also beneficial for your puppy's long-term health and behavior as a family friend.

There are more and more products coming to market that use more natural ingredients to keep bugs at bay. Seek them out and give careful consideration to using them instead. Think about how these products are produced, the packaging they're in, and other ways that they may be a poor choice not only for your pup, but for the planet as well.

The Green Indoors

Walk through any aisle of dog supplies and you'll see an explosion of cute, colorful, cushy toys and beds. If they are washable and durable, fine, but if your dog delights in ripping the seams or chewing holes in them so he can have a "Polyfill party," steer clear. As mentioned earlier, Kongs, Nylabones, and sterilized bones are better options. Destructive puppies will find lasting comfort in beds that don't have foam fillings.

The Green Outdoors

Can you picture yourself, your puppy, and your family enjoying an afternoon in your yard, playing on a lush lawn bordered with thriving bushes and flowers, anticipating the cook-out you have planned for later in the day? Sounds great, doesn't it? The problem is that there are lots of things in your yard that you might want to have look perfect but may be hazardous to the health of all of you.

To achieve that "picture-perfect" moment where everything looks great, people are encouraged to fertilize their lawns, apply weed killer, spray for bugs, and spray to kill or prevent any diseases on our bushes and flower gardens. If this has been your line of defense, before letting your puppy and family romp away in the yard, reexamine the products you're using. What are their cautions for dogs? For children? What's in the sprays you use on various parts of your lawn and garden? How do those products affect the natural flora and fauna of the area you live in? Your yard may look great, but the price you pay for it may be the health of the living beings it's intended for.

Going green outdoors means paying attention to the number and type of products you use or things you do to sustain a potentially unnatural environment. For example, do you live in a place where keeping grass green means watering it almost daily? Are you and all your neighbors doing that? Think about how much water you're using in the neighborhood. Is the water falling on grass and plants that have been chemically treated to thrive? Where is the run-off going and how might it be affecting other life forms?

Know Your Place

Keeping a green yard doesn't mean it has to be barren and ugly. When you understand what might grow best where you are and you take into consideration the effects that your pup will have on your yard (wearing down a path, digging, creating urine or feces stains), you can create a space that works for you and your pup instead of against you.

That means talking to a local plant supplier about the kinds of things that are easy to grow. It may mean creating a pebbled path along the fence line or planting a foot or so away from it so your dog can walk or run there without damaging the landscaping. It means that if your pup likes to dig, instead of constantly getting after him to stop, you choose a spot in the yard where it's appropriate for him to do so, and you put in a sand box for him. And it means training him to do his business in a particular spot that you can monitor for stains, and picking up after his bowel movements.

When a green(er) mindset starts to kick in for you, you'll notice all sorts of things in your piece of the great outdoors that could be more eco-friendly. A propane grill is less polluting than a charcoal one; there are green-friendly materials now for everything from deck surfaces to patio furniture; choose toys that are longer-lasting than many of the cheap plastic ones sold at discount stores; and so on.

Green Travel

A puppy who loves to travel and gets to go a lot of places will be well-socialized and adaptable to all kinds of situations and events in his life. If you anticipate traveling with your puppy, as discussed in detail in Chapter 20, there are ways to do it in as green a way as possible.

The first is to be sure you always have biodegradable poop-scoop bags with you. It is both inconsiderate and harmful to not pick up after your dog unless you are in a very remote area. Even national parks that allow dogs require that they be kept on leash so they don't disturb the park's ecosystem. Cleaning up after your dog is part of leaving a park in the same condition in which you found it.

Another way to travel greenly is to consider how far you want to go with your dog in the car. It may sound adventurous to visit a park that's thirty miles away, but if your car doesn't get great gas mileage, you should probably just go to the one that's five miles away—or the one that's within walking distance. So long as your pup is with you and getting exercise, she won't notice.

ALERT!

If your plans involve overnight stays, do your research to be sure that any accommodations you choose along the way are pet-friendly—an added bonus would be a pet-friendly lodging with a green bend. More and more lodgings are promoting their conservation efforts, and supporting them is good for everyone.

Consider the supplies you need for your pup while on the road. Bring those from home and resist buying more. Also bring along a few old towels that you can use to dry your dog after a swim, or protect your car seat, or spread over a hotel blanket to keep it clean. Minimize your use of paper towels and anything that's instantly disposable. Get one of those green shopping bags that so many stores offer now and use it as your pup's supply bag for the car, filling it with old towels, an extra cotton leash, a collapsible (and reusable) water bowl, and copies of your pup's veterinary records.

Raising Green Awareness

As the caretaker for a puppy who will hopefully be by your side for a decade or more, it is your responsibility to understand your pup's position and potential in the world. The advice in this book is intended to lead you in the right direction, to help you in making the best decisions relative to the overall care of your pup.

There's always more, just as a childrearing guide only scratches the surface of the reality of rearing a confident and contributing member of society. If the information in this book energizes you to want to provide top-quality care, then you may discover that the choices that seem so plentiful in the places where you shop for supplies or go for advice may in fact feel limited. Do they provide fresh foods? Do they have a selection of bedding made from recycled materials? Do they have collars and leashes made from organic cotton or hemp? Are the grooming tools made well, and do the shampoos and other treatments for skin and coat contain all-natural, non-irritating or non-polluting ingredients? Can you find biodegradable poop-scoop bags?

QUESTION?

How can I learn more about going green?
There are lots of websites on the subject of living a greener life, and applying some of the tips to how you raise and care for your pup makes a lot of sense. At green fairs held around the country, you can meet manufacturers of green products, listen to speakers on a variety of subjects, and meet like-minded people. All great resources for making a difference and staying motivated.

If your search for healthier, greener products takes you away from your local pet store, or large chains, you may want to let them know. People love to spoil their pets and feel like they're providing the best for them, and more and more that means the kinds of eco-minded products mentioned in this chapter. Pet supply stores should be leading the pack in bringing these to consumers. Work with your store managers to see what you can do to help them and your community.

APPENDIX A

Resources

Owning a puppy brings you instant membership into the worldwide community of fellow dog owners—a passionate group, for sure! There are numerous organizations, books, magazines, and online communities associated with the care and keeping of your canine companion. This appendix lists some of the largest and most established, and can serve as a base and a springboard for discovering others.

Registries

The American Kennel Club

The most famous organization that represents purebred dogs in the United States is the American Kennel Club. Established in 1884 to advance the interests of purebred dogs, today the American Kennel Club recognizes more than 150 breeds in seven groups (Sporting, Non-Sporting, Working, Herding, Terrier, Hound, and Toy) as well as a host of breeds in the miscellaneous category.

The AKC is a nonprofit organization whose members are not individual dog owners, but breed clubs. The AKC oversees the establishment of recognized breeds in the United States, and also enforces the standards by which breeds are judged. To carry out its many functions, the AKC maintains offices in New York City (where it was founded) and Raleigh, North Carolina.

American Kennel Club
51 Madison Avenue
New York, NY 10010
or
5580 Centerview Drive
Raleigh, NC 27606-3390
www.akc.org

The United Kennel Club (UKC)

The United Kennel Club was founded in 1898 by Chauncey Z. Bennett. The UKC registers more than a quarter-million dogs each year. UKC is the second oldest and second largest all-breed dog registry in the United States. They are located in Kalamazoo, Michigan.

The UKC, like the AKC, sponsors events of many kinds, from dog shows to a host of performance events. The UKC is made up of over 1,000 different clubs that oversee several thousand licensed annual dog events. Many of their events are very easy to enter and compete in, promoting owners to show and compete with their dogs, as opposed to hiring professional trainers or handlers.

United Kennel Club
100 East Kilgore Road
Kalamazoo, MI 49001-5598
www.ukcdogs.com

The American Rare Breed Association (ARBA)

The mission of the American Rare Breed Association is to serve and protect what are considered rare breeds of dogs in the United States. This includes promoting and educating the public dog fancier about 130 or more breeds from around the world that are not now recognized by the American Kennel Club.

American Rare Breed Association
100 Nicholas Street NW
Washington, DC 20011
www.arba.org

The Canadian Kennel Club (CKC)

Much like the AKC, the CKC is the primary registering body and over-seer of the sport of purebred dogs in Canada. Many Canadians who want to compete in the United States register their dogs in both clubs. Much like the AKC, the Canadian Kennel Club is devoted to encouraging, guiding, and advancing the interests of purebred dogs and their responsible owners and breeders in Canada.

Canadian Kennel Club
Commerce Park
88 Skyway Avenue, Suite 100
Etobicoke, ON M9W 6R4
Canada
www.ckc.ca

The Kennel Club (UK)

Founded in 1873, the primary objective of the Kennel Club is to promote in every way, the general improvement of dogs. The Kennel Club is able to offer dog owners an unparalleled source of information, experience and advice on dog welfare, dog health, dog training and dog breeding.

The Kennel Club
1-5 Clarges Street
Piccadilly
London W1J 8AB
www.thekennelclub.org.uk

The Fédération Cynologique Internationale (FCI)

Currently based in Belgium, the Fédération Cynologique Internationale was created in 1911 with the aim to promote and protect cynology and purebred dogs by any means it considers necessary. The founding nations were Germany, Austria, Belgium, France, and the Netherlands. The Federation disappeared due to the first World War and in 1921, the Société Centrale Canine de France and the Société Royale Saint-Hubert re-created it. The new articles of association were adopted on April 10th, 1921 and on March 5th, 1968, the FCI got the legal personality by decree. Today the organization sponsors two of the world's largest dog shows: The European Dog Show and the World Dog Show.

Fédération Cynologique Internationale
Secrétariat Général de la FCI
Place Albert 1er, 13
B—6530 Thuin
Belgium
www.fci.be

Pet Advocacy and Therapy Groups

The American Society for the Prevention of Cruelty to Animals (ASPCA)

The ASPCA is one of the most active pro-pet groups in the world. A nonprofit company, the ASPCA sponsors countless numbers of groups and events to protect animals' and pet owners' rights. The ASPCA has attempted to reduce pain, fear, and suffering in animals through humane law enforcement, legislative advocacy, education, and hands-on animal care.

The ASPCA was founded in 1866 by a diplomat named Henry Bergh. Today, the ASPCA supplies a number of different services to pet and animal lovers all across the country. They are perhaps best known for helping shelter strays and foster adoptions.

ASPCA
424 East 92nd Street
New York, NY 10128-6804
(212) 876-7700
www.aspca.org

The Humane Society of the United States (HSUS)

The Humane Society of the United States (HSUS) is another of the nation's largest animal-protection organizations. HSUS promotes the "humane treatment of animals and to foster respect, understanding, and compassion for all creatures." The HSUS uses such venues as the legal system, education, and legislation to ensure the protection of animals of all kinds.

The HSUS was founded in 1954 and currently has nine major offices in the United States. Unlike the ASPCA, the HSUS does not have any affiliate shelters. The HSUS mainly concerns itself with wildlife protection, companion animals, and animal research violations. However, they do sponsor many events for pet owners and do encourage pet rescue (adoption).

Humane Society of the United States
2100 L Street, NW
Washington, DC 20037
www.hsus.org

The American Humane Association (AHA)

Based in Englewood, Colorado, and founded in 1877, the American Humane Association (AHA) is a welfare organization involved in assisting both animals and children. These days the AHA oversees the treatment of animals on movie and television sets and is working to establish standards for dog trainers, among many other things.

American Humane Association
63 Inverness Dr. East
Englewood, CO 80112
www.americanhumane.org

Delta Society

The Delta Foundation was established in 1977 in Portland, Oregon, under the leadership of Michael McCulloch, MD, and Leo K. Bustad, DVM, PhD, dean of a veterinary college and a pioneer in human-animal bond theory and application. From the beginning, Delta provided the first comprehensive training in animal-assisted activities and therapy to volunteers and health care professionals, and it continues to develop standards-based training materials. It is committed to its mission to improve human health through service and therapy animals.

Delta Society
P.O. Box 1080
Renton, WA 98057
www.deltasociety.org

Therapy Dogs International (TDI)

Elaine Smith founded TDI in 1976 to create an organization dedicated to regulating, testing and registering therapy dogs as well as their handlers. Through this process, they are better prepared and able to assist in visits to nursing homes, hospitals, and other institutions where therapy dogs are needed.

Therapy Dogs International
88 Bartley Road
Flanders, NJ 07836
www.tdi-dog.org

Training and Behavior

The Association of Pet Dog Trainers (APDT)

Founded in 1993 by Dr. Ian Dunbar, the APDT has grown to become one of the largest dog-training organizations in the world. It is committed to developing better trainers through education, and offers individual pet dog trainers a respected and concerted voice in the dog world, promoting dog-friendly dog training to the veterinary profession and the public.

Association of Pet Dog Trainers
150 Executive Center Drive Box 35
Greenville, SC 29615
www.apdt.com

The International Association of Canine Professionals (IACP)

IACP was founded by Martin Deeley to promote the highest standards of professional and business practice among canine professionals including, but not limited to, dog trainers, veterinarians, groomers, kennel managers, and pet sitters. It also is a great resource to locate a qualified canine professional in your area.

The International Association of Canine Professionals
P.O.Box 560156
Montverde, Fl. 34756-0156
(407)469-2008
www.dogpro.org

National Association of Dog Obedience Instructors (NADOI)

Founded in 1965 to promote modern, humane training methods and at the same time elevate the standards of the dog-training profession, NADOI members need to demonstrate that they have attained certain skills and knowledge through testing measured by their peers. The NADOI's mission is to endorse dog obedience instructors of the highest caliber; to provide continuing education and learning resources to those instructors; and to continue to promote humane, effective training methods and competent instructors.

National Association of Dog Obedience Instructors
PO Box 369
729 Grapevine Hwy
Hurst, TX 76054
www.nadoi.org

Health

American Veterinary Medical Association (AVMA)

A convention of veterinary surgeons in New York in 1863 led to the foundation of the United States Veterinary Medical Association. It was created to serve as a resource for veterinarians across the country. In 1889, the name was changed to the American Veterinary Medical Association. Today there are over 75,000 members. The AVMA serves the veterinarians who care for the nation's millions of pets of all kinds, as well as those who serve in medical research, prevention of bio and agro terrorism, food safety and who contribute to scientific breakthroughs throughout the world.

American Veterinary Medical Association
1931 North Meacham Road, Suite 100
Schaumburg, IL 60173-4360
www.avma.org

Animal Poison Control Center

Since 1978, the ASPCA Animal Poison Control Center (APCC) has been the premier animal poison control center in North America. The center, an allied agency of the University of Illinois, is the only facility of its kind, staffed by twenty-five veterinarians and thirteen certified veterinary technicians. Located in Urbana, Illinois, the specially trained staff provides assistance to pet owners and veterinarians pertaining to toxic chemicals and dangerous plants, products and substances twenty-four hours a day, seven days a week.

(888) 426-4435
www.aspca.org

The American Kennel Club Canine Health Foundation (AKC CHF)

Founded in 1995, The AKC Canine Health Foundation is currently the largest nonprofit funder of exclusively canine research in the world. The foundation works to develop significant resources for basic and applied health programs with emphasis on canine genetics to improve the quality of life for dogs and their owners. The foundation funds research and supports canine health scientists and professionals in their efforts to study the causes and origins of canine diseases in order to formulate effective treatments.

www.akcchf.org

PennHip for Diagnosis of Hip Dysplasia

PennHip stands for University of **Penn**sylvania **H**ip **I**mprovement **Pro**gram, and is a not-for-profit program. It involves a special technique that assesses the conditions of a dog's hips to determine the severity of current or developing hip dysplasia. The information is saved in a database that continues to grow and serve veterinarians trying to understand and treat this condition.

www.pennhip.org

Recommended Reading

It's not possible to list all the helpful publications available for dog owners—and there are more that come out every year. But this list is a great starting point. Enjoy!

General

The Complete Dog Book, by The American Kennel Club (Howell Book House)

The Complete Dog Book for Kids, by The American Kennel Club (Howell Book House)

Dogs Never Lie About Love: Reflections on the Emotional World of Dogs, by Jeffrey Moussaief Masson (Three Rivers Press)

The Intelligence of Dogs, by Stanley Coren (Free Press)

Pack of Two, by Caroline Knapp (The Dial Press)

The Quotable Dog, by Greg Snider (Contemporary Books)

Spotted in France, by Gregory Edmont (Rodale)

Green Dog, Good Dog: Reducing Your Dog's Carbon Paw Print, by Dominique De Vito (Lark Books)

Adoption and Rescue

Adopting a Dog: The Indispensable Guide for Your Newest Family Member (W.W. Norton & Co.)

Successful Dog Adoption, by Sue Sternberg (Howell Book House)

Your Adopted Dog: Everything You Need to Know About Rescuing and Caring for a Best Friend in Need, by Shelley Frost & Katerina Lorenzatos Makris (The Lyons Press)

Health

Dog Owner's Home Veterinary Handbook, by Delbert G. Carlson, DVM, and James M. Giffin, MD (Howell Book House)

The Everything Dog Health Book, by Kim Campbell Thornton (Adams Media)

Feeding Your Dog for Life: The Real Facts About Proper Nutrition, by Diane Morgan (Doral)

The Goldsteins' Wellness & Longevity Program: Natural Care for Dogs & Cats, by Robert S. and Susan Goldstein (TFH Publications)

The Holistic Health Guide: Natural Care for the Whole Dog, by Doug Knueven, DVM, CVA, CAC (TFH Publications)

Training and Behavior

Bones Would Rain from the Sky, by Suzanne Clothier (Grand Central Publishing)

The Culture Clash, by Jean Donaldson (James & Kenneth Publishers)

Before and After Getting Your Puppy: The Positive Approach to Raising a Happy, Healthy, and Well-Behaved Dog, by Ian Dunbar, PhD, MRCVS (New World Library)

Dr. Dunbar's Good Little Dog Book, by Ian Dunbar, PhD, MRCVS (James & Kenneth Publishers)

Don't Shoot the Dog, by Karen Pryor (Bantam)

Dual Ring Dog, by Amy Ammen and Jacqueline Frasier (Howell Book House)

For the Love of a Dog: Understanding Emotion in You and Your Best Friend, by Patricia McConnell, PhD (Ballantine)

Hip Ideas for Hyper Dogs, by Amy Ammen (Howell Book House)

Surviving Your Dog's Adolescence, by Carol Lea Benjamin (Howell Book House)

Training in No Time, by Amy Ammen (Howell Book House)

The Everything® Dog Training & Tricks Book, by Gerilyn J. Bielakiewicz, Bethany Brown, and Christel A. Shea (Adams Media)

Little Dogs: Training Your Pint-Sized Companion, by Deborah Wood (TFH Publications)

On Talking Terms With Dogs: Calming Signals, by Turid Rugaas (Dogwise Publihing)

Pet Loss

The Loss of a Pet, by Dr. Wallace Sife (Howell Book House)

When Your Pet Dies, by Jamie Quakenbush (Simon & Schuster)

Magazines

AKC Gazette and **AKC Family Dog**
Publications of the American Kennel Club
www.akc.org

Bloodlines Journal, Coonhound Bloodlines, and **Hunting Retriever**
Publications of the United Kennel Club
www.ukcdogs.com

Canine Review and **Dogs in Canada**
Publications of the Canadian Kennel Club
www.ckc.ca

Dog Fancy, Dogs for Kids, Dogs in Review, and **Dog World**
All from Fancy Publications
www.animalnetwork.com

Bark Magazine
The Modern Dog Culture Magazine
http://thebark.com

Dog and Kennel Magazine
From Pet Publishing
www.dogandkennel.com

Dogs Today
Britain's Biggest and Best Dog Magazine
www.dogstodaymagazine.co.uk

Kennel Gazette
A Publication of The Kennel Club
www.thekennelclub.org.uk

Whole Dog Journal: A Monthly Guide to Natural Dog Care & Training
A Publication of Belvoir Publications
www.whole-dog-journal.com

Glossary

B

You'll soon find out that the dog world has a language of its own, just like so many other hobbies and pastimes. And as your puppy grows and you start becoming more active and involved in his life, you'll want to learn some of the language of dogs, too. For example, it's helpful to know what certain body parts are called when you're trying to talk to a veterinarian about where you think your pup is experiencing pain. This glossary should help you better understand and communicate about your pup's world.

Abdomen

Sometimes used interchangeably with "tummy" to describe the area between the chest and hindquarters, where the ribs end and there is a tuck toward the hind end.

Agility

An exciting and action-packed sport for dogs and their caregivers. It involves the dogs being directed to negotiate an obstacle course that includes jumps, weave poles, tunnels, and other things while being timed.

Albino

A dog with white hair and pink eyes is called albino. The condition is genetic.

Almond-shaped eyes

When the tissue around the dog's eyes is elongated, it gives the eye an almond shape and appearance.

Anal sacs

The two sacs located just inside the rim of the anal sphincter and on either side of the rectum. The anal sacs distribute scent when a dog defecates, but they can become impacted, leading to discomfort and even infection.

Ankle

A dog's ankle is called a hock.

Badger

A coat color that describes a combination of white, gray, brown, and black hairs. Also referred to as beaver.

Bait

Something used to gain a dog's attention during training or while performing. This is often a piece of food or a special toy.

Balance

When a dog appears symmetrical and in proportion all over, he is described as balanced. It is the condition of having all body parts in harmony.

Bay

The sound a hunting dog makes while on a scent. Typically a long bark or howl.

Beady eyes

A description of eyes that are small, round, and glittering.

Beard

The hair that grows longer and thicker on the muzzle (nose), especially from the lower jaw.

Bench show

A dog show where the dogs must stay on a "bench" to be observed by attendees of the show instead of leaving when they're not in the ring. While many dog shows were once benched, there are only a few that retain this tradition. One is the Westminster Kennel Club show in New York City in February.

Best in Show

The honor bestowed upon the single dog that wins from among all others entered at a particular show.

Best of Breed

The honor bestowed upon the dog (male or female) that wins from among all others of its breed at a particular show.

Best of Opposite Sex

The honor bestowed upon the male or female dog that does not win Best of Breed in its breed at a particular show. For example, if the Best of Breed winner is a male dog, then Best of Opposite would be a bitch, and vice versa.

Bite

The way the jaws meet when the mouth is closed. There are four types: scissor, level, undershot, or overshot.

Bitch

The term used to describe a female dog.

Blaze
A prominent white stripe that runs down the center of a dog's face.

Blue
A term used to describe the color of a coat that is a diluted shade of black.

Bone
While this is the substance known to make up the skeleton, it is also a term used to describe a dog's substance in proportion to its overall size.

Breed
A dog developed to have certain characteristics that hold through generations of breeding.

Brush
A term used to describe a bushy tail like that of a fox.

Canines
Besides describing dogs themselves, these are also teeth. Specifically, those located on the upper and lower jaws that are large and pointed.

Cat foot
The kind of foot where the toes are short, rounded, and tight, like that of a cat.

Champion
A title given to a dog or bitch that has won a certain number of points in specific classes at dog shows. Abbreviated as "Ch." in front of a dog's name.

Character
That which defines the breed as typical, including its general appearance, expression, and individual nature.

Claw
Another term for toenail.

Clip
The way a dog's coat is trimmed to give it an appearance typical of its breed.

Coarse
A term used to describe a dog that lacks elegance or refinement.

Coat
The hair or fur that covers a dog.

Cobby
A term used to describe a short-bodied and compact dog.

Cocked ears
Those that are erect but semi-pricked so that only the tip is bent forward.

Conformation
The way the dog conforms to its breed standard through its form, structure, makeup, and arrangement of body parts.

Crest
The area at the back of the neck that is arched.

Croup
The part of the back directly above the hind legs.

Crown
The topskull of the dog.

Cry
The sound that hounds make when they're trailing a scent.

Curled tail
One that comes up over the dog's back.

Dam
The female dog that is a puppy's mother.

Dewclaw
The "fifth toe" that's on the inside of the leg. Dewclaws are removed on some breeds when puppies are very young.

Dish faced
A concave appearance of the foreface when viewed in profile.

Dock
A procedure that shortens a dog's tail by cutting it. Done when puppies are very young.

Dog
A term that collectively references male and female members of the canine species, it is also used specifically to designate a male instead of a female.

Double coat
A coat type that constitutes a softer, denser "undercoat" along with a harsher "topcoat" which, in combination, protect a dog from weather extremes and things like burrs and prickers.

Drive
The action of the hindquarters to propel a dog forward.

Dual champion
The title that's accorded a dog who has attained Championships in the conformation ring and in field trials.

Ear flap
A term used to describe the leather (skin) of the ear.

Ectropion
A genetic condition in which the lower eyelid rolls outward, away from the eyeball. (Opposite of entropion.)

Entropion
A genetic condition in which the lower eyelid rolls inward, toward the eyeball. (Opposite of ectropion.)

Estrus
The part of the female dog's heat cycle during which ovulation occurs.

Feathering
The longer hair that grows on different parts of the body, including the ears, legs, tail, and tummy.

Fetlock
The term used to describe the wrist or pastern of the dog.

Flank
Also called the coupling, this refers to the part of the body between the last rib and the hip.

Flecking
Irregularly shaped spots or markings that distinguish the look of the coat.

Flews
Pendulous skin at the corners of the mouth, responsible for drooling in some breeds.

Foxy
A reference to the expression of a dog or the appearance of its head so that it appears sharp and pointed, like a fox.

Furnishings
The excessive hair on some breeds that covers extremities, particularly the head and tail.

Gait
The term used to describe how a dog moves; the pattern of its footsteps or speed of its movement.

Gay tail
Description of a tail held high.

Get
Another word to describe the puppies whelped by a dam.

Groups
The division of the breeds as determined by the American Kennel Club. There are seven of them: Sporting, Working, Toy, Terrier, Herding, Non-Sporting, and Hound.

Hackles
The hair on the back of the neck and along the back that goes up when a dog is frightened or angry.

Halo
The ring of black around the eyes of some breeds.

Handler
The person who shows or works the dog in competition.

Haunches
The area of the hips.

Haw
The membrane visible in the inner corner of a dog's eye. More prominent in some breeds than others.

Heat
Another word to describe the part of a female's reproductive cycle when she is in estrus.

Hindquarters
The back end of a dog that includes the pelvis, thighs, hocks, pasterns, and rear feet.

Hock
The canine term for ankle—where the hind leg forms the joint between the metatarsus and second thigh.

Inbreeding
The breeding of closely related dogs.

Incisors
The six teeth on the upper jaw and six teeth on the lower jaw that are between the canines and form the bite.

Kiss marks
A reference to the tan spots that are on the cheeks and over the eyes of some breeds.

Kissing Spot
Another term for the "lozenge" that is on the head of particular breeds, notably the Cavalier King Charles Spaniel and Blenheim variety of the English Toy Spaniel.

Knee
Called the stifle on the dog.

Lead
Another term for the leash or piece of equipment used to walk or lead a dog.

Leather
The area of the outer ear that forms the flap of the ear.

Leggy
A description of a dog that is particularly tall.

Litter
The term used to describe the group of puppies whelped by a particular dam.

Loin
The area between the ribs and pelvis that is associated with the lumbar portion of the vertebrae.

Lolling tongue
A tongue that protrudes from the mouth.

Lozenge
The more technical term for the kissing spot.

Markings
Reference to the white areas against a colored background on a dog's coat.

Mask
The area on the face that is darker and forms a mask.

Milk teeth
The first teeth in a puppy's mouth. These fall out when the adult teeth come in.

Mustache
The longer hair that grows on the upper lip.

Muzzle
The part of the face that is in front of the eyes and includes the jaws and nasal bones. It's also the name of the piece of equipment that can be put over this area to keep a dog from biting or eating.

Neuter
The umbrella term for removing the reproductive organs of a dog (castration) or bitch (spay).

Nictitating membrane
The technical term for the third eyelid.

Obedience trial
The formal competition in which dogs work to obtain points ("legs") toward an obedience title.

Occiput
The point of the skull that is all the way in the back.

Otter tail
Typically used to describe the tail of the Labrador Retriever—thick at the root and then round and tapering.

Overshot
A term that describes when the upper jaw extends over the lower jaw.

Pads
The soles of a dog's feet.

Parrot mouth
An extended overshot jaw.

Pastern
The part of the foreleg (metatarsal bones) between the wrist (carpus) and the foot, and the part of the hind leg (metatarsal bones) between the ankle (hock) and the foot.

Patella
Another term for kneecap.

Pips
The tan spots that are above the eyes of most breeds that are black-and-tan in color.

Prick ear
The term that refers to the erect carriage of the ear with a pointed tip.

Propeller ears
The term that refers to the carriage of the ears when they stick out horizontally.

Prosternum
The point of the breastbone.

Rat tail
A tail that is thick at the base and covered with curls and then loses the curls as it tapers to a point.

Ring tail
The carriage of the tail that goes up and around, almost in a circle.

Roll
A term used to describe the fold of skin that goes across the top of the nose as well as the movement of a dog with short legs and a rounded ribcage.

Rudder
Another word to describe the tail.

Ruff
The thicker hair that grows around the neck, like a mane.

Saber tail
Tail carriage that forms a semicircle.

Scissors bite
The "classic bite," when the outer tips of the lower incisors line up with the inner tips of the upper incisors.

Sclera
The white membrane that surrounds the cornea of the eye.

Screw tail
The spiral formation of a naturally short, twisted tail.

Shanks
The technical term for the thighs.

Sire
The male dog that fathered a litter of puppies.

Slew feet
The term used to describe when feet stick out instead of forward.

Snow nose
When a normally black nose becomes streaked with pink in the winter or when it's cold.

Stack
The positioning of a dog in the show ring to show off its stance.

Star
The term used to describe a white mark on the forehead that is neither too small nor too large.

Sternum
Another word for breastbone.

Stifle
On the hind legs, the stifle is the knee, or joint between the two thighs.

Stop
The part of the foreface where the muzzle meets the skull between the eyes.

Stud
A male dog used for breeding.

Thorax
The part of the body enclosed by the ribs.

Topcoat
The part of the fur that constitutes the outer layer; usually harsh.

Topline
The area between the withers (behind the neck) to the tail that defines the dog's outline.

Type
The characteristics that, in combination, contribute to the unique appearance of a particular breed.

Undercoat
The part of the fur that constitutes the layer closer to the skin; usually soft and downy.

Undershot
When the lower jaw extends past the upper jaw.

Variety
A further refining of a type of breed by the AKC or other breed registry. Nine AKC breeds have varieties: Cocker Spaniels (by color); Beagles (by size); Dachshunds (by size and coat type); Bull Terriers (by size); Manchester Terriers (by size); Chihuahuas (by coat type); English Toy Spaniels (by coat type); Poodles (by size); and Collies (by coat type).

Veil
The hair that hangs over the eyes from the forelock.

Webbed feet
A foot in which the toes are connected by a membrane; typical of water-retrieving breeds.

Whip tail
A straight and pointed tail that's carried straight out stiffly.

Whorls
Hair that grows in a circular or ridged pattern, like that of the Rhodesian Ridgeback.

Withers
The point behind the dog's neck that is the highest part of the shoulder.

Wolf claw
The dewclaw on the hind leg.

Index